The
EVERYTHING
Gardening Book

Dear Reader:

You can grow the most beautiful flowers, delicious vegetables, tasty herbs, and sweet berries and fruits in your backyard and around your home grounds, wherever you live. All you need to know is in this exciting book.

I've been growing plants of all types since I was in 4-H and won my first gardening prize when I was twelve years old. Ever since those good old days I've enjoyed growing a wide range of plants and crops. I've written several dozen books about gardening, been a nationally syndicated garden columnist in hundreds of papers for more than twenty-five years, and done radio and TV features as "Doctor Plant."

In this book I'll share with you many growing secrets I've learned from veteran gardeners and other top experts. Gardening is America's number-one family hobby and continues to grow in popularity. I hope you'll dig in with family and friends, plant and enjoy your own gardens, and share what you learn from this book and your gardening experience with many others. My living and writing theme is down-to-earth for everyone across America: Let's grow better together!

Your gardening friend,

Allan A. Swenson

The EVERYTHING® Series

Editorial

Publishing Director	Gary M. Krebs
Managing Editor	Kate McBride
Copy Chief	Laura MacLaughlin
Acquisitions Editor	Eric Hall
Development Editors	Lesley Bolton Michael Paydos
Production Editor	Khrysti Nazzaro

Production

Production Director	Susan Beale
Production Manager	Michelle Roy Kelly
Series Designers	Daria Perreault Colleen Cunningham
Cover Design	Paul Beatrice Frank Rivera
Layout and Graphics	Colleen Cunningham Rachael Eiben Michelle Roy Kelly Daria Perreault Erin Ring
Series Cover Artist	Barry Littmann
Interior Illustrator	Argosy Publishing
Insert Photography	© PhotoDisc, Inc

Visit the entire Everything® Series at everything.com

THE
EVERYTHING
GARDENING BOOK

Grow beautiful flowers, delicious
vegetables, and healthy herbs—
right in your own backyard

Allan A. Swenson

Adams Media Corporation
Avon, Massachusetts

To every gardener who helps another grow better.

An Everything® Series Book.
Everything® is a registered trademark of Adams Media Corporation.

Published by Adams Media Corporation
57 Littlefield Street, Avon, MA 02322 U.S.A.
www.adamsmedia.com

ISBN: 1-58062-860-5
Printed in the United States of America.

J I H G F E D C B A

Library of Congress Cataloging-in-Publication Data
Swenson, Allan A.
The everything gardening book / Allan A. Swenson.
p.   cm.   (An everything series book)
ISBN 1-58062-860-5
1. Gardening. I. Title. II. Series: Everything series.
SB453 .S894 2003
635–dc21

2002014686

This publication is designed to provide accurate and authoritative information with regard to the subject matter covered. It is sold with the understanding that the publisher is not engaged in rendering legal, accounting, or other professional advice. If legal advice or other expert assistance is required, the services of a competent professional person should be sought.
        —From a *Declaration of Principles* jointly adopted by a Committee of the American Bar Association and a Committee of Publishers and Associations

Many of the designations used by manufacturers and sellers to distinguish their products are claimed as trademarks. Where those designations appear in this book and Adams Media was aware of a trademark claim, the designations have been printed with initial capital letters.

This book is available at quantity discounts for bulk purchases.
For information, call 1-800-872-5627.

Contents

International Vegetable Favorites / 131

Enjoy Blooming Beauty / 145

Landscape Basics for Beauty and Benefits / 161

Landscape Fruitfully / 177

Berry Tasty Gardens / 189

Spice Up Your Life with Herbs / 199

Acknowledgments

Thanks to many gardening experts and hundreds of friends who shared their knowledge, ideas, tips, and advice with me so I may share their experience, wit, and wisdom with you.

Top Ten Things You Will Learn
After Reading This Book

1. Save time and reduce the risk of strain by choosing the right tools for the right projects.

2. Understanding the growing seasons will help you know when to plant for maximum life and abundant harvests.

3. By learning which plants are right for your climate and soil structure, you can ensure healthy, long-lasting garden pleasures.

4. Poor soil can be improved with do-it-yourself compost.

5. Plants can be protected by knowing how to recognize disease and control harmful pests.

6. Add homegrown taste to family meals by growing and preserving culinary herbs and spices.

7. Reap the benefits of science with methods for making the most of hybrid plants and vegetables.

8. Delicious meals can be found in your own backyard by growing delicious fruits and vegetables for cooking and preserving.

9. Get back to nature with organic gardening.

10. Impress your neighbors by creating a fun and exciting gardening theme in your own backyard.

Introduction

▶ GARDENING HAS DEEP ROOTS. You can trace it back to the Garden of Eden, the Hanging Gardens of Babylon, and many other famous gardens around the world. Today, gardening is America's most popular family hobby. More than 85 million gardeners actively cultivate flowers, vegetables, fruits, and herbs each year, enjoying the fresh air, healthful exercise, and nature's response to their talented touch. Join the masses and get growing with the many projects you'll find in this book. As you perfect your growing skills, you will be able to proudly demonstrate the results of your own "green thumb" for friends and neighbors to appreciate.

In this book you'll discover a wide range of great gardening adventures from growing glorious and fragrant flowers to producing fresh vegetables for delicious meals. You'll learn secrets of berried treasures and fruitful mini-orchards. You'll discover how to spice up your life with herbs and brighten the indoors with appealing houseplants.

As you dig in and begin growing better, you'll learn how to fertilize plants to make them grow bigger, stronger, and more abundant. You'll also discover how to encourage beneficial insects to do away with the harmful ones so they don't bug you or your plants. And there's a lot more. Many gardening experts from top plant breeders to veteran horticulturists have willingly shared their years of experience. You'll be able to use those tips and secrets to make your gardens your pride and joy.

You'll find new growing horizons with multipurpose trees and shrubs for attractive outdoor living areas that also boost your property values. If you live in a condominium or apartment, you'll discover how to enjoy container gardens, plant a window box, and create blooming beauty in pots, tubs, baskets, and barrels for your porch, patio, or balcony.

And you won't have to do it alone. Gardening is often thought of as a solitary pastime, but it can be a social activity as well. Community garden plots are places where people meet, share ideas, and build new friendships. Gardeners are a happy bunch. They gladly answer questions and offer ideas—along with their plants and friendship—to all who share their love of the land.

Many gardeners have become involved in the worthwhile Grow a Row for the Hungry program, which was launched by the Garden Writers of America. Millions of pounds of produce have been grown and donated to food shelters and pantries. Other types of gardens have sprouted as well. In Therapy Gardens, for example, dedicated gardeners have helped older, ill, and troubled people find their way back to healthier lives. Biblical gardens featuring flowers, vegetables, and herbs mentioned in the Scriptures have begun taking root in churchyards and home backyards.

It has been well said that great oaks from tiny acorns grow. You'll find more great growing truths and delights when you dig into gardening because it has so many dimensions. With this book in hand, you can discover a new world of wonder. You have as many possibilities as you wish to enjoy when you pick up a spade, dig into the ground, and plant your seeds. Gardening does indeed offer great growing opportunities in many worthwhile ways. Ⓔ

Chapter 1

Dig In for Great Growing Fun

Gardening gets more exciting and fun every year. The blooming beauty and fragrance of flowers and the tasty herbs, vegetables, and fruits from your backyard are just a sampling of the benefits of this avocation. This chapter will introduce you to the benefits, trends, and sheer enjoyment that are available while gardening.

The Many Benefits of Gardening

From an aesthetic standpoint, gardens offer you dramatic opportunities to enjoy colorful, fragrant flower displays of all shapes and sizes. From a tastier standpoint, you can treat yourself and your family to the best eating ever. Delicious new hybrid vegetables will turn your mealtimes into dining events. You can spice up your culinary endeavors with homegrown herbs. Berries are another sweet treat that you can easily grow in your backyard. Attractive landscaping can make your outdoor living more enjoyable and also boost your home value. Shrubs, trees, and flowers make your property more desirable as they grow in beauty year after year.

Enjoying Fragrant Gardens

One of the sweetest delights of gardening is enjoying the fragrance of flowers. Too often this joy is overlooked as we choose flowers and shrubs for color, display, and other purposes. This year, focus on fragrance and you'll be pleasantly rewarded every time you step outdoors. Some plants have subtle perfumes while others smell fruity or spicy or flood the night with sweet aromas.

To have a sweet smelling garden from spring to fall, you can choose from a wide assortment of fragrant plants. This spring, pick from a dazzling array that includes lily of the valley, syringa, clematis, old-time roses, and viburnum.

Paths, walkways, outdoor dining areas, or quiet sitting nooks are ideal spots for fragrant flowers. These plants can also deliver their pleasures from window boxes or containers on patios and decks. Keep in mind which way the winds blow and try to site plants upwind so their perfume drifts with the breeze where you want it. Many garden centers offer a variety of plants with a long bloom period. From French lilacs in spring to sweet autumn clematis in fall, consider the value of fragrant plants as you plan your garden this year. They add a pleasing element to your landscape and life. Some of the best seed choices include the following:

- Carnations
- Fragrant nicotiana

- Lavender
- Mignonette
- Various pinks
- Stocks
- Sweet pea

You can also plant biennials such as dame's rocket, sweet William, and English wallflower and herbs like ornamental basil and rosemary. With these flowers and plants, you'll enjoy the sweet smell of success in your garden.

When planting a garden for fragrance, it is wise to concentrate the most fragrant plants near areas where you are likely to spend time outdoors, especially in the early morning or evening. That's when most fragrant plants are at their peak.

Eating Healthfully

Fresh veggies are another gardening treat. There is no doubt that ripe juicy tomatoes plucked right from the vine are one of the tastiest rewards. So is sugar-sweet corn. Tastier living is one major reason that gardening has become America's number-one family hobby.

Small plots and backyard gardening provide richer supplies of healthier food. There are more vitamins in freshly picked vegetables and fruits than in those that have been delayed in shipping from the farm to the supermarket to your kitchen.

Vegetable gardeners are always asked: "Why do you spend so much time and effort growing your food when it is available at the grocery store?" There are probably as many answers to this question as there are vegetable gardeners. While there are significant intangible physical and spiritual benefits to be gained from the vigorous exertion involved in coaxing food from the soil, the tangible benefits are the easiest to describe. Homegrown food is the freshest. The freshest vegetables are also the most nutritious. They are picked ripe with their full complement of vitamins intact.

Another key point, especially today, is that homegrown food is the safest. These days everyone is aware of the various issues surrounding the production of food. Important strides have been made in regulating and minimizing the use of pesticide products in food production, but there are still concerns about residues on store-bought produce. As a gardener, you have many options for pest control that include alternate methods and a wide choice of materials. In this book you'll learn how to grow safe vegetables while ensuring a healthy level of pest control.

FACT

Unlike store-bought produce, backyard-grown vegetables and fruits are picked at their peak ripeness. Anyone who has plucked a ripe, sun-warmed tomato or crisp sugar snap pea and eaten it while standing in the garden knows what fresh really tastes like.

Adding a Little Flavor to Your Days

You can also spice up your life with herbs. Many herbs are hardy, easy to grow, and even bear lovely blossoms. Others add fragrance to gardens and rooms. Indoor herbs like basil, dill, and thyme can add a delicious fragrance to every room in your home. However, their best quality is their flavor. Even a small pinch of one herb or a leaf of another can make meals come alive. You can sprinkle herbs on salads, soups, and stews or blend them with gravy and sauces. Another nice advantage is that you can enjoy herbs year-round. (To discover new taste horizons, you'll find tips about herbs in Chapter 16.)

Some herbs are easily grown indoors in pots or tubs, allowing you to snip some for flavoring whenever you wish. Herbs can also be picked and dried from your outdoor gardens, enabling you to add them to recipes all year long.

Having Tuneful Landscapes

Gardening can also be a musical experience. Songbirds sing for their supper in properly planted landscapes. Encourage insect-eating birds, and they will reward you with their singing as they help win your battle with nasty bugs, naturally. The more insect-eating birds you can attract, the more bugs they will eat. Tree and cliff swallows, swifts, wrens, and flycatchers are a good gardener's friends.

Juncos, kinglets, and song sparrows feast on scale and other minute insects. Warblers sing for their supper and make quick work of worms and weevils. Scarlet tanagers, vireos, flycatchers, and phoebes dine on moths. Flycatchers and chimney swifts are nature's mosquito-control specialists. Thrashers, meadowlarks, bluebirds, and mockingbirds all do their duty on grasshoppers, worms, caterpillars, and other unwanted insects.

Providing birdhouses, baths, nesting boxes, and shelves are only part of the picture. You and the birds can enjoy attractive shrubs, flowers, trees, vines, and windbreaks as well. Flowering shrubs and plants provide seeds, berries, and nuts. Check with your local Audubon Society for the best tips to attract insect-eating birds.

According to bird authorities, a swallow can gulp 1,000 insects in a single day. And the ever-busy house wren accounts for hundreds of spiders and caterpillars daily.

FACT

Boosting Your Property Value

One of the major advantages of landscape gardening is that it can add significantly to your property value. Realtors in various parts of the country and college researchers have conducted numerous surveys, and the good news abounds. By improving your landscaping, you can add 6 to 10 percent to the value of your home.

Veteran gardeners offer these words of wisdom to new homeowners: Plant trees and shrubs the first year. As these plants grow larger and more beautiful year after year, they will add to the value of your property.

The Gardens of the Future

More gardeners are refocusing on new looks to realize even more benefits from their gardens. Informal gardens have been popular for the past decade. Looking ahead, many leading arborists, horticulturists, and landscape designers believe that this next century will move away from the so-called cottage gardens and toward more formally designed gardens.

Classic Gardens

Taking an overview of the classic gardens that have been celebrated throughout the ages can provide insights into what the future may hold. Classic gardens are still very much appreciated today.

Longwood Gardens and Kew Gardens are just two magnificent gardens that can be partially reconstructed in your backyard. Here in America we can find classic structured gardens at Thomas Jefferson's Monticello and a classic vegetable garden at George Washington's Mount Vernon. Some of their elements are easily reproduced, as are those in other famous public and private gardens. You'll find lots of worthwhile arboretums to visit listed in Appendix B; they offer an abundant harvest of garden design ideas.

FACT

Water gardening, one of America's fastest growing garden trends, emulates Asian gardens, where water has long been appreciated as a soothing element, especially in crowded cities.

Statuary and Ornaments

Garden statuary and furniture is another element of the classic garden that seems to be gaining popularity as well. As you look ahead to discovering new gardening adventures, consider using containers of all sorts for portable color displays during the season. Think about where you can feature pergolas, statuary, and ornaments. There are many other elements you can adopt from classic gardens, including neatly clipped hedges, topiary designs, ponds and fountains, seats or benches, hanging baskets, and even sunken and walled gardens with arbors and rockeries.

Formal versus Informal

Kitchen gardens, or cottage gardens, often have their own space, usually as convenient spots to grow veggies and herbs for tasty meal making. However, as more people try to create dramatic garden displays, they realize that informal cottage gardens, depending on the artistry of the gardener, are often difficult to maintain because they tend to ramble and overgrow.

A more formal garden, bed, or border with a distinct and defined pattern can be more easily managed. A formal garden has a pattern, which can be filled in with plants and color. The gardener can design colorful tapestry gardens that delight the eye and the nose.

However, you don't have to abide by the rules of informality or formality; they can be combined. A formal garden has an outline, much like a fancy cake. Vines, which are informal, can tumble over structured walls. Plants can spring up informally from permanent stepping stones and structured paths. Gardens like these look as if they are bathed in plants, but the structure is still evident.

Chapter 13 provides basic ideas for better gardening design. *The Everything® Lawn Care Book* also provides dramatic ideas for using lawns as part of your overall plantscape designs.

Your Own Fruitful Landscape

Perhaps the greatest joy of gardening is the delicious bounty you can harvest from a fruitful landscape. The fact is berry bushes and fruit trees deserve a place in every landscape. Nothing beats the taste of freshly picked sun-ripened blackberries, blueberries, raspberries, and strawberries. Berry bushes are versatile, and newer varieties offer larger, more luscious berries, which naturally lead to pies and homemade jams.

Try a Mini-Orchard

Many gardeners overlook fruit trees because they worry that they don't have the space and they believe that caring for fruit trees is difficult. That's just not true. Today's dwarf and semi-dwarf fruit trees require very little space and yield ample quantities of full-size fruit. New, prolific, and disease-resistant varieties are readily available to make the culture of a home mini-orchard very easy and rewarding.

Two key mail-order nurseries—Stark Bro's and Miller Nurseries—offer the widest range of fruit trees and berries. Their addresses are given in Appendix C, and you can also visit their Web sites at *www.starkbros.com* and *www.millernurseries.com*, respectively.

New Trends Offer Ideas

Gardening has gained popularity even though time to garden seems increasingly scarce. Today's gardeners are demanding more color, stronger fragrances, and year-round beauty from their plants. Trying to find ways to meet these demands leads to new trends in gardening, which of course leads us to more ideas.

Bright Colors in Demand

For a decade or so, muted colors and pastels were popular. However, by the late 1990s, gardeners worldwide began to favor brighter colors. Plant breeders noted that trend and began developing brighter colored varieties in blue, chartreuse, coral, hot pink, lavender, orange, orchid, purple, red, and yellow.

Container Gardening Is Popular

Container gardening is a major trend around the world, and it's also gaining ground in America. People are using more containers in creative ways. Try container plantings in doorways and on decks, balconies, or terraces. Or use potted plants in your landscape as structured focal points or movable accents to lead the eye to the garden beds.

Fragrance Is "In" Again

As any gardener will attest, the nose knows what smells good. For many years, plant breeders concentrated on larger, more beautiful blooms, especially with roses. In the process they sacrificed fragrance. Gardeners spoke out, and loudly. They wanted perfume again!

FACT

In plant hybridizing, breeders often have to give up something to get something. Hybridizers successfully crossbred plants to gain bigger blossoms or greater disease resistance, but they lost natural fragrance in the process. Today, flower hybridizers are coming full circle by breeding to bring back long-lost common scents.

Foliage Gains Attention

Another major trend is the focus on the texture, shape, and pattern of plants. Flowers may be fleeting, but foliage is there all season. Gardeners are now mixing the textures, colors, heights, and sizes of distinctive leaves to achieve dramatic effects. Even green foliage comes in endless hues, and more plants feature bicolored leaves. Garden experts point out the values of contrasting leaves that are matte or shiny, big and broad, small and feathery, leathery or soft, smooth-edged or raggedy. These foliage factors combine to create a living tapestry, however they're mixed.

Year-Round Beauty Wanted

Many gardeners focus on the outdoor growing season. However, people are also admiring the altered winter landscape. For this they want more plants and hard elements such as fences, stones, stonework, walls, statues, arbors, columns, and benches that heighten visual interest during the colder months. Hellebore roses have climbed in popularity. So have shrubs with colored bark of distinctive shapes and growth patterns.

Short on Time

With little extra time available, some gardeners become impatient, wanting to see instant or speedier results. One solution may be to buy pregrown plants. More mail-order seed firms and nurseries, as well as local garden centers, are providing pregrown plants. Bulbs, perennials, and even shrubs that are nearly full grown are available at retail stores.

Natural Gardening Is Gaining Friends

Pioneer Americans lived by an old adage: Waste not; want not. Somewhere we lost track of that wisdom. Natural gardening is as old as recorded history and as new as you wish to make it in your backyard.

Today, millions of Americans are thinking about the values of natural foods, natural tastes, and natural gardening. Many fellow gardeners are rediscovering that better nutrition and a calmer, happier, and more productive life go hand in glove with natural vegetable gardening. Even with a small plot of ground, you can enjoy bountiful, nourishing harvests all season long. In the past few years, vegetable seed sales have been posting new records. You'll find useful down-to-earth basic information on natural gardening in Chapter 9.

Chapter 2

Pick Your Garden Pleasures

Veteran gardeners delight in expanding their growing horizons year after year as they cultivate more productively and create more glorious plantscapes. You too can open the door to your own exciting gardening experience. This chapter will give you a sneak preview of some of the adventures awaiting you as either a veteran or first-time gardener.

Grow Multipurpose Trees and Shrubs

Flowering shrubs are obviously much larger than most perennials, so they are great choices for maximizing color and adding lots of fragrance. Most shrubs are generally low maintenance. They provide winter "structure" plus early spring greenery. You can even focus on growing some with distinctive shapes, bark forms, colors, and textures that have appeal when leaves have fallen. Here are some of the favorites based on recent polls I've conducted. Not all may grow in your area so no matter how much you may like their looks, check with local garden authorities to be sure those you prefer can grow well in your locale.

Allan Swenson's Great Growing Commandment #1:
Understand what growing conditions plants need and provide them to ensure they grow to their fullest potential.

Many native deciduous azaleas have highly fragrant flowers in pastel pinks, yellows, and white. These varieties include the coast azalea, the sweet azalea, and the swamp azalea.

Box-leaf azara has small but richly fragrant flowers that smell of white chocolate in late winter and spring. It prefers sun but tolerates partial shade.

Carolina allspice or sweetbush has dark red 2-inch flowers in summer. It likes sun or partial shade.

Daphnes, especially Carol Mackie and Somerset, have super fragrance from small white or purplish flowers in late spring. Many other daphne species are highly fragrant, especially garland flower and winter daphne.

Gardenias are long-blooming evergreen shrubs that produce white flowers in summer with extraordinary fragrance. These are mainly southern plants.

Lilacs are rightfully gaining popularity again. There are hundreds of varieties of this popular 8- to 10-foot-high shrub. Among the most highly fragrant as well as disease-resistant choices are Henri Robert, excel, vauban, and Miss Kim for northern areas. In southern areas, horticultural zones 8 and 9, you must choose heat-tolerant lilac varieties such as big blue, blue skies, and lavender lady.

Mock orange is a showy delight. Most species and varieties of this old-fashioned favorite have strongly scented showy white flowers in early summer.

Koreanspice viburnum has powerfully fragrant small white flower clusters in spring. It likes sun to partial shade. Ask your local garden center for some of the different types.

Witch hazel is a treat, too, with long-lasting spidery yellow, orange, or red flowers that open in winter. It prefers part shade or sun.

Sometimes vines fit a landscape better than shrubs, especially when they grow up barren walls, sides of buildings, or fences. Here are some good multipurpose choices.

Clematis in a variety of colors is good for zones 5 through 8. Most of the large, showy hybrid clematis are not scented, but the following species are all richly scented and can be vigorous climbers up to 15 feet or more: *Clematis armandii, Clematis flammula,* and sweet autumn clematis that produce masses of star-shaped white flowers in late summer through autumn.

Honeysuckle is wonderfully fragrant, including Etruscan, common honeysuckle, and Italian honeysuckle.

Variegated kiwi vine has white flowers in early summer and grows 15 feet tall.

ALERT!

Allan Swenson's Great Growing Commandment #2:
Pull small weeds regularly so they don't steal nutrients and water from good plants.

Enjoy the Most Flavorful Vegetables

Every year many more tasty vegetables are introduced. One reason is that plant companies are wandering the world in search of new plants to introduce to attract more mail-order customers. Plant breeders also have been exceptionally busy hybridizing even better vegetables.

Veteran gardeners often like to experiment with new varieties and compare them to their old favorites. That's one way to make new and tasteful discoveries in your garden. The National Garden Bureau and All-America Selections are constantly evaluating new varieties of vegetables under different growing conditions nationwide. Their ongoing studies help home gardeners produce even more abundantly. Here's a preview of some of the newest and best veggies.

Bean–Bush yin yang is traditionally used in Latin American dishes and stews. This delicious and vivid black-and-white variety is best used as a "shell" or "dried" bean, but it can be eaten green when very young.

Bean–Pole helda is a 58-day climbing bean that produces over a long period and yields more in less space when allowed to climb on a tepee or fence. It is a great yielder of big, 9-inch–long, flat-sided Romano pods that have an absolutely wonderful flavor.

Cucumber–Diva is an All-America Selections winner. All female flowers mean a potential for higher yield for this slicing cucumber with tender skin, sweet flavor, and crisp texture. You can begin harvest in about fifty-eight days.

Lettuce–Hyper red rumple is an early-maturing (45 to 55 days) variety. The deeply savoyed leaves on this loose-leaf variety exhibit a wonderful, plum-colored, blistery appearance. This plant tends to spread to 12 inches while only reaching a height of 5 to 6 inches and represents a truly unique addition to any salad.

Pea–Sugar snap sugar star is an improved version of the original stringless sugar snap pea, sugar daddy. In trials, sugar star has provided great tasting pods that harvest one to two days earlier than sugar daddy. This variety is an excellent garden addition for flavorful recipes.

Pepper–Super heavyweight is the biggest, heaviest, thickest-walled, sweetest bell pepper introduced to date. It is great for giant stuffed peppers. The pepper fruits turn gold when mature.

Squash–Summer super zuke is a zucchini you do not have to pick small. You can harvest these substantial fruits at 12 inches long and over 3 inches wide. Use them grilled or baked in stews or fresh in salads.

Tomato–Agriset 8279 grape has a funny name but is a sweet, bite-size grape tomato that bears twenty-plus fruits on large indeterminate-type plants in seventy-five days. The small, bright red grape-size fruit are firm and are rated highly for their texture, flavor, and crack tolerance.

ALERT!

Allan Swenson's Great Growing Commandment #3: Buy the best hybrid seed varieties to grow the most beautiful flowers and prolific vegetables.

Use Garden Labor Savers

Everyone is pressed for time today, but we still have an urge to garden. Here are twelve useful tips for saving time by growing more productively.

1. Mow your lawn regularly. Too often we create extra work by planting in areas that require hand trimming. Avoid irregular plantings and trees and fences in the middle of lawns.
2. Use flexible plastic edging sunk in the soil where flowerbeds and borders merge with lawns. This edging keeps grass and other plants in their proper places.
3. Edge lawns with brick, flagstone, or other dividers to make neat borders and reduce hand trimming, weeding, and clipping.

4. Keep tools sharp. Soil sticks to dull, dirty hoes and shovels. Dull pruning shears and saws make cutting difficult and can tear bark. Spending a few minutes each winter cleaning and sharpening tools saves hours when garden activity is busiest.

5. Plant ground covers, ivy, various creepers, myrtle, and similar plants to solve slope problems. These plants will cover the ground and save mowing time.

6. Select new trees and shrubs carefully. Learn about their mature height and shape so they won't overgrow their location. Choose natural dwarf shrubs, such as spreading junipers instead of taller types, to reduce pruning time.

7. Remember: An ounce of prevention saves hours of cure for insects and diseases. Just a few minutes spraying gardens to thwart pests avoids the anguish of fighting major battles against bugs later.

8. Let sprinklers do the watering. Bubbler and soaker hoses are handy to water shrubs, trees, beds, and borders well. Rotating and traveling sprinklers water the lawn while you do other things. A timer is handy to turn water on and off automatically, allowing you to save both water and money.

9. Use mulch; it's one of the best garden labor savers. Try spreading old leaves, compost, shavings, bark chips, grass clippings, or black plastic. Mulch helps smother weeds and retain soil moisture. It looks attractive and saves hours of weeding, watering, and general care.

10. Plan ahead. Jot down important dates to do specific garden jobs next year.

11. Grow wildflowers instead of grass. It's a popular new trend. Wildflowers are hardy, require little care, and save gas and mowing time while they provide blooming beauty along property borders, on slopes, and other difficult spots.

12. Use controlled-release fertilizers that provide plant nutrition over the entire season so plants thrive and you don't need to add fertilizer so often during the growing season.

Allan Swenson's Great Growing Commandment #4:
Give vegetables a balanced fertilizer diet regularly so they grow most productively.

Cultivate Youthful Fellowships

Gardening offers a new world of sharing, especially with youngsters; it helps them grow better in their new hobby and in life. Gardening teaches responsibility and opens doors to lifelong avocations. You'll find many suggestions in Chapter 19, but as a starter, here's one of the best ideas that has sprouted in years.

Growing More Than Plants

We all know that many students don't really enjoy learning chemistry or math, among other subjects, but experience has shown that they all seem to like growing plants. The logical answer is to use this activity to teach other subjects that students may not be as enthusiastic about. And that is exactly what the National Garden Bureau, the National Science Foundation, and the National Gardening Association accomplished.

These three organizations funded a joint venture to donate commercially produced growth chambers called GrowLabs to selected elementary schools around the United States. In addition to the growth chambers, the three companies contributed supplies such as seeds and growing media.

FACT

The GrowLab unit is 52 inches wide by 23 inches deep and 39 inches tall. It fits on a tabletop and has a metal frame that holds two 4-foot light fixtures with special grow lights and plastic trays to hold plants. There is a 24-hour timer to control the lights, a climate control tent to regulate humidity, and a guidebook to help the teacher get the most from having a GrowLab in the classroom.

Bring In the Professionals

Although the program provides lesson plans for using the GrowLab to teach a variety of subjects through experimentation, the National Garden Bureau also arranges for a seed company professional to adopt the designated classroom or school, provide advice, and visit the classroom to answer questions.

Professionals like Nona Wolfram Koivula, executive director of the National Garden Bureau, who are involved with the classroom projects, report that they have been a very rewarding experience. Koivula was impressed with the enthusiasm and intelligence of the students; as they began growing plants, other subjects began to fall into place for them.

The nationally recognized gardening leader points out that growing plants enables students to see beyond the plants themselves. She notes that students readily see that plants not only provide food but also fabrics and building supplies. In the process, students learn that the climate can help or hinder agriculture and that not every place has the best soil for plant production.

Koivula noted that depending on what a classroom teacher does with the GrowLab program, students can also learn about business from growing and selling plants. They have to use math and other subjects including selling methods and record keeping.

ALERT!

Allan Swenson's Great Growing Commandment #5:
Recycle organic matter into compost to improve your soil and enrich your garden.

Teachers Praise the Program

Alan Roth, a teacher at Washington State School for the Blind in Vancouver, reported that the GrowLab has provided a variety of lessons for students in grades six, seven, and eight. Roth notes that some of his students who are totally blind learned spatial awareness by standing up after watering the plants and hitting their heads on the lights. He also learned not to put his briefcase near the GrowLab because it can get watered. Roth is convinced that the GrowLab also teaches responsibility; if the plants die because someone forgot to water them, other students urge better care. He believes that the project ties together math, biology, chemistry, and social studies as well. Not only do kids develop a healthy self-esteem by growing good plants, they receive praise from their classmates.

At the William Beye Elementary School in Oak Park, Illinois, fourth grade teacher Jan Weerts has used a GrowLab for two years. What began as two large social studies and science units allowed the class to study the prairie and rain forest, grow flowers and vegetables, and learn about food.

FACT

The National Garden Bureau considers children's gardening to be one of its most important missions. The nonprofit organization intends to continue donating GrowLabs to schools through the twenty-first century. For more information about the GrowLab and other educational programs, write to the National Gardening Association, 180 Flynn Avenue, Burlington, Vermont 05401.

Think International Flavor Favorites

Gardening is growing globally. One way to learn more about the wide world of gardening is on the Internet. As you discover how to grow plants from other countries, you'll learn more about the cultures and their cuisines. And that leads to tastier eating, naturally.

Not many years ago, futurists talked about how modern-day workers could counterbalance their "high-tech, low-touch" work lives with "high-touch, low-tech" activities like gardening. The opportunity to be involved in an activity that requires planning, creating, touching, feeling, tasting, and smelling is a natural balance to a day spent using a computer. The futurists were right. Gardening continues to be one of America's favorite activities.

Internet Garden Connections

There are a growing number of gardening information sites on the Internet that can provide answers, display color illustrations, help with planning, and sell you a wide variety of supplies and tools. (Check out Appendix C for a list.)

If you don't have access to the Internet, call your local library or a computer store for locations of public computers. For a fee, you'll be able to surf the Net.

Using Search Engines

Unless you have visited a site before, chances are you may not know how to reach a certain place or company or even what's out there. You are not alone; that is why there are marvelous things called search engines. These sites are starting points for finding places to go when you don't know a lot about what you are looking for.

Although there are several search engines out there, three popular sites are Yahoo! at *www.yahoo.com*, WebCrawler at *www.webcrawler.com*, and Google at *www.google.com*. Once you contact these sites, type the word *garden* or *gardening* in the Search box provided and a whole list of gardening sites will pop up. If you want to contact a particular company, type in the name and as much address information as you have.

ALERT!

Allan Swenson's Great Growing Commandment #6:
Plant an extra row of vegetables to donate to your local food pantry.

Here are some leading garden firms and their Web site addresses with brief notes about what they offer.

W. Atlee Burpee Co. at *www.burpee.com*—You can order a catalog, seeds, plants, and supplies, and hook up with other sites.

The Cook's Garden at *www.cooksgarden.com*—You can order a catalog, seeds, and supplies for the American kitchen garden.

Johnny's Selected Seeds at *www.johnnyseeds.com*—You can order a catalog and flower, herb, and vegetable seeds, get growing advice, and see photos of some varieties.

Nichols Garden Nursery at ✍ *www.nicholsgardennursery.com*—You'll find international vegetables plus herbs and rare seeds. Order a catalog, seeds, and supplies, and get recipes and a garden tip of the week.

Park Seed Co. at ✍ *www.parkseed.com*—You can order seeds and supplies, e-mail customer service to get growing advice, and find links to other sites.

You can explore the great growing world whenever and wherever you wish. Opportunities to expand your growing horizons abound today. Finding them is easier than digging into the ground. You can do it with a click of your mouse.

ALERT!

Allan Swenson's Great Growing Commandment #7:
Always read and heed complete label directions before using any pesticides.

Learn the Value of Gardening Therapy

Horticultural therapy dovetails perfectly with the current emphasis on mind-body healing according to Charles Sourby. He has taught many classes on this important aspect of gardening, including a major program at the New York Botanical Garden. His insights are especially worthwhile because they reach the deepest roots of gardening.

According to Sourby, his key program explores the healing of the soul that gardening offers. He points to biblical gardens, Asian gardens, and the writings of ancient and current mystics, which he believes are intertwined. In his talks and programs, Sourby notes that connecting with soil, seeds, and gardens leads people to the presence of God and the mysterious rhythm of healing and growth. He uses this approach in his horticultural therapy programs.

Spiritual Garden Focus

Another of Sourby's theories is also worth further consideration. Many people in senior housing, rest homes, and nursing facilities have deep and abiding religious faith. He notes that plants that are mentioned in the Bible are a living link between people of those distant times and people today. Plants played a significant role in the Bible. Many scriptural references describe the beauty of flowers; the flavors and uses of foods, herbs, and fruits; and the importance of trees for building homes. Using scriptural references, Sourby can help people relate the biblical plants that they grow in their gardens to spiritual experiences. This is another focus of his horticultural therapy programs.

Allan Swenson's Great Growing Commandment #8:
Try growing wildflowers for a carefree, natural growing experience.

Fresh Air and Sunshine Help

Just growing plants can be beneficial, Sourby explains in his classes. Fragrant, tasty herbs planted in beds and borders can entice people to get up from their beds or chairs, go into the garden, smell the flowers, and taste the herbs. Sourby believes there is great value in such experiences that lift people from their worries and remind them of happier times. In addition, the physical activity of planting seeds, smelling flowers, and tasting herbs and fresh vegetables can give ailing people a new enthusiasm for life. Gardening gives them something to look forward to each day beyond taking medication, watching TV, or just sitting in their rooms.

Growing vegetables also provides daily exercise, a project, and some time in the sunshine and fresh air, all of which have therapeutic value, Sourby believes. One of the keys is making gardening simple by using easy-to-grow plants like lettuce, tomatoes, and squash. Container gardens—just a pot, bucket, or tub with a few plants—can be rewarding, giving people their own little garden on a windowsill, balcony, or doorway.

Allan Swenson's Great Growing Commandment #9:
Lend a hand to children, helping them dig in and grow better in many worthwhile ways.

Many people experience the deepest sense of peace in the solitude and safety of the garden. Sourby believes that people associate green with nature's cycles; it is the emblem of new growth. Water symbolizes purity and rebirth; its cleansing properties are both literal and metaphorical. In the presence of water, people feel invigorated and strengthened by nature's resilience and beauty, even as the soft, quiet motion calms them.

Gardening Philosophy for Thought

Charles Sourby is a thoughtful, dedicated, devoted gardener who teaches the therapeutic value of gardening. Over the years, he has shared many aspects of his gardening philosophy with me and with many others. Here are a few of his key thoughts for your thoughtful reference:

- People find solace in the permanence of nature, but a garden's eternal character derives from the very fact that it is always changing.
- In their everyday lives, people may grudgingly accept change. In the garden, however, they nurture and celebrate its stunning beauty.
- Just as humans balance change and pressure in an endless variety of ways, plants lace together a myriad of forms and designs across the garden as time goes by.
- Like a composer, a gardener can orchestrate the sound of the garden, planting the notes to elicit musical responses from the vast world of insects and animals as well as other sources such as water, wind chimes, or rustling grasses.
- A seat or a bench sets up a vantage point that outlines the boundaries of the garden, limiting vistas and defining the space as distinct from other places.

ALERT!

Allan Swenson's Great Growing Commandment #10:
Count your blessings every day as you create a more beautiful, tasteful, healthier world, wherever you live.

Sourby's inspiring thoughts and focus are well worth considering in our frenzied world today. Perhaps he has recaptured some of the essence of the ancient monastic gardens. Perhaps his ideas can lead you to design a quiet spot for meditation and inspiration!

Chapter 3

E **Expand Your Growing Horizons**

The gardening world has been growing in many delightful and delicious directions. More specialty firms have sprouted and taken root. In addition, you can expand your gardening horizons with heirloom varieties, exotic international favorites, new and productive hybrid varieties, and enjoy greater success than ever before.

The National Garden Bureau

The National Garden Bureau (NGB) is one of America's reliable gardening information sources. Sponsored by leading seed companies, this group focuses on spotlighting growing trends and providing down-to-earth help for gardeners. They offer hands-on information on how to decorate your outdoor living space with the beauty of flowers and the value of raising vegetables. Their focus is providing advice about growing from seed, whether old favorites, the newest hybrid, or open-pollinated varieties. They also help gardeners with advice on purchasing the best flower and vegetable bedding plants and prestarted plants.

As a major organization dedicated to helping people grow better, this group also sends out many useful news releases to garden writers nationwide. There are more than 1,500 members of the Garden Writers Association of America whose articles appear in many magazines, newspapers, and garden club newsletters. Keep your eyes open for news, tips, and ideas from NGB in local media. Clip and save to have the latest updates, news of best varieties, award-winning flowers and veggies, and good growing pointers, too.

The National Garden Bureau is a nonprofit organization. You can reach them at ✑ *www.ngb.org*. The Web site provides gardening tips and links to member seed firms that provide sources for plants and their own growing advice. You can also focus on the gardening help offered by individual seed companies and plant firms. Many colorful, informative free catalogs are offered. Take advantage of that pool of gardening knowledge. Besides, when winter winds wail and your green thumb begins to itch, garden catalogs arrive to give a preview of another great growing year. Enjoy that experience!

Get Free Information

Let your fingers do the walking and you'll become an expert gardener. Catalogs include more than just details about plants. They provide a wealth of great growing ideas, tips, and advice. They also provide vistas of new plants introduced from around the world. In today's interconnected communications world, you can reach out and harvest an abundance of knowledge.

Many top horticulturists and expert gardeners work for leading mail-order seed and nursery firms. Many mail-order firms add helpful tips for growing plants, when to pick veggies, and how to use herbs and also sometimes publish recipes in their catalogs. Some gardeners clip and save what they want in their own loose-leaf binders, which is a convenient way to collect the tips you want for handy reference each year.

You can tap into top gardening talent at dozens of colorful, informative Web sites on the Internet and print out pages of valuable information. There's a wealth of data in cyberspace to be harvested. Pick what you wish and it is yours! Even if you don't have a computer or connection to the Internet, all schools and libraries do. Many libraries give free or low-cost classes on using computers and help you learn the skills to reach around the world to pick out the information you want.

If you haven't surfed the Web for great gardening ideas and advice, you're missing bushels of useful information and hundreds of free pages about every aspect and type of gardening. In addition, you can probably find new gardening friends and swap ideas and maybe even seeds and plants. Think globally and grow locally.

Be aware that you can also dial toll-free numbers for expert personal answers to your garden questions from various firms. You often can find those phone numbers in their catalogs. Equally helpful, you can get free answers by e-mail from experts at many seed, plant, and garden product firms.

Mail Order Gardening Association

The Mail Order Gardening Association (MGA) is the world's largest group of companies that specialize in providing garden products via mail order and online. At MGA's periodically revised Web site, ✐ *www.mailordergardening.com*, you can find smart shopper tips and what to do when your order arrives. They also have more than 130 members who offer illustrated catalogs packed with tips and ideas.

The best thing about this site is the impressive list of member companies categorized by type of product: annuals, perennials, fruit trees, garden supplies, and fertilizer. There are twenty-six companies listed under "bulbs" alone!

Click onto a company name and up pops a short description of the catalog's offerings, phone number, and address. Click on the hotlink and you're instantly connected to the catalog's homepage. This Web site is a great place to start when you want to see just how many garden seed, plant, product, and accessory firms are online. You also can find toll-free numbers for companies that will respond to your gardening questions.

Garden.com

Garden.com bills itself as the "ultimate resource for everything gardening," and it just might be. There are buckets of information on subjects ranging from composting to planting perennials, and there's always a handy tip of the day. These tips are added periodically. Regularly scheduled "chats" enable you to converse with expert gardeners. The regional garden section is very useful for getting growing tips that are applicable to your area. You can also buy just about anything you have ever wanted to plant or use in your garden.

Gardening Magazines

Naturally you can also subscribe to such fine and useful magazines as *Horticulture*, *Fine Gardening*, *Sunset*, and others. Libraries usually have one and often several different gardening magazines available. Check out articles on new varieties, gardening products, and ideas. You may even meet other gardeners at the library who will share their love and knowledge of gardening with you.

The Bulb Lady

Bulb gardening is growing in popularity and the Bulb Lady, Debbie Van Bourgondien, has a colorful, useful Web site at *www.dutchbulbs.com*. Here you'll find timely articles about virtually every kind of bulb. If the feature articles don't answer your question, just ask the Bulb Lady. She'll e-mail you a personalized answer. This site features a colorful, informative catalog of bulb plants assembled in one convenient place. The catalog can also be ordered by mail.

Tools of All Types

When you need just the right tool or piece of equipment and can't find it locally, check the Gardener's Supply Company site ✍ *www.gardeners.com*. This site features the fine merchandise found in their printed catalogs and periodically includes online bargains. In addition, you can search an extensive Q&A library of helpful gardening information. If your question still hasn't been answered, you can e-mail the staff and receive a response within forty-eight hours. Or drop them a line at ▣ 128 Intervale Road, Burlington, Vermont 05401, and request their catalog. Other good mail-order firm catalogs for tools include Burpee, Park Seed, Mellinger's, Charley's Greenhouses, Miller Nurseries, and Johnny's Selected Seeds. Their addresses are given in Appendix C, which contains a snail mail checklist of my favorite mail-order firms offering a wealth of gardening information in their free catalogs.

FACT

Thomas Jefferson once wrote: "The greatest service which can be rendered any community is to add a useful plant to its culture." By that standard, the Thomas Jefferson Center for Historic Plants Web site, ✍ *www.monticello.org*, is a natural treasure that every gardener should visit.

Grow Forward with Old-Time Plants

You can grow forward with new hybrids in your garden or find historic heirloom plants and conduct revealing and rewarding research about them as you expand your gardening knowledge. If you love old-type gardens, visit some of the Old World places and historic sites listed in Appendix B. As the focus on heirloom and grandma's garden treasures expands, many mail-order firms are locating and offering some of the best varieties of the century. (See Appendix C for a list of addresses.)

It's a new trend worth trying. At ✍ *www.monticello.org*, you can browse through a library of articles about Thomas Jefferson's gardens or look through an online catalog for an eighteenth-century suggestion for your own garden. An impressive selection of seeds, bulbs, plants, and trees is available.

Gain Global Gardening Tips

Sometimes it pays to look beyond America's borders to learn some very ancient gardening secrets. Take a trip to the Holy Land by Internet. You can visit a 650-acre Biblical Garden Preserve in the Holy Land at ✍ *www.neot-kedumim.org.il*. This is a labor of love, recreating an extensive preserve with the flowers, herbs, vegetables, fruits, trees, and some of the fauna mentioned in the Scriptures. With a click of the mouse you can take a virtual walk on various trails, see glorious photos of plants, and broaden your horizons.

For herb gardeners, there's ✍ *www.wholeherb.com*. You'll find a host of worthwhile ideas and a bountiful harvest of tasty recipes to try. Fruitful gardens are also gaining popularity. Stark Bro's at ✍ *www.starkbros.com* and Miller Nurseries at ✍ *www.millernurseries.com* are two of America's foremost fruit and berry suppliers. Their sites are tasteful sources for information about fruit trees and berry bushes. Topics ranging from planting and pruning to harvesting and controlling pests is at your fingertips.

For organic gardening, which is immensely popular today, call up Organic Gardening at ✍ *www.organicgardening.com*. They're America's experts and advice is plentiful. As you surf the Web, you'll find hundreds of articles, information pages, and other material you may wish to save. Most sites allow you to download and print out pages of helpful ideas, tips, and advice.

Try Test Plots of Special Plants

You can really soar into new growing experiences with exotic plants. More seed firms are offering special heirloom varieties that have been rediscovered, which is encouraging some home gardeners to test those old favorites and even try their hand at crossbreeding new varieties. There seems to be a bit of the scientist in many home gardeners today.

Another excellent source for special plants are the many specialty plant associations that you can find on the Internet. Just enter the names of exotic or special plants on Google or another search engine. Specialty plant associations welcome inquiries and are looking for new members. If you have knowledge or plants to swap or share, there's a growing world awaiting you today.

ALERT!

Be aware that there are special rules governing shipping plants to different states. You should always check with the county extension agent or state plant inspection office before becoming involved in shipping plants. Insects or diseases may be in soils or on plants, and plant inspection rules make sure such problems aren't spread around the country.

Garden Clubs and Guilds

Keep an eye out for local garden club, church, and service club plant and garden supply sales in your area. Often members grow many extra seedlings and have root cuttings and a variety of garden items to sell each spring as fundraising projects for their organization. Ask around. You may discover nearby clubs that you can join to really expand your gardening knowledge in your own backyard.

Watch local newspapers, too. You'll probably see notices of local clubs, plant sales, perhaps even courses given by the county extension office—a gold mine of garden know-how. That's their job, helping farmers and gardeners to grow better. Call them up, attend meetings, and get free flyers, brochures, and specific how-to literature. County extension offices are affiliated with your state land grant college. Each year most land grant colleges offer courses and have open house events for gardeners. Tap into your local and state experts.

Depending on your interests, there are dozens of specialty garden clubs, guilds, and organizations. One way to find them is to ask your local librarian for a directory of Specialty Garden Clubs and Societies. You'll be amazed at what you find.

FACT

To receive a Garden Catalog Guide, send $2 by check or money order to the Mailorder Gardening Association, ⌨ Dept. SC-AS, P.O. Box 2129, Columbia, Maryland 21045. This guide also lists dozens of garden firms with toll-free telephone numbers, advice hotlines, e-mail addresses, and Web sites to browse through at your leisure.

Ask Around Town

In this fast-paced world of high-tech wonders, people tend to think in terms of e-mail, Web sites, chat rooms, and other multimedia avenues of communication to have their questions answered. But sometimes it is far easier to just ask around. Local garden centers are in business because the owners probably love gardening and know which plants do well in your area. Naturally they want you to buy seeds, plants, and supplies from them. In exchange, they can provide you with an abundance of valuable gardening information. So can local nurseries.

You get to see the colors and shapes and sizes of flowers, shrubs, and other plants in season. Seeing them lets you visualize how they will look in your garden. And you can find out which really *will* grow in your area. Sometimes those that have great appeal in colorful catalogs just don't thrive or even survive in your horticultural zone. That's a big reason to shop for information and garden products and plants locally.

Major chains have been expanding their garden centers as well. A few years ago, many chain stores simply stocked up with plants for the garden season but didn't always have someone who could give advice about them. Times have changed. Many veteran gardeners say there is nothing quite like a homegrown garden center or nursery owner for good advice. However, today more chains are hiring men and women with gardening savvy. Stop, ask, tune in, and make your own decisions. Compare advice, too. Many different gardeners have different approaches and degrees of experience and expertise to offer. Ⓔ

Chapter 4

Tool Up Well and Wisely

Pick the right tools for the job and your gardening gets easier every time you dig into a growing project. Today you have a wide array of basic tools plus gadgets, mowers, sweepers, and power equipment of all types. This chapter gives you an overview of the best tools for your gardening activities and key reasons for choosing them.

Digging Devices for Easy Gardening

How you go about gardening is up to you, your budget, and, in all likelihood, a spousal debate on a shredder versus a new refrigerator. Keep in mind, gardening today doesn't need to be primitive dig-by-hand grunt work. Tool up to enjoy outdoor chores. For whatever size or type of garden you have, some tools are basic, others are useful, some are handy for special jobs, and others are a luxury. But all are nice to have.

Every gardener has his or her choice for must-have tools. The list usually increases just before spring, about the time those colorful, tempting seed catalogs arrive.

Good Tools Are Essential

For the serious gardener, a checklist of basic tools is helpful. At the top of that list should be a good, reliable lawn mower. The mower does not have to be expensive, but it should be made by a reliable firm and have a solid, sturdy frame and an adjustable cutting height.

Beware the bargain lawn mowers that show up in special spring sales. They may be inexpensive, but too often they are lightweight and poorly made. They just won't hold up for years of lawn mowing, as a sturdier mower will. Shop around and remember that in gardening as in life, you get what you pay for.

As every professional contractor knows, good tools are essential. For gardeners, a spade, shovel, rake, spading fork, hoe, and hand trowel should be on the list of basic tools. Again, look for sturdy, well-made tools. Cheaper, lighter tools may last for a few seasons, but they probably won't give you the service you deserve and will get from quality tools.

I hope you'll be gardening for many seasons, so consider your tools a one-time, permanent investment. Good tools are a sound investment. They can take a pounding. They have a better "feel" when you are using them. And you can sharpen them each winter so they will work better in the spring.

Somehow, cheap tools tend to feel like junk. Treat yourself to good tools and you'll enjoy gardening more. In shopping for gardening tools, people sometimes get carried away by the colorful ads in the Sunday newspaper supplements. It pays to check old, reliable suppliers, including reputable firms like Sears. Their Craftsmen tools are rated as some of the best available for sturdiness, durability, and quality as well as reasonable cost.

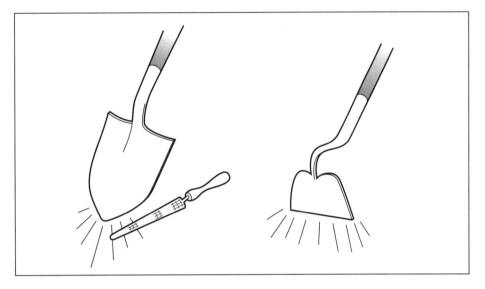

▲ Keep gardening tools sharp to ensure safety and efficiency.

FACT

Did you know that people are buying more garden and household tools than ever before? Statistics also reveal that more people are buying plants and becoming involved in all phases and types of gardening.

Listing the Basics

Here is a list of the typical tools you should have. You will find them useful, particularly on special projects. Logic dictates that you focus on your garden plans and invest in the tools that you will need most. As you expand your growing horizons, you can add to your list, including tools that are designed for special projects such as planting bulbs or close cultivating around plants with shallow roots. As you comparison shop, jot down prices next to each tool.

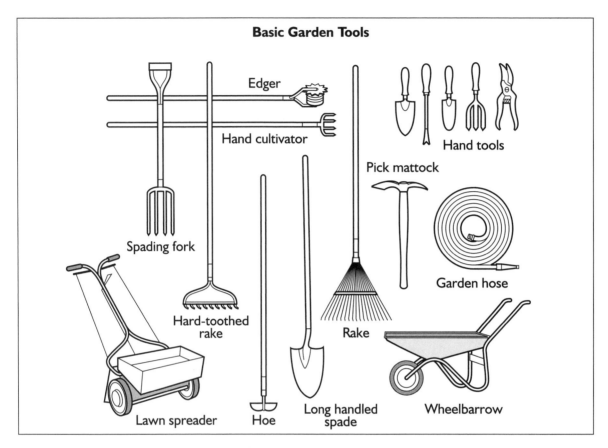

Basic Garden Tools

Edger

Hand cultivator

Hand tools

Pick mattock

Spading fork

Garden hose

Hard-toothed rake

Rake

Lawn spreader

Hoe

Long handled spade

Wheelbarrow

▲ The right tools make gardening easy

▶ BASIC GARDEN TOOLS

- Ax
- Cord: 100-foot ball
- Cord: Heavy-duty 500 feet
- Cultivator: Four-tine type
- Hand cultivator
- Hand rake
- Hand shears: The grass clipping type
- Hand shears: Heavy-duty pruners
- Hand trowel

- Hoe
- Metal file: For sharpening tools
- Pick or mattock
- Pruning saw
- Rake: Firm, fixed tines (metal)
- Rake: Flexible tines (metal or bamboo) for leaves
- Shovel: Long handle

- Sickle
- Sledgehammer
- Spade: Round point digger
- Spade: Square blade
- Spading fork: D-handle
- Spading fork: Long, straight handle
- Weeder bar: Weed cutter
- Wire brush: For cleaning tools

The Amazing Tiller

Shovels are handy, spades are fine, but give me a tiller any old time. That is not quite an old English verse, but it pins the point. After a lawn mower, a rototiller should be your next power investment. Here's why. Want to renovate a lawn that is only 50 by 100 feet? How many times will you turn a spade to prepare a seedbed that size? A good tiller will do it in an hour or so.

FACT

An 8-horsepower Troy-Bilt tiller earned its $1,400 cost in one season for a local gardener. He put in ten flower beds, 125 feet long and 6 feet wide, in one weekend. The flowers he grew and sold at his roadside stand paid for the tiller and left him a profit. Every year since, he's grown dollars and his tiller's gotten a thank-you pat on the chassis.

Tillers Make Life Easier

Veteran gardeners say that a solid, variable-speed, forward and reverse rotary tiller is the most useful power equipment purchase you can make after a lawn mower. A rototiller makes gardening easier from turning under sod and making new beds to cultivating areas during the growing season.

A sturdy, reliable rotary tiller takes the strain out of more gardening hours than you would care to count over the years. It is a friend indeed. Rotary tillers till, aerate, cultivate, and deep plow. They perform these functions quickly, efficiently, and with little effort. That sure saves the back! However, as useful as rototillers are, veteran gardeners realize that it is important to focus on the basics, those tools that you will use most often for your garden and landscape projects.

Tiller Shopping Tips

There are tillers with straight blades and those with blades that curve slightly at each end. The latter type will perform best in most situations. It cuts through old sod, is more effective in turning surface material, and loosens soil better.

When you shop for a tiller, consider carefully what you want it to do. If you intend to turn under sod and churn heavy soil to mix in humus, you probably need a higher horsepower tiller. Think about the areas where you will be gardening. In most cases, there will be corners and odd spots that require tight turns. Insist on a reverse drive or gear on the tiller. Remember, you can more easily back out under power than lift, tug, and haul a heavy machine back into the proper position.

Slow and fast speeds are helpful, too. Some units have variable speeds based on the throttle. Others have ranges at different settings. Be sure to ask for a demonstration or trial. Find out about the warranty period for a tiller or any major piece of equipment; you want to know your rights to return it or get repairs if needed.

Pay Attention to Your Tiller

Tillers require periodic attention. Drive shafts take a beating in rocky or clay soils. Engines can heat up as dust and dirt clog air intakes. Change oil and air filters as specified, and lubricate all parts that require it.

Be sure to try out new power equipment before putting it to work. A strong tiller, mishandled, can walk away from its new owner and chop down half a row of valuable plants. Some machines have built-in safeguards to prevent this, but some don't. In general, when you lower the handles, the tiller bites deeper into the earth. When you raise the handles, it cultivates and moves forward. Using the wheels that attach to most units will ensure light cultivation and minimum deep digging. The depth gauge is helpful, but it takes some experience to get the "feel" of using a rototiller properly. Your best bet is to get a feel for how it works for deep tilling and cultivating by trying it out in areas that aren't too important.

Memorize this sentence: "I will read the owner's manual before I try to use my power equipment." Repeat it and heed what the manual says. You'll save yourself grief and enjoy better gardening when you use your power equipment as it was designed.

Time-Saving Tools

Americans seem busier than ever these days. Perhaps it's a sign of the times. Perhaps it's also a sign that people should slow down, dig in, and grow better in gardens and in their lives.

Power equipment does fit into the busy gardener's tool checklist. Depending on the extent of your gardens and future growing plans, you can add the power tools that best fit your needs. A riding mower is one delight, especially if you have a large lawn. In addition, a riding mower lets you drive around your property in comfort while enjoying the blooming beauty and plantscapes that are part of your growing world.

If you have a large property, consider buying a shredder. Finely chopped or shredded organic matter composts faster because smaller pieces decay more quickly. Although a rotary mower can be used on leaves, mulch, and grass clippings to grind them for soil improvement, a shredder may be more useful on larger pieces of ground. Improved machines are now available that shred, grind, and practically pulverize any organic materials put through them; depending on their horsepower, that includes small pieces of brush and saplings.

Power Equipment Adviser

Think power and you can get a lot of work done without a backache. Of course, don't forget your budget and family priorities. Logic says that people should only purchase what they really need.

This section contains a few tips for getting the most out of your power equipment.

Keep the blades on your rotary mower sharp for better cutting and nicer-looking lawns. Rotary mowers cut by the whirling action of the blades. If allowed to become dull, blades may still cut but you'll notice that an eighth to a fourth of the grass blade tip is torn. Moisture evaporates more easily from bruised grass leaves, so you'll notice that in a day or so, grass cut with a dull rotary mower will have a brownish haze. Use the bagger attachment to your lawn mower. It is a marvelous tool that will keep your lawn clean of clippings. And you'll be able to put those clippings to use as mulch or to make compost. That's a big plus because every time you recycle organic matter to make compost or let mulch decay, you gain improved soil condition.

Look for a simple adjustable cutting height in a mower. Some mowers require an engineering degree to change the cutting height. You will want to cut lower in spring and more frequently when the grass is growing rapidly. Then, as summer heat arrives, raise the cutting height to give grass a better growing advantage in drier conditions.

If a lawn is growing very fast, mow at a higher level one day and at a lower level a day or so later; that way you won't shock the grass by cutting too much off at once. If that sounds like extra work, think what good exercise it is for you, and you don't even have to visit a health club.

ALERT!

Never attempt to unclog the exhaust chute area of a mower until the mower is shut down and the spark plug wire is disconnected. One pull on the blade to free an obstruction could start the mower and cut off your fingers or hand. It also pays to let the mower cool down. Too many people have burned themselves on hot exhaust pipes.

Shopping for Garden Tools

It pays to shop around. Craftsmen tools are popular for their quality and durability. Other chain stores, including hardware chains, offer their own brands. Try visiting garage and lawn sales; you may find exceptional bargains. Families move every year for business, personal, or retirement reasons. As a result, perfectly sound tools are often available at a fraction of their retail cost. Many veteran gardeners have filled in their tool wish list with top-quality tools in excellent condition that they found at yard sales.

Also keep an eye on classified ads. Oftentimes you'll spot that one piece of equipment you've always wanted. Before you rush to purchase it, however, remember that some equipment is sold because it isn't working right. Be sure to do a "test drive" and ask for a demonstration. If you need a rototiller, try it out. You may quickly realize that it is too cumbersome to handle, doesn't turn or dig well, or may be too small to handle your jobs. When you buy tools, buy a good sharp metal file as well. It will help you sharpen your tools, and you will sweat less while gardening. Sharp tools are safer, and they cut, dig, and till more easily.

Paint bright red, yellow, or other colored bands on the handles of your tools, or use plastic tape. That way, you will be more likely to spot them if you leave them somewhere on your property. More important, you can spot them at a neighbor's house if they've been borrowed.

Add up your own checklist and it may seem a bit much. Your best bet is to buy what you really need for the projects you have in mind. Wait for off-season sales to get the extra items you would like to have. One veteran gardener has his wish list on the visor of his car. As he spots bargains at yard sales or at stores, he has a handy reference to check which tools he needs or wants.

Improvising

There are some useful tools that you can even make yourself. If you want a narrow cultivator or tiller to use between plants in narrow rows, pick out an old metal rake at a barn sale. Cut off the outer ends with a hacksaw, and you have a 6-inch-wide mini-rake. The same idea applies to a hoe. In close plantings and for special cultivation jobs, a V-shaped hoe is perfect. You can buy one, but you can also cut an old square hoe to suit your needs.

You don't have to wait to get just the right item. Americans are noted for their ability to improvise. Nature also is most helpful, for example, by providing branches that need pruning. Those pruned branches serve well to support early peas. Use branches as stakes for marking garden rows or as trellises for pole beans and other climbing vegetables or flowers.

Sliced 6-inch slabs of trunk can provide a temporary stepping stone path in your garden or a trail through a wet area. Naturally wood will eventually rot, but sometimes it helps to have a temporary pathway and log slices can give you one.

Tools can do double duty. Paint or wrap tape around a tool handle at 6-inch intervals, and you've just created a handy measuring tool for planting, marking rows, or measuring space. You can lay the tool down when spacing bulbs or transplanting seedlings.

When you want poles for fencing or making trellises, think like a farmer. Locust, cedar, and redwood are strong and resist decay. Locust and cedar normally grow fast and tall, which makes them ideal for use as stakes, posts, and poles. All you have to do is trim off the branches. If your neighbor wants a vacant lot cleared, for example, you may be able to get good poles just by asking. Then you can tie these saplings together at the top like tepee poles to let pole beans and peas climb. This tepee makes the beans and peas easier to pick, too.

Garden Aids to Consider When Shopping

A handcart, wheelbarrow, or garden trailer to pull with your riding mower or garden tractor should be an early purchase. Many gardening friends have learned through experience that a large-wheeled, high-sided garden cart is especially practical. The things you usually carry—such as peat moss, mulch hay, or bags of fertilizer—are reasonably light but bulky.

To mark rows in your garden, wind stout cord or heavy parcel twine on a sturdy stake. Heavier cord stays taut when you stretch it between stakes. A simple reel mounted on the stake makes retrieval easy with a few spins.

When your garden space is limited, plan to grow up not out. Vertical gardening is easy. Tomatoes, peas, beans, and vine crops can and will climb. You can plant closer if you train plants on a fence, within a wire cylinder, or up a trellis.

Tomatoes, squash, and cucumbers grow well within wire cylinders. You can make the cylinders with heavy-duty farm fencing or even chicken wire stapled around wooden supports. You can accomplish the same thing by putting four poles in a 2-foot square and attaching stapling wire at intervals around them.

FACT

A wire frame that fits the inside contour of the garden cart, trailer, or wheelbarrow is a big help when raking autumn leaves. Make one of lath with chicken wire so it folds up for storage.

Sharing and Renting Tools

At this point, as you compare the tools and equipment that are necessary with those you desire, add up the total cost. Include the extras on your wish list, too. Consider where you might pare costs a bit or improvise for special uses. Or, consider pooling with family and neighbors. Each person could buy a different special tool to share. That spreads the cost out and since gardeners like to share ideas, tips, and advice, as well as brag about successes, sharing tools is also worthwhile.

As much as gardeners love their toys and tools, there is a matter of dollars and sense. If you only need to till in the spring, it is much cheaper to rent a tiller than invest $1,000 or more and then have to maintain and store it as well. Salespeople at lumber yards report that many premade sheds are sold to store tillers, mowers, grinders and shredders, power sprayers, and a host of other pieces of garden equipment. Renting and hiring equipment might be more practical for you.

Taking Care of Your Toys

When the gardening season is over, or at least the outdoor part, set aside a weekend or two for cleanup. Put your tools in order and hang them where they belong. If one or two are missing, check with neighbors—maybe you loaned them out. Repair any broken handles, splits, or cracks. Sand and repaint any splintery wood. Then clean the tools and apply a light coat of oil to all metal parts. This maintenance will ensure that you and your tools are ready for the first flush of spring.

FACT

To lift heavy things in the garden, be sure to bend at the knees and lift. Do not bend over from the waist; you'll risk pulling or straining back muscles. If in doubt, ask your doctor about the correct way to lift heavy weights to protect your back and other muscles.

Power equipment needs extra care. Read the owner's manual for each machine. Here is a basic checklist to help get the job done well:

- Drain the oil after the engine has been warmed up, then refill it for storage.
- Disconnect the spark plug wires on all gas engines.
- Drain the gas tank to avoid accumulation of gummy deposits that could clog the engine next year.
- Remove the air cleaner and wash it with kerosene or materials recommended in the manual; replace if needed.
- Clean all dirt, debris, clippings, and old grease from all areas. Use a wire brush to clean all matted grass and debris from under rotary mowers. Paint the underside with a light coat of oil and oil all moving parts.
- Check the manual and grease all points indicated; add a little grease on chain drives.
- Remove blades from rotary mowers and have them sharpened.
- Wire-brush or scrape all rusty areas and repaint if needed.
- Check the entire machine for loose screws, bolts, wiring, and anything that might need repair. (Consult the owner's manual for a parts diagram.)
- Order any replacement parts when you check your machines and put them to bed at the end of the gardening season.
- Store your tools and equipment in a protected area, away from children, if possible.
- As time permits and parts arrive, complete all repairs so your equipment is ready when spring sprouts and is maintained to give you many years of useful, productive life.

Chapter 5

Understand Your Garden Ground

Good gardening begins with an understanding of several basic points: You must pick your site well, become familiar with your growing conditions, and plan thoughtfully. This chapter will help you master these basic points to achieve the success you deserve.

Pick the Right Site

The best first step for gardening success is to pick the right location. Most plants need at least six hours of sun each day. Your garden area also needs water to give thirsty plants their needed drinks each week. You also need room to work the area so you can make garden miracles happen.

Examine your garden areas at different times of the day to see how the sun flows over it. Note where tall trees or buildings cast their shadows at different times. Remember that it is best to plant fragrant flowers upwind so their sweet scents drift to the areas where you'll be sitting, entertaining, or enjoying your flower gardens.

In areas near tall trees or paved area runoffs, you'll need to make adjustments such as extra fertilizing and directing excess water or street pollution away from the garden areas. Keep beds running north and south, when possible. That way each row has an equal amount of sunlight.

FACT

Southern exposures are best. After that, experienced gardeners prefer eastern, then western, and finally northern exposure plots. Avoid areas where shadows from trees or buildings block the sun for too long each day.

If you have slopes, consider contour planting with rows along the hill, not up and down. By following the contours of the land, you'll avoid losing topsoil and mulch during rainstorms. Also avoid nearby hedges or trees with shallow roots that draw water and nutrients from the soil. If you do naturalized plantings or grow near tree roots, plan to test the soil and fertilize periodically to nourish your flowers properly.

Understanding Your Soil

Look at your soil. Slice a profile with a spade. See how much topsoil you have and whether it is crumbly loam, sand, or clay. No matter what you find, you can improve it. You'll find useful tips for improving any kind of soil in Chapter 6.

An understanding of soils and how to improve them is basic to improving growing conditions, wherever you live and garden. Regardless of what you have, from clay to sandy soils or even construction debris and fill soil, it can be improved. Nothing happens overnight. However, by making improvements year by year, you can see amazing results. The key is organic matter. Soil changes through continuing decomposition of organic materials. Fortunately, the raw materials to improve soil are abundantly available.

Make a mental note that healthy soil lets you grow healthy plants. That's important in your pest control efforts. Insects dislike healthy plants! They prefer sickly, weak plants. Keep plants healthy and you'll thwart bugs naturally.

The bacteria and fungi in your living soil are vital contributors to soil formation because they live on animal and plant residues, which they break down from complex compounds into simpler forms. Nitrogen-fixing bacteria, for example, in the nodules of legumes, actually fix, or transfer, nitrogen from the atmosphere and help make it available in the soil for future plants.

Soil comes in various colors, types, and quality. Don't let the color fool you. Black soil can actually be low in nutrients. Reddish sandy soils can actually be good growing soils. No matter where you live or what soil you have, you can improve it and upgrade the growing conditions. Your basic objective is to aim for a balance in structure, texture, and porosity. Good gardening is a matter of balance.

All soils have several things in common. They contain organic matter, water, air, and minerals. The proportion of these elements may vary, but a soil's components remain essentially the same.

Get Your Hands Dirty

No matter where you live or what you find when you begin digging a garden, keep in mind a basic truth: All soil can be improved. Sometimes just a little effort will work wonders. Other times you may need a multiyear plan. Start by getting a feel for your soil. Crumble a handful of soil in your hands. If it crumbles freely, you are feeling the ideal texture.

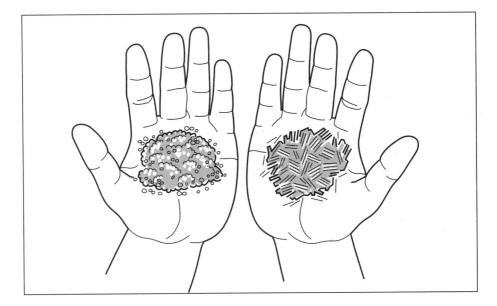

▲ Feel the soil. If it is wet, sticks together, and has clumps, it needs help. If it is sandy, you need to build up the organic matter in it. Nutrients are important, but the consistency of the growing medium is also important. The more you can rebuild soil to a granular feel, the better your garden will grow.

Heed the Advice of Locals

Reputable nurserymen and garden centers are aware of problem soil in your area. Ask for their recommendations for improving your growing ground. They usually want your business for seeds, plants, and trees and will answer questions honestly. It is up to you to know the questions to ask. There are riches in any soil, but they must be unlocked to produce a productive, bountiful garden.

ALERT!

Be aware that some homebuilders and developers may backfill poor soil around new home foundations. This soil can be rocky or heavy clay or whatever else they removed when digging the house foundation. Ask neighbors what they saw when your new home was being built. If it is poor, backfill soil, you may need the help of a local landscape contractor to replace it.

Compost Is a Vital Key

If you have sandy or clay soil, you can improve it with compost. That's one of the easiest, most effective ways to make garden ground more productive. You can turn organic matter into usable compost in just fourteen days.

Soil, like the plants that grow in it, is alive! Millions of bacteria, fungi, and microorganisms inhabit it. There is a close relationship between the amount of life in the soil and its basic fertility. The tiny animal life reduces complex organic substances such as sugars and proteins to simpler chemical forms like carbon dioxide, nitrates, and water. In this way, nutrients are again made available for plants. Successful gardening is directly related to the use of compost for enrichment of the soil. The better the compost, the better the soil.

Any soil can be improved with compost, even the hard, caked subsoil often found around new home developments. The addition of organic matter or humus through composting is the best and least expensive way to improve your soil. Topsoil contains from 2 to 8 percent organic matter by dry weight. You should continue to add organic matter every year in order to keep improving your soil bank. A good average application is about 1 inch of organic matter or humus from compost for every 4 inches of topsoil.

ALERT!

Avoid using diseased plants for compost. Despite the fact that natural heating in the center of the pile may and usually does kill most disease organisms, there are still some risks. For example, don't use peony tops if they are infected with botrytris blight or iris leaves if iris borers are a problem.

Ideally, compost that is in the process of becoming that rich, dark humus you want will not have a seriously objectionable smell—at least not to good gardeners! Many actually like the smell of soil enrichment in action. Of course, in any decomposition of organic matter, there is an odor. Also, compost pits aren't very attractive. Try putting yours in an out-of-the-way location or screen the area from view with a fence, hedge, or shrub.

▲ A good screen for compost piles

Selecting a Site

Choose a site convenient to water so you can periodically wet down the pile or pit to keep it moist. A shady area is good, but avoid low areas that collect rain and remain soggy. Bacteria that help make compost into good humus require ample moisture, air, and oxygen.

Making a Compost Pit

The next step is to construct the pit or pile. Air circulation is important because the more air that circulates through and around the pile, the faster decomposition will occur. Turning a compost pile with a spading fork is hard work, but it's necessary. It is worthwhile to have at least two piles of compost since it is in flux at all times. That way you can use finished compost from one while making more humus in the other.

Almost any organic material can be composted with the simple Indore method. This method was developed and practiced in England by Sir Albert Howard, father of the modern organic movement. It is the most practical, efficient, and widely used method for both small and large gardens.

The Basics of the Indore Method

The Indore method involves the simple layering of various materials. Start with a 6- to 8-inch layer of green organic material. Do not let the word *green* fool you. Grass clippings or dried leaves may be brown, but they are considered green matter in the terminology of organic gardening.

Over this first layer of green material (clippings, leaves, old weeds, and vegetation pulled from the garden), add a 2-inch layer of manure. Your goal is to add nitrogen to speed up the decaying process. Cow, horse, sheep, and poultry manure will do the job if you can get them locally. Today many garden centers and chain stores also have bagged manure.

The next layer in your compost pile should consist of an inch or two of garden soil. Spread that evenly to ensure effective interaction. Next, add a 1-inch layer of mixed-rock phosphate and limestone, and top it off with manure or a soil covering a few inches thick. You can usually get these materials from local garden centers or garden departments at modern chain stores.

You can build a small pile, just 4 feet wide, 4 feet long, and 4 feet high. Most gardeners find it desirable to have several smaller piles so they will be in varying stages of action and can be used as finished compost.

FACT

With the keen interest today in natural gardening, you can probably find compost-making kits through local garden centers. Many types have bins and tumblers that you can fill and then turn a crank to mix the organic material.

Watering and Spading

Keep the compost pile moist. As you apply the layers, sprinkle them with water. The material going into the pile should be moist, especially if you're using dry leaves, grass clippings, and other dry materials. When you have finished building the pile, leave a depression on the top to catch rainwater that can then trickle down through the layers.

If you are in a drought period, water the compost pile once or twice a week because two types of bacteria—aerobic and anaerobic—will be at work in your compost. Aerobic bacteria need air circulation in order to do their job. Anaerobic bacteria work more slowly and proceed without much aeration of the pile. Turning the pile by fork or spade or otherwise providing improved aeration will quicken the entire process. Spading means work, but only two or three turnings are needed before the humus is ready.

Consider building the pile around several pipes with holes through them. This method lets air penetrate, helps the heat build up as decomposition occurs, and saves your back from turning the pile. There are many other ways to accomplish similar results. Compare notes with neighbor gardeners.

Compost Activity

The elevation of composting material off the ground allows freer air circulation beneath and provides one of the easiest ways to speed up decomposition. This elevation can be done using cinder blocks, which are handy and do not rot. Space them around the area on which you will build the pile: one block, one space, one block, and so on.

Place a layer of plastic-coated fencing on the cinder blocks. Be sure to leave spaces for that vital air circulation.

Bacteria, of course, are the microscopic helpers in any compost-building activity. They are beneficial to inoculate the pile as it is built. You can buy soil bacteria cultures from various sources, but the easiest way to meet this need is to save the remnants of a previous compost pile and add some of it to the new pile. The bacteria will thrive, multiply, and go right to work.

▲ Building a compost pit using cinder blocks

Spring and summer are the best times for making compost. Sun, rain, and warm weather speed the process. Not much decay takes place in winter, so don't expect much decomposition of organic material until spring.

ALERT!

Never use treated railroad ties or attempt to treat the wood you use for making a compost bin with chemical preservatives. Contamination from unwanted chemicals could cause problems for your garden plants. Don't risk chemical pollution.

Field Composting

If you have room and can afford to wait for the slower, but easier-to-make compost to cure, you will find that field composting is ideal. Basically it is a layering method that needs no building or pit or special pile. As you gather green matter, apply it in layers to the heap. Keep adding more until you have a satisfactory 4- to 6-inch layer. Then add manure or other nitrogen-containing materials to speed up decomposition. Add more green matter until there are several layers.

By the following year, providing you take the time to turn the field pile, you will have good humus. Even if you do not turn the pile, you can expect this field composting method to yield good humus in time.

Composting is a continual process that works like a charm. The remnants you apply to the newer piles help inoculate them with more bacteria to keep the microorganism level in high gear.

Compost Materials

Just about any type of vegetation and organic matter can be put to use to make compost. You can turn garbage into humus with little effort: vegetable parings, tops of carrots, radishes, beets, corn husks, pea pods, and the outer leaves of lettuce and cabbage. Any type of organic household vegetation can be composted.

Many towns now prohibit the burning of leaves and brush, and that can be a bonus for gardeners. Some towns collect the leaves and dump them at a sanitary landfill or city dump, and more are actually composting such materials. Sometimes you can sign up to get free or very low cost compost from your town. You can also collect leaves from your own yard, let neighbors pile their leaves in your compost heap, or even help yourself to the weekly town leaf pickup.

Leaves of all types can be added to the compost pile. All weeds, extra leaves and stalks from your vegetables, grass clippings, hay collected from highway mowing, or bales of old, spoiled hay from farms make excellent source material. In all soil-improving activities, keep in mind that you are aiming for balance: balance of organic materials and balance with nature. The more variety you put into the compost, the more variety of nutrients you will obtain from the cured humus. The reason is that some plants take up more of one nutrient than another. The nutrients absorbed are transmitted throughout different parts of the plants: in roots, fruits, stems, and leaves. It follows that by using the roots and stems of some plants and the leaves and stalks of others, you will add different amounts of various elements to your compost.

ALERT!

Do not use kitchen wastes such as animal fats and bones. They decompose slowly and attract dogs and other animals. They also turn rancid and stink up the area.

Mulch Is a Marvelous Aid

Mulch is a naturally good idea. It is a simple, effective, and practical way to begin recycling nature's bounty for better gardening. Just count the reasons to be grateful for this natural discovery. You'll agree with millions of gardeners that mulching pays in many ways:

1. Mulch preserves moisture in the soil.
2. Mulch smothers weeds.
3. Mulch decays to improve soil condition.
4. Mulch helps prevent erosion.

Mulch is indeed a natural gardening bonanza. Next to composting, mulching is the single, most vital natural gardening activity.

Mulch Materials

Most of the necessary materials are easily available wherever you live, and most are free. The list of materials is endless. Consider for a moment grass clippings, leaves, chopped or ground brush and twigs, and pine needles. Basically, mulch is any material you can find as a protective covering for the soil, including straw, hay, ground corncobs, peat moss, sawdust, shavings, composted refuse you or neighbors make, and even gravel, sand, or stones. Mulch may also include peanut hulls, ground bark, redwood chips, layers of newspapers covered with grass clippings, and whatever will decompose to add nutrients to the soil. You can also use black plastic coverings and any other materials that stop weeds and help soil retain moisture.

Focus first on organic materials that break down and recycle into the earth. Whatever material you use and apply depends of course on what you have available and what works into your budget and gardening goals. If you like to see dark rich-looking soil around shrubs and trees and along garden rows, you can opt for peat moss, ground sphagnum moss, or chipped bark and wood chips. Well-decayed sawdust is darker. Redwood chips and pine bark also look nice.

Dry lawn clippings are fluffy when first spread. You can gather them from the baggers on your power mower. After a few rains, they tend to form a thin, compact layer. Grass clippings do decompose, and you can add more layers as you mow your lawn each week.

Gravel, stone chips, or even flat stones can be used as a substitute for organic mulch. They provide weed control, function as stepping stones, and hold early-season heat in the soil.

ALERT!

There are drawbacks and basic problems with some materials. Wood chips and cellulose materials draw nitrogen out of the soil, so you must compensate by adding higher nitrogen fertilizer to your garden ground.

Stop Weed Thievery

Controlling weeds is a tiresome annual chore. You can pull, cultivate, or till them away, but some weeds are frustratingly persistent. They also may leave seeds in the ground just waiting for you to till. Then the seeds sprout, grow, and rob your plants of the nutrients and moisture they need.

No doubt, weeds rob you and your garden. They compete for needed moisture from the soil, depriving other plants and shrubs of those essentials for good growth. Weeds may also host harmful insects that will cross over to attack your vegetables and flowers. Luckily, proper mulching can stop weed growth effectively. It smothers the seedlings, prevents other seeds from sprouting, and encourages those useful underground allies, earthworms, to work their wonders in the soil around your plants.

Mulch is more than a weed control effort. It is a simple, worthwhile way to improve your soil for long-range garden performance improvement.

Try Permanent Mulching

Many natural gardeners prefer permanent mulching, which is like composting right in your garden. As organic mulch materials decay, they continue to produce humus. To plant flower seedlings or bulbs, just move the mulch and plant. When seedlings are up and growing well, apply mulch around them to thwart any weeds.

At the end of a garden season, you can leave mulch in place or till it under to further improve soil texture, condition, and fertility. Because mulch materials may not be readily available in large quantities, selective mulching fits better into most garden plans.

Compost is your best mulch. As you create compost and humus, it provides an attractive, more useful mulch because it already contains some nutrients. In addition, the original composting process, which generates high temperatures in compost piles, also destroys many weed seeds.

Keep one thought in mind with all types of mulch. It is usually necessary to add a nitrogen source to the mulch. Some mulches, wood shavings and wood chips especially, require extra nitrogen to assist in decomposition and in maintaining the balance of fertility you need for optimum plant growth. Rotted manure or pelleted fertilizer with high nitrogen analysis also works.

As much as you find mulch an important asset, don't get carried away. Apply only a sufficient layer to prevent weed growth during the summer. If the mulch compacts, it may keep water from penetrating properly to the soil. Your best rule of green thumb is to apply only thin layers of dense mulch at a time and add more as the old mulch decomposes. Leaf mold, peat moss, sawdust, and wood chips can be applied to a depth of just a few inches. Grass clippings, old mulch, hay, straw, and other types of fluffy mulch can be applied 6 to 8 inches thick.

Note the Nutrient Values

Peat moss is probably the most readily available and most common mulch. Your best, cost-efficient bet is to buy the biggest bales or bags available. Although peat moss has no nutrient value, most other mulch materials do. For example, lawn clippings provide about 1 pound of nitrogen and 2 pounds of potash for each 100 pounds of dry clippings.

Researchers have also found that leaf mold or shredded leaves can provide nitrogen content as high as 5 percent. Alfalfa or clover hay is higher in nitrogen than orchard grass or timothy because these legumes have nitrogen-fixing bacteria in their root nodules. That is why farmers prefer alfalfa or clover hay to provide a high protein value for their livestock.

ALERT!

Don't mulch the soil when it is excessively wet. Molds can start below the mulch surface, and the trapped moisture combined with heat can cause hidden mold problems. You may also contribute to damping-off diseases on seedlings if you mulch before they have true leaves and a strong roothold.

Chapter 6
Nourish Your Soil

Garden soil is not just the place you grow plants. Soil is your plants' life support system. In this chapter you'll have an opportunity to dig into the good earth, learn more about it, and discover how you can improve it for great growing success.

Soil Basics

When you take care of your soil, it will take care of you and your plants. The basic principle for productive gardening is improvement of the soil. The better the humus and the soil conditions you can build, the better your plants will grow. Healthy soil enables you to grow healthy plants. There is one key factor that stands out in this effort: Insects dislike healthy plants! They prefer sickly, undernourished plants. It makes sense to focus on that when you build fertile growing ground.

QUESTION?

What's in the soil?
Soil is composed of weathered rock and organic matter, water, and air. However, the hidden "magic" in a healthy soil is the life— the small animals, worms, insects, bacteria, and microbes—that flourishes when the other soil elements are in balance.

Continuous Improvement

An understanding of soils and how to improve them is basic to improving growing conditions, wherever you live and garden. No matter what you have, from clay to sandy soils, from backfill around a new development home to soggy spots in your land, soil can be improved. You can make it fruitful with a simple, careful, and continuing improvement plan. The emphasis is on "continuing." Nothing happens overnight. But you can make immediate and useful improvements today. Then just continue on that natural soil-building process month after month, year after year. The results will astound you.

Get to Know Soil

Soil comes in various types and qualities. An understanding of basic soil formation and composition is essential to your efforts to work with nature in creating an optimum growing environment for your plants. With the exception of rugged mountains or arctic areas, soil covers the earth. It may be many feet deep, as in the fertile soils of Iowa and parts of the Midwest. It may be shallow, as in the desert areas of the Southwest or forested land of northern horticultural zones.

Soil comes in a variety of colors. It may be red as the soils of Hawaii and parts of the red shale soils of the Mid-Atlantic States. It may be black as the soils of the Dakotas. In coastal areas and certain portions of inland states, it may be quite sandy, the result of deposits from glaciers eons ago. In some parts of the country, you'll be confronted with clay soils, as thick and sticky as Louisiana gumbo soils. No matter where you live or what soil you find there, you can improve it, rebuild it, and upgrade your growing conditions.

Soil Terms

It helps to understand the terms used, from groups and types to textures and structures. As you read this book and identify what you have, you can better understand the ways to improve it.

> Too little porosity hinders plant growth because as soil compacts it forms hardpan layers on or beneath the surface that cause roots to rot. Without pore space, roots can't penetrate to find water and nutrients and won't thrive.

Texture refers to the size of the majority of particles making up the soil. It ranges from microscopic clay particles to small stones and gravel. Soils are generally categorized using these terms:

- **Clay soils:** Stony clay, gravelly clay, sandy clay, and silty clay
- **Loam soils:** Coarse sandy loams, medium sandy loams, fine sandy loams, silty loams, and clay loams
- **Sandy soils:** Gravelly sands, coarse sands, medium sands, fine sands, and loamy sands

Building structure and texture includes replenishing organic matter and using proper cultivation practices. Make no mistake about this fact: Soil is very much alive. To keep it alive and healthy, there must be pore space, known as porosity. Water, nutrients, roots, and air move through this pore space. When you look at a handful of soil, it looks like, well, soil. But about 25 to 50 percent of what you hold in your hands is actually pore space. A greater percentage of pore space can mean possible water loss, leaching of nutrients from the upper layers, and excessive nitrogen release.

Elements of Soil

All soils have several things in common. They contain minerals, organic matter, water, and air. The proportion of these elements may vary, but the components remain essentially the same. Approximately half the soil in your garden consists of small pieces of weathered rock that have slowly been broken down by wind, rain, freezing, thawing, and other chemical and biological processes through the years.

Organic matter is the partially decomposed remains of soil organisms and plant life, such as lichens and mosses, grasses and leaves, trees, and all other kinds of vegetative matter, including the decayed mulch or compost you have added. Organic matter makes up a small portion of soil—about 5 to 10 percent. However, it is essential because it binds soil particles into porous granules that allow air and water to move through the soil. Organic matter also retains moisture. Humus holds up to 90 percent of its weight in water and absorbs and stores nutrients. Most important, organic matter is food for microorganisms that are vital to healthy soil formation.

ALERT!

Avoid stepping in growing beds or compacting the soil with heavy equipment; in other words, driving over it with a garden tractor. Never work the soil when it is very wet. This practice can damage its structure.

A healthy soil is about 25 percent air. Insects, microbes, earthworms, and all soil life require this much air to live. The air in soil is an important source of the atmospheric nitrogen used by plants. Note that well aerated soil has plenty of pore space between the soil particles. Fine soil particles such as clay or silt have tiny spaces between them that are too small for air to properly penetrate. Hence, plants don't grow well. Soil composed of large particles like sand has large pore spaces and contains plenty of air. Too much air, however, can cause organic matter to decompose too quickly. It is important to ensure a balanced supply of air in your soil by adding plenty of organic matter.

Healthy soil will also contain about 25 percent water. Water, like air, is held in the pore spaces between soil particles. Large pore spaces allow rain and irrigation water to move down into the root zone and then also into the subsoil. In sandy soils, spaces between soil particles are so large that gravity causes water to drain down and out very quickly. That's why sandy soils dry out so fast. That also explains why fertilizer will leach down into the subsoil and not benefit plants.

Your Soil's Profile

Every soil has a profile. Layers in this profile are called horizons. The profile is represented by a series of layers in a vertical section that descends to the parent or bedrock below. In this profile you'll find the history of the soil and its formation.

Horizons of the profile differ in color, structure, porosity, and consistency. In shallow soils, these horizons may only be an inch thick, sometimes less. You may also find soil horizons several feet deep. Usually, however, the horizon will be a foot or so thick. You can cut a soil profile with a spade to examine it and learn some basics of what you must deal with in your gardening efforts.

ESSENTIAL

Take a spade and slice the soil in a trench, pit, or large hole. Cut it clean on one side to reveal the horizons. You will be able to see the topsoil, subsoil, and below. Try this in different areas, and you'll be surprised at the differences you may find just around your home grounds.

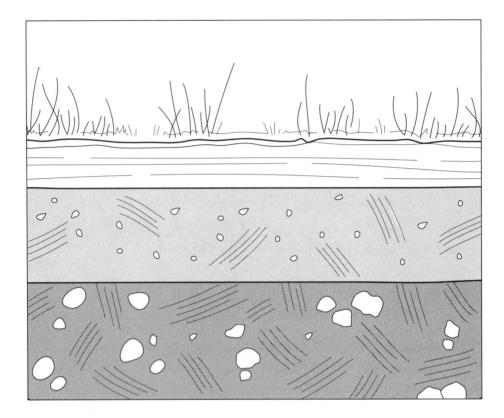

▲The three main layers of the soil profile

Three Basic Horizons

Soil scientists list the three master horizons simply as *A, B,* and *C.* In some cases there is a merged horizon known as an *AC* profile. Where erosion has been at work or where humans have misused and depleted the soil, or through a combination of these factors, the upper horizons may be gone.

True soil is the combined *A* and *B* horizons that form the major portion of the soil profile. In these layers, life is moving because the soil is truly alive. Millions of bacteria and fungi, plant roots, small insects, and animals are busy at work. Learning to achieve a balance with them, with nature, and with the life processes already in the soil is essential to obtaining the bountiful results you want.

Wind, water, and weather all contribute to the initial formation of any soil. Bedrock freezes and thaws, becomes wet and dries out. In this natural ongoing process, bedrock cracks and fractures. Over thousands of years, this continuing movement results in the first phases of soil formation.

Plants Help the Soil-Making Process

Plants add to the process. Bacteria, fungi, tiny lichens, and moss begin to grow. These tiny primitive plants gain a foothold in the crevices. As roots find their way into cracks, they produce more plants and die. In the process, they deposit the first organic matter. Over the centuries, this process continues slowly, ceaselessly.

As organic matter accumulates, it too changes. Rain falls and water carries elements to the lower levels, helping to break down minerals in the parent material. New compounds are formed as air, water, and other elements interact and combine.

FACT

If you wish to continue your study of soils, many books are available that provide a depth of knowledge. You may find the subject fascinating. Some gardeners have become so interested in soil that they switched careers and became landscaping contractors to cash in on their knowledge of the good earth.

Additions and Losses

Most gardeners are concerned only with the soil they can call their own. Of that soil, the upper portion deserves your closest attention, since it is this growing medium and level that contains the material available for your garden plant use. The upper soil levels are, naturally, subject to the elements. Rain falls and carries carbon dioxide into the soil from the air. Rainfall also transports valuable minerals dissolved from humus, sand, and rock particles. The minerals decompose slowly, constantly, reacting with water and other minerals to form new compounds. This process goes on every day, helping to build soil and the needed nutrients for future plants.

In the process, additions and losses occur as well. Clay particles, minerals, and soluble salts tend to be leached to lower levels. As they move downward, they are deposited in the *B* horizon where the roots of plants can absorb them.

Changes in soil formation and depletion occur at varying rates. In general, organic matter decomposes more rapidly. Minerals decompose more slowly. As plants grow, some of these materials are used and returned in the natural cycle of growth, death, and decomposition. The plants that grew or grow on the land determine to a large degree the types of organic matter in the soil.

It's Alive!

Your soil is filled with living organisms, mainly in the upper plant-growing areas. The action of plants and their roots, insects, worms, animals, bacteria, and fungi help mix soil horizons. Normally, leaves, grasses, twigs, and humus are found at the surface, with fibrous roots lower in the horizon. As stronger plant life develops, the deep roots pick up nutrients from lower levels and redeposit them on the surface.

Bacteria and fungi in your living soil are vital contributors to soil formation. They live on animal and plant residues. They break down complex compounds into simple forms. In the nodules of legumes, nitrogen-fixing bacteria, for example, actually fix nitrogen from the atmosphere and help make it available in the soil for future plants. You can learn a lot by observing your soil.

Creating Balance

All soils can be improved with the proper treatment. Your early goal should be to aim for a balance in structure, texture, and porosity. The word *balance* is important to consider. Nature is a matter of balance, in the food chains of animals and in the food growing from soils. Excesses are what throw people and plants out of balance in life. Pick up a handful of rich warm soil in the spring. If it crumbles freely in your palm, you are approaching the ideal. Naturally, there are unseen factors, such as nutrient levels, in balance in the soil. But the consistency of the growing medium is of underlying importance.

The closer you have or can rebuild soil to a granular feel, with clusters of soil that easily shake apart, the better your garden will grow. The better the soil, the less chance of erosion, providing you follow proper cultivation practices.

Erosion Can Hurt Gardens

Soil erodes in several ways. Heavy rains on unprotected sites will carry away topsoil. Left unchecked, gullies develop. You can see examples of this in your travels, often along highways. Happily, highway departments now realize the value of ground cover and vegetation to hold soil in place and preserve it. Wind can blow away the fine, light surface soil, too. Dust storms still occur in parts of America today.

For practical purposes, water erosion is the main problem confronting home gardeners. That doesn't mean just erosion on sloping garden land. America's proclivity to pave driveways, parking lots, and playgrounds denies rain a way to soak into the earth. A heavy rain across asphalt driveways or parking areas can lead to erosion problems on nearby garden areas.

FACT

The dust bowl phenomenon that occurred on the Great Plains in the early 1930s is a prime example of overused, abused soil that just blew away and left farmers helpless and homeless. Too many moved on, repeating the same cycle on new land.

Soil Conservation Pointers

Contour farming has proved that soil can be held in place and erosion avoided on sloping or hilly land. If you have a hilly area, you can profit by using contours. Leave a 2- to 3-foot grass strip every 6 to 10 feet running parallel with the contour of the land. These strips will act as minidams to slow the rapid runoff of surface water. Ground covers, such as vetch or clover on steep slopes, and myrtle, pachysandra, or ivy will retard erosion. Knowledge of how water moves over, through, and into the soil will help you resolve problems that excess rain and irrigation may cause.

Be wary about buying "topsoil" or "loam" as a quick-fix approach to lawn and garden building. Less-than-honest contractors may offer rich-looking topsoil or so-called loam at low prices. On occasion, they obtain this good-looking dark soil by dredging silt in rivers and ponds and mixing it with sand. If you use it, you may compound your problems.

Improve Soil Structure

Here are some basic tips for improving your soil. They can serve as your quick reference checklist as you dig in to grow better.

Improving Clay Soil

- Work 2 to 3 inches of organic matter—old mulch, finished compost, or even peat moss—into the surface of the soil
- Add at least 1 inch more each year after that
- Add organic matter in the fall, if possible
- Use permanent raised beds to improve drainage and keep foot traffic off the growing area
- Minimize tilling and spading
- Never till or try to cultivate the soil when it is wet

Improving Sandy Soil

- Work in 3 to 4 inches of organic matter such as well-rotted manure or finished compost
- Mulch around your plants with leaves, wood chips, bark, hay, or straw to retain moisture and cool the soil
- Plan to add at least 2 inches of organic matter each year
- Grow cover crops or green manures

Improving Silty Soil

- Add 1 inch of organic matter each year
- Avoid soil compaction by unnecessary tilling and walking on garden beds
- Consider constructing raised beds, which are also easier to maintain

Test Your Soil

A professional soil test gives you a wealth of information about your soil—most important, the pH and amount of different nutrients. Local cooperative extension service offices usually offer a professional soil-testing service that is low cost with results specifically focused on location. If this service is not available, you can also have your soil tested by an independent soil lab. Many garden centers offer them or can direct you to a local source. Soil test results usually rate the levels of soil pH, phosphorus, potassium, magnesium, calcium, and sometimes nitrogen.

More labs now offer tests for micronutrients such as boron, zinc, and manganese. Trace minerals are important to plants, too. However, unless plants show nutrition problems, you probably won't need micronutrient testing. To add micronutrients, try adding organic fertilizers or commercial blends that have microelements listed on the label. Organic fertilizers such as greensand and kelp meal usually have micronutrients to help where soil is deficient in them.

Green manures and cover crops planted in fall and turned or tilled under each spring help improve soil and can also add small amounts of nutrients.

To get the most accurate test results, take a soil sample from each garden area, including your lawn, flower garden, and vegetable garden. Each area needs different nutrients for the type of plants you grow. Spring and fall are the best times to do soil tests because the soil is more stable. You can then incorporate any recommended fertilizers your garden ground needs.

Know Soil Chemistry

Yes, you must pay attention also to the acidity/alkalinity chemical balance, which varies in different soils. Different plants need different acid or alkaline growing environments. The addition of manures, minerals, and trace elements also plays a part. So does the mechanical treatment of your garden ground.

QUESTION?

What is soil pH?

The pH level of your soil indicates its relative acidity or alkalinity. A pH test measures the ratio of hydrogen (positive) ions to hydroxyl (negative) ions in the soil water. When hydrogen and hydroxyl ions are present in equal amounts, the pH is said to be neutral (pH 7). When the hydrogen ions prevail, the soil is acidic (pH 1 to pH 6.5). And when the hydroxyl ions tip the balance, the pH is alkaline (pH 6.8 to pH 14).

Match Soil pH to Plant Needs

Most essential plant nutrients are soluble at pH levels of 6.5 to 6.8, which is why most plants grow best in this range. If the pH of your soil is much higher or lower, soil nutrients start to become chemically bound to the soil particles; this makes them unavailable to your plants. Plant health suffers because the roots can't absorb the nutrients they need to feed the plants.

To improve soil fertility, you need to put the pH of your soil within the 6.5 to 6.8 range.

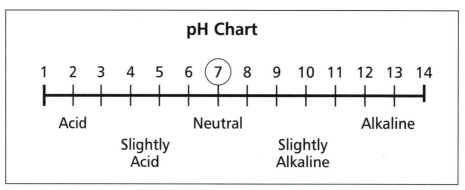

▲ Using a pH chart to determine the acidity of soil

You can't, and shouldn't, try to change the pH of your soil overnight. It is better to alter it over one or two growing seasons and then maintain it every year thereafter. Liberal application of organic matter is a good idea because it helps moderate pH imbalances.

Correcting Acidic Soil

If the pH of your soil is less than 6.5, it may be too acidic for most garden plants. Learn what plants need. For example, blueberries and azaleas require acidic soil.

The most common way to raise the pH of your soil and make it less acidic is to add powdered limestone. Dolomitic limestone will also add manganese to the soil. Apply lime in the fall because it takes several months to alter the pH of the soil.

FACT

Soils in the eastern half of the United States are usually on the acidic side. That's just the way it is and you can blame it on Mother Nature if you wish. Lime is the easy way to "sweeten" acid soil.

Wood ash from wood stoves also raises pH and works more quickly than limestone. It also contains potassium. However, if you add too much wood ash, you can drastically alter the pH and cause nutrient imbalances. For best results, apply wood ash in the winter and no more than 2 pounds per 100 square feet every two to three years.

Solving Alkaline Soil Problems

If your soil pH is higher than 6.8, you should acidify your soil. Soils in the western United States, especially in arid regions, are typically alkaline. This too is a gift from Mother Nature. Add ground sulfur to acidify your soil. You can also incorporate naturally acidic organic materials such as conifer needles, sawdust, peat moss, and oak leaves.

Know the *ABCs* of *NPK*

You will always see fertilizer expressed in numbers such as 10-5-5 or 10-20-10. Many different types of fertilizer are available today. The numbers refer to the percentage by net weight of each nutrient. *N* for nitrogen is always the first number. *P,* which stands for available phosphorus, is always the second number. The third number is *K* and stands for soluble potash. In other words, a 5-10-5 fertilizer contains 5 percent nitrogen, 10 percent available phosphorus, and 5 percent soluble potash. Labeling laws allow only the immediately available nutrients to be listed.

Basically that formula means that a 100-pound bag contains 20 pounds of nutrients. Inert carriers, which ensure that fertilizer ingredients are spread more evenly, constitute the remaining 80 pounds. Since different plants require different levels of nutrition, commercial fertilizers have a wide range of compositions, depending on what the manufacturer puts in the formula.

It helps to know what these nutrients contribute to plant growth. Each nutrient has a specific purpose. When you understand them, you'll be more in tune with what makes your garden grow.

FACT

Nutrient analysis for organic fertilizers tends to be low. The nutrients gradually become available to plants over a period of months or even years.

Nitrogen

Nitrogen is the key element for vegetative growth. It promotes strong and healthy leaves, stalks, and stems. In fact, it is vital for all green leaf tissue. Nitrogen fosters the development of proteins, called growth builders, in plants. Without this essential element, you'll see yellowed foliage and stunted growth.

Too much nitrogen can also cause problems. Oversupply encourages excess leaf and stem growth at the expense of flower and fruit formation. Leafy plants such as corn are big users of nitrogen. So is grass. As a result, the formulas for lawn fertilizers have high first numbers (16-6-4, 20-10-10), indicating that nitrogen is high in proportion to the other elements.

Phosphorus

Phosphorus is vital for prolific flower development, good fruit set, and seed production. It is also required for proper development of plant sugars. You do want sweet-tasting squash, tomatoes, and corn, don't you? Then you should be concerned with the proper balance of phosphorus, the sugar-encouraging nutrient in your fertilizer.

Lack of phosphorus is easily spotted. Plants are stunted and have a yellowed look. This appearance may appear similar to nitrogen deficiency, but look again. The distinctive purplish color around the edges of the leaves and between the leaf veins means there is a phosphorus deficiency. Equally important, root development is retarded when phosphorus is insufficient. Leaves may fall and plants may fail to flower. If phosphorus is out of balance with other elements, you can use super-phosphate to adjust the soil nutrient balance.

Potash

Potash or potassium, the *K* in the formula, promotes strong, healthy roots. It also aids in seed production. Potash quickens the maturity of crops and may help in disease resistance. Yellowish mottling indicates potassium deficiency. In severe cases, foliage loss occurs and roots won't develop well. Fruit set is poor when potash is low.

The Key Elements

Nitrogen, phosphorus, and potassium are the key elements. Today, there are many quality fertilizers in granular and liquid preparations. The labels will tell you which crops to use them on. Some are designed for fruits, others for flowering plants, and others are more general purpose. Ask the specialists at your garden center about them. Sometimes it pays to use several types for the kinds of plants that you have. There are also fertilizer spikes that you can drive into the soil around trees to nourish them.

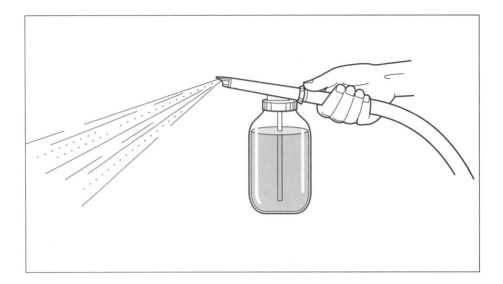

▲ Using garden hose sprayers to apply fertilizer

Get to know the *ABC*s of fertilizer and you'll discover what a big difference it can make in stronger, more beautiful, and productive plants.

Chapter 7

E Help Gardens Grow Right

Whatever your reasons for growing a garden, you certainly want to give it your best effort. If you know a bit more about how plants grow and develop, you'll be better able to take care of them, and they'll reward you for your efforts. This chapter will give you the know-how you need to help gardens grow right.

A Plant's Life

One of the major differences between plants and animals is that plants make their own food. To produce this food, a plant needs light energy from the sun, carbon dioxide from the air, and water from the soil. If a plant is lacking any of these ingredients, photosynthesis, the plant's food-making process, will slow down or stop. Eventually the plant will die.

Basically, photosynthesis relies on chlorophyll, a green pigment found in plants. The foods, which include the sugar made during photosynthesis, become available to the plant as they are changed to energy. The plant uses this energy to build new tissues and grow.

FACT

Photosynthesis can be described in this way: Water + energy from the sun + carbon dioxide from the air = carbohydrates or food + oxygen + water. Plants are vital because they take in the carbon dioxide that all animals exhale and give us oxygen, which we must have to live.

Transpiration Is Vital

Transpiration is the upward movement of water through a plant's roots, stem, and leaves. Water evaporates from tiny holes called stomates in the plant's leaves. Then the plant pulls water upward from the roots. Nutrients, the fertilizer elements in the soil, enter the roots with the water and move to wherever they are needed in the plant.

Some of the water is used in plant cells for photosynthesis, but more than 90 percent of the water that enters in the roots is ultimately lost through the stomates. That water loss acts like a giant air conditioner, which accounts for the ability of large trees to cool the air around our homes—yet another reason to have extensive landscaping for outdoor living enjoyment.

Five Factors for Plant Growth

Five key factors influence a plant's growth. If any factor is less than ideal, it will limit growth. Smart gardeners manage a plant's environment so their plants have a good balance of all the necessary ingredients.

The acronym *MANTLE* is an easy way to remember the five key environmental factors for good plant growth. *M* is moisture, *A* is air, *N* is nutrients, *T* is temperature, and *L* is light. Put these together and you have our environment *(E)*.

1. **Moisture is essential for plant life**. It is used to move nutrients throughout the plant and helps control its temperature. It is the major part of living cells.

2. **Air is made up of many kinds of gases including nitrogen, oxygen, and carbon dioxide.** Oxygen is rarely a limited element. Plants usually give off more oxygen than they use. However, in a tightly closed greenhouse, the lack of carbon dioxide can limit plant growth.

3. **Nutrients refer to the need for and use of basic chemical elements in the plant.** A lot must happen before a plant can take up and use a chemical element like nitrogen, phosphorus, or potash. The three elements plants need for growth that are drawn from the air and water are carbon, hydrogen, and oxygen. There are six nutrients found in the soil that plants use in large amounts. These macronutrients are calcium, magnesium, nitrogen, phosphorus, potassium, and sulfur.

4. **Temperature is important to plants.** They have a comfort zone, much as people do. Extreme temperatures, both cold and hot, can stunt growth. Hardiness refers to a plant's ability to withstand low temperatures, and plant breeders have worked hard to perfect new varieties that can take low winter temperatures.

5. **Light, both quantity and quality, has a major effect on plant growth.** Light quantity is the amount of sunlight plants receive, and it varies with the seasons. Most annual flowers and vegetables need lots of sun every day to perform at their peak. Light quality refers to the color or wavelength of the light that reaches the plant surface; it affects growth and the formation of flowers.

Most plants need full sun, but some can tolerate shade. Others thrive in cooler weather, and some must have heat to prosper. Because plants differ in their hardiness to withstand winter, breeders work hard to perfect varieties that can mature more quickly and set fruit for harvest or vegetables to pick in a short season. Frost has always been a challenge. In late spring, frosts kill newly sprouted seedlings. Early fall frosts kill off tender veggies or berries before we get to enjoy them.

FACT

Sometimes plants can get nutrients through their leaves if a dilute solution is sprayed on them. This is called foliar feeding, a popular new process using hose-end sprayers with fertilizer solutions. Much of the runoff gets into the soil where nutrients in the solution are absorbed by the roots.

Determine Your Horticultural Zone

One of the key elements to guide you in selecting which plants will grow in your area is the horticultural zone, a carefully calculated system of zones of temperature ranges that determine plant growth. You'll find important notes on the zones in all mail-order catalogs and usually on the tags of plants you purchase locally. For example, if a plant will grow in zones 6 to 4, that tells you that the plant will grow in the cooler areas of the country, which is where those zones appear in the U.S. Department of Agriculture Hardiness Zone Map (✎ *www.usna.usda.gov/Hardzone/*).

Get an Indoor Jump on Spring

Every gardener faces the same question: When is the best time to start seeds indoors to get a jump on spring and gain precious weeks of growing time? That's an important consideration. Nobody wants vines full of green tomatoes when an early frost kills the vines before most of the tomatoes ripen. Or, you only get to enjoy a few sweet melons!

▲ MAP OF NORTH AMERICAN TEMPERATURE ZONES

ZONE KEY

1 2 3 4 5 6 7 8 9 10 11

Determine the Frost-Free Date

Find the date that the last frost is normally expected in your area. Ask veteran gardeners or garden center owners. Timing is everything if you want to grow most abundantly.

If you need help determining your spring frost-free date, call your county extension agent who can tell you for certain. The county extension offices keep local records, which is what really counts where you live and garden. Once you have that probable frost-free date, count backward from that date to determine the number of weeks you should start seedlings indoors for the crops you intend to grow.

You can check with the National Climatic Data Center on the Internet to determine usual frost-free dates in various parts of the United States. Veteran gardeners report that this data predicts the last spring frost date with about 90 percent accuracy. The center's Web site is ✑ *http://lwf.ncdc.noaa.gov/oa/ncdc.html*.

The Seed

Seeds are made up of three major parts: the embryo, the endosperm, and the seed coat. The embryo is actually an immature plant in an arrested state of development. It will eventually grow to form a full-grown plant. The endosperm is the built-in food supply for the plant. It is made up of proteins, carbohydrates, and fats. The seed coat is the hard outer covering that protects the seed from disease and insects and also prevents water from entering the seed and causing it to germinate and grow before it should.

Tips For Seed Starting

You have many advantages when you start your own plants from seeds. One is that you can grow interesting varieties that often are not offered in chain store garden departments. Mail-order catalogs offer you lots of other choices, including disease-resistant vegetables and flowers that are especially valuable because they have a built-in genetic value.

By sprouting your own seedlings, you get a multiweek jump on spring. You'll have sturdy seedlings ready to plant outdoors when the weather is right. That head start gives your plants many extra weeks toward maturity, especially when you have a short outdoor season.

Some plants grow better than others. Surefire vegetables include broccoli, cabbage, cauliflower, cucumbers, leeks, lettuce, melons, peppers, pumpkins, and tomatoes. Good annual flowers are alyssum, cosmos, marigolds, and zinnias. Perennials include Shasta daisies, columbines, and hollyhocks. Wherever you buy your seeds, read the package directions to get the best information about starting seedlings indoors.

Before you begin planting seeds, assemble your supplies: containers, soil mix, and seeds. Starting seeds indoors isn't an expensive process, especially if you recycle food containers. Give some thought to that and you'll be off to a good natural start to get your gardens growing right.

ALERT!

Use pure water for starting seeds in pots or trays indoors, especially if your city water is full of chlorine and fluoride. A gallon or two of spring water is a good bet to help start your seedlings without chemical contamination.

Use the Best Soil Mixes

Growing seedlings for transplanting outdoors is fairly easy, but it does require some dedication and skill. To start seeds, you can use prepackaged seed starter mixes from stores. They are inexpensive and free from disease organisms and weed seeds. Most gardeners prefer buying growing media from garden stores because it is free of disease and insects, which reduces the potential for damping off or spreading a common fungal disease.

It is best to start seeds with seed starter mixtures not potting soil. Avoid using garden soil; it may contain disease organisms that will affect young seedlings. Garden soil tends to cake and doesn't allow water to drain properly. There are many brand-name seed-starting mixes on the market. In addition, you can find kits of mixes in trays and a variety of peat pots, Jiffy 7 cubes, and other seed-starting aids.

Seed Starter Steps

Here are seven basic steps to start seeds in order to produce transplants for your outdoor gardens. Be sure to time your planting so seedlings will be ready and hardened off for garden planting time. Check your calendar to be sure you know when it is safe in your area to plant outdoors, after the last usual frost.

1. Make holes in the bottom of containers for drainage, unless you have a unit that features proper draining, so you avoid overwatering.
2. Fill containers with moist growing media until it overflows and tap it down gently. Soil should be level with the top of the container.
3. Make rows 2 inches apart and ¼ inch deep. Sow tomato and pepper seeds 2 to 3 seeds per inch and other seeds as instructed on the seed packs.
4. Cover seeds with starting mixture no deeper than twice its thickness and pat it down lightly. Many gardeners prefer to place a sheet of newspaper on top of the newly planted tray to keep in the moisture that helps seeds germinate.
5. Place your container in an area that will keep soil 65° to 75°F.
6. Check every few days to see when seedlings emerge. Then remove the cover and place containers in full sunlight.
7. When the seedlings are sturdy, transplant them into other containers to prevent overcrowding. This also helps them develop a well-branched root system. Use only the most vigorous seedlings. Handle them gently by their leaves not by the stems. Replant the seedlings slightly deeper than they grew in the tray.

As your seedlings continue to grow, water each container regularly to keep soil from drying out. You should also use a dilute fertilizer starter solution to give young plants a boost of nutrients.

Windowsill Seedlings

As more gardeners begin windowsill seedlings to gain weeks of growing time, which leads to more abundant veggie crops, many handy windowsill planter kits have been introduced. You can find them in the garden departments of chains such as Home Depot, Wal-Mart, True Value, Trustworthy, and others, as well as at local garden centers. Mail-order catalogs also feature a variety of kits from simple ones to those with heat mats and miniature greenhouse systems.

Some avid gardeners have bought or built coldframes or hotbeds, attached to basement windows, as a place for seedlings to start early. You can find a variety of devices of all sizes, shapes, and prices at garden centers and in mail-order catalogs. They are only really useful for a few weeks, which probably isn't practical for many gardeners. Nevertheless, there it is. Now you have some research about them just in case you plan to be an active gardener for many years.

FACT

Photoperiod, the length of day and night, affects flowering and other events in some plants. Most flowers need at least six hours of sun a day to perform well. So do most veggies.

It helps to know when you should start seeds indoors to have seedlings at the safe outdoor planting time in your area. Once you determine when that is, you can plan your seed-starting projects. For convenience, here's a handy list for popular plants:

- **12–14 weeks:** Chives, coleus, impatiens, leeks, onions, pansies
- **8–12 weeks:** Alyssum, cole and cabbage crops, peppers, petunias, snapdragons, and other hardy annuals
- **6–8 weeks:** Eggplants and tomatoes
- **5–6 weeks:** Cockscombs, marigolds, zinnias, and other tender annuals
- **2–4 weeks:** Cucumbers, melons, okra, pumpkins, and squash

ALERT!

Melons, cukes, and squash can be difficult to transplant. They are best started in individual peat pots that can then be placed directly in the ground. Roots will grow right though the sides and bottom of the pot.

Transplanting Tips and Tricks

Before you plant seedlings outdoors, they should be "hardened off." While they were growing indoors they had warm conditions, unlike the changing temperatures they will have in the outdoor garden. Toughen your seedlings before moving them outdoors. About one week before the plants are to go outside, start acclimating them to the harsh conditions of the garden world. On a warm spring day, move pots or containers of transplants to a shaded, protected place for a few hours. Each day, unless the weather is really terrible, gradually increase the plants' exposure to sun and breeze. Take plants indoors if temperatures dip below 40°F.

At the end of the week, leave them out overnight; then transplant them into the garden. When the time is right for planting outdoors, after the danger of frost has passed, prepare the ground by digging or tilling a few days before transplanting. It helps to transplant on a cloudy day in late afternoon or early evening. Water the plants in their containers a few hours before transplanting them into the garden.

Dig a hole large enough to hold the rootball. Set the plant slightly deeper than it was growing in the container and at the recommended spacing according to the seed packet. Press the soil firmly around the roots of the transplants and pour about a cup of starter fertilizer solution around the plant. You can make a starter solution by mixing the fertilizer recommended for that plant at half strength. If you have grown seedlings in individual pots, be sure the top of the pot is covered. Otherwise it could wick moisture from the soil and slow the plant's progress rooting in the garden soil. Instead of liquid starter solution, you can use a circle of slow-release pelleted fertilizer in a band around the transplants to give them a nutrition boost.

Handle plants carefully and avoid disturbing the roots or bruising the stems. If you're transplanting from trays, be sure the mix is moist and there is a large rootball area of soil mixture around the plant to avoid transplant shock.

Recycle Food Containers for Garden Use

Recycling provides free gardening aids for good gardeners. This section will give you some ideas on what you can do with everyday food containers such as milk cartons and jugs, ice cream and yogurt cups, egg cartons, and even plastic glasses. Save and wash ice cream cups and sticks from Popsicles. Add planting soil and sow a few seeds in each cup.

With a crayon or felt-tip pen, mark on the container the variety and the date planted. Or use Popsicle sticks to mark the variety, date planted, and other information. They also make handy stakes; just staple the empty seed packets to them. If you use them to mark garden rows outdoors, put the empty seed packet in a plastic bag so it won't get soggy and hard to read. Seed packets provide important tips for thinning and transplanting.

▲ Using Popsicle sticks to keep track of plantings

Plastic Containers as Planters

Recycle milk containers. Cut one side from a quart or half-gallon container. Fill it with seed starting mix. Cut the side you removed to make dividers within the milk carton. When seedlings are tall enough to transplant or plant outdoors, slit the sides of the cartons and gently slide out the root cube to avoid disturbing tender roots.

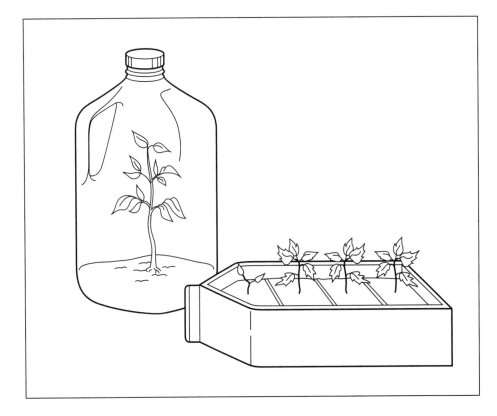

▲ Using cardboard and plastic milk containers as planters

Milk cartons have other uses as well. Carefully cut off the bottoms an inch or two high. Use them as plant saucers to keep water from staining windowsills or tabletops. Enjoy butter or margarine on toast each morning, but save the containers. These, too, can be used for seed starting or as containers for cuttings and transplants.

◀ Using plastic containers for starting seeds

Egg Cartons as Starter Trays

Composition egg cartons offer great potential as seed starter trays. Simply remove the top and fill the egg areas with seed starting mix and seeds. Pinch off the smallest, weakest seedlings in each unit after they are an inch or two tall. When ready to transplant, moisten the tray and gently scoop out the seedlings to plant outdoors.

Save Plastic Cups and Containers

Save clear plastic drinking cups. Use them with ice cream cups or similar smaller food containers to make miniature terrariums. These little containers are ideal to hold high humidity as you start to slowly germinate seeds or to give cuttings a better habitat for setting roots.

Clear plastic and glass jars serve the same purpose, providing a greenhouse effect over tubs and pots that you use to start seedlings or to grow transplants from cuttings of favorite plants. Be sure you don't put them in hot, direct sun. North or west windows are better to avoid overheating tiny plants.

Create Cutworm Barriers

Cutworms are pests that can be a problem in any garden. They love to topple young tomatoes, cabbages, broccoli, and other tender, tempting seedlings. Simply cut regular quart or half-gallon milk containers in 3- to 4-inch sections to make cutworm barriers. Press them upright into the ground around the base of seedlings and forget about cutworm damage.

Handy Row Greenhouses

If you want to get into the outdoor garden early but are worried about continuing cold weather, consider row greenhouses. Cut wire coat hangers with pliers and form them into hoops. Then, insert them into the ground. Slit plastic dry cleaners' bags and place the plastic over the wire hoops to provide shelter for the seedlings from late spring chills. Make furrows along each side of the row and tuck the plastic in, cover the edges and ends with soil, and you have an inexpensive row greenhouse. The plastic traps warmth during the day and stops late frosts from killing tender seedlings.

On especially hot days, lift the side for ventilation to let excess heat escape. You want to protect your plants from chills, but you don't want to cook them. Once you have your transplants in the ground, water them and water twice more during the next week if you have less than 2 inches of rain. Remove hot caps and row covers when plants become crowded and the warmth of spring has arrived.

FACT

Save original seed packages with tips about thinning seedlings and other useful information. Put them in zippered plastic bags and staple them to Popsicle sticks or row markers. This trick helps you identify which variety you planted where and gives you quick access to growing tips.

Plan Succession Plantings

A proven way to extend your vegetable harvest is succession planting. For instance, since members of the cabbage family prefer cool weather, plant them early. Then plant seeds in pots or other garden spots so you have new plants coming along. As you harvest early vegetables, simply transplant the growing seedlings to that empty place and put it to continuing productive use. It isn't necessary to use the same plant. The point is to keep the space in your garden as productive as possible throughout the growing season.

By midsummer it pays to replant those cool season–loving plants that can grow well into the fall. After a few years, you'll probably have developed your own system and gardening timetable. Keep records, of course, to get a feel for the timing of planting, replanting, and stretching the growing season.

Make a Yearly Project List

First, learn and record the typical frost-free dates for your area. Then, check maturity dates for all your vegetables since they are most impacted by growing schedules. Second, buy short season–maturing vegetables if you need them. Start seeds indoors to gain four to eight weeks of growing time that will give you sturdy seedlings that leap ahead when planted in their outdoor garden spots.

Don't Forget Tilling

Once you have these dates and plans in mind, make a master gardening project checklist for yourself. Consider fall plowing or tilling, either with your own or rented equipment or hire it out to a contractor. This early preparation ensures that weeds and old crop residues will be turned under to improve soil condition with organic matter and a basic seedbed will be ready for spring planting. April showers may bring spring flowers, but you should never till or dig wet soil. Fall tilling provides a good planting bed that may only need some light raking and smoothing before spring planting.

Note Results

Record the times you do various garden projects and also note the results. That's another simple way to stay tuned to Mother Nature in your area. If your area usually has a summer drought, perhaps you should plant earlier and add succession crops later to work around the dry period. Or, purchase the necessary drip irrigation, soaker hoses, or other watering equipment at year-end sales to save money and have the equipment you need to beat droughts.

Know Harvest Dates

One point that is often overlooked by many people is vacation time. Too often eager gardeners plant without thinking of when veggie crops will be ready. Mark your planned vacation in your gardening calendar. Check back on the expected maturity dates for your prized crops. If vacation falls then, ask family and friends to pick and enjoy some of the veggies, while saving others for your return. That way the crops won't over-ripen and spoil.

Swap Gardening Chores

Also, remember that weeds have a way of taking over gardens during vacations. Part of your long-range plan should be to swap gardening chores with friends and neighbors. Naturally, using mulch and pulling young weeds early will help prevent a weed takeover while you are on vacation. But it also pays to have a friend check out your garden and do some necessary cultivation and harvesting so your garden stays neat, tidy, and as productive as it should be.

Once you have a plan, not just in mind but written down, your gardening experiences will progress smoothly and yield a better and more productive garden.

Chapter 8
How to Beat Bugs

Pest control is much easier when you spot problems early before serious damage is done or populations build up. Smart gardening is based on an understanding of nature's interactions. This chapter will help you beat harmful bugs more easily and successfully in a variety of ways.

Plan a Pest Control Program

A successful pest control plan should focus on the best ways to beat bugs and plant diseases without having to wage all-out war. Some plans make use of natural pest control materials. Others take advantage of modern pesticides that are effective and reasonably safe to use. By looking at your pest problem realistically, you can focus on the key points:

- Use companion planting, crop rotation, and other methods to stop pest problems
- Save time and money by avoiding excess use of pesticides
- Use good bugs to beat bad ones
- Protect the environment by working to create a balance of nature in your home grounds

American home gardeners often use more pesticides per square foot in their gardens than farmers do in their fields. The rationale seems to be that if a little pesticide is good, more will be better. That's not true and can be a big mistake. For one thing, pesticide overuse may leave harmful residues, make handling plants hazardous, and harm beneficial insects, birds, and pets.

FACT

A **pesticide** is used to kill a pest whether it's an insect, rodent, fungi, or weed. An **insecticide** is a chemical used to kill insects.

Growing public concern about pesticide overuse has benefited everyone. More gardeners are realizing that picture-perfect vegetables aren't necessary and that plants can withstand a fair amount of damage yet still produce a good crop of tasty food or wonderful flowers.

Take Care of Your Plants

Insect pests and plant diseases are a challenge for every gardener. If you think of your garden as an ecosystem that has its own natural balance, you'll realize that some damage to plants can be a signal that your plants need more attention.

Not every insect is an enemy. Some are pollinators. Others break down organic matter. Some are beneficial predators that feed on the real enemies. Effective techniques such as physical barriers, traps, and specific biological agents are available to help you protect your garden and still maintain a safe, harmonious natural environment.

Pests Don't Like Healthy Plants

Insects and diseases usually attack unhealthy plants. Your best bet for preventive control is to take good care of your plants. Build up healthy soil by adding organic matter to your garden every year and improving nutrient levels, soil structure, and water-holding capacity. Be certain your plants get adequate amounts of water and all the nutrients they need. Use mulches, so your valued plants don't need to compete with masses of weeds for water and nutrients. Pull a few weeds every time you visit the garden. Thin seedlings, so the plants are not overcrowded.

Practice Periodic Garden Cleanup

Garden cleanup is the logical first step to solve growing problems. Remove old squash and cucumber vines, tomato plants, and similar debris after the harvest. Many insects winter in such debris and get an early start on your plants the following spring. Many plant pathogens also live in the soil year-round. So, remove and dispose of any diseased or infested plants.

Cultivate the soil in the fall to expose any eggs, larvae, or pupae to birds and cold temperatures. Remove weeds regularly since they can also harbor insect pests.

ALERT! Never use any diseased plants or parts in compost. Even when compost piles heat up as decomposition progresses, disease organisms may survive and can then transmit diseases when you spread the compost or humus. Your best bet is to burn or otherwise destroy diseased plant parts, including nests of insects such as caterpillars in trees or shrubs.

Consider Crop Rotation

Many insects and disease-causing organisms winter in soil near host plants. Crop rotation reduces insect damage and minimizes soil-borne disease organisms. Wait at least two years before you plant the same or related crops, such as broccoli and cauliflower, in the same spot. Tomatoes, potatoes, and onions are particularly vulnerable to problems when planted in the same place year after year. Crop rotation also keeps soil nutrients in balance over time.

Try Companion Planting

Some plant combinations thwart insects. See Chapter 9 for more details. But in a nutshell, here's the way it works: Plants complement or protect one another in various ways. For example, marigolds have a natural resistance to insects, so planting marigolds as a border around the garden or among vegetables seems to discourage insects and adds color to the veggie patch.

QUESTION?

What are insectary plants?
Insectary plants attract and host beneficial insects. From there, the beneficial bugs wander afield to prey, eat, and control harmful garden pests. Beneficial bugs include ladybugs, praying mantis, and green lacewings.

Some herbs also help. For example, basil is beneficial to tomatoes; carrots grow well with leaf lettuce, and their roots exude a substance that helps peas. Organic gardeners say that members of the allium family, such as onions and garlic, effectively deter pests that attack roses.

Some plants have the opposite effect and seem to inhibit one another's growth. For example, tomatoes and members of the brassica family, including broccoli and cabbage, do not grow well when planted together.

Recognizing Insect Problems

Veteran gardeners keep watch for anything that doesn't look normal. By spotting bug problems early, they can stop the problem faster and easier. Take a tip from the veterans and you'll be far ahead when it comes time to do battle with the bugs.

Here are the signs and signals to watch for on your daily inspection.

Chewing insects chew off parts of a plant or mine into plants. Symptoms are ragged leaves, holes in fruits and seeds, bumps and abrasions in leaves, wilted or dead plants, and the presence of the worms. Examples are cabbageworms, tomato hornworms, armyworms, grasshoppers, and Colorado potato beetles.

Sucking insects feed on growing plants by piercing the skin and sucking sap from cells. The insect remains on the outside of the plant. Symptoms are usually off-color and misshapen foliage and fruit. Examples are aphids, scale insect, squash bugs, and leafhoppers.

Internal feeders are harder to spot. Many of your worst pests feed within plant tissues and are harder to control with insecticides. Symptoms are wilting, weak-looking, stunted or dead plants. Examples are the European corn borer, squash vine borer, and various leaf miners.

Underground insects do their dirty deeds belowground where it is almost impossible to spot them early. Symptoms are wilting, weakened plants, stunted growth, and dead plants. Examples are wireworms and cabbage maggots.

Insects feeding in one of these four ways cause about 95 percent of direct injury to plants.

Integrated Pest Management

After following the basic ideas for cleanup, rotation, and improved plant varieties, think about IPM, or Integrated Pest Management. IPM strategies have been proposed by various garden advisers including master gardeners, cooperative extension agents, horticulture instructors, and nursery and garden center professionals. (You might also hear another phrase, Plant Health Care or PHC, from home landscape maintenance and design professionals and certified arborists.)

FACT

Both strategies, IPM and PHC, have the same goal: to educate gardeners and landscapers so they can maintain their gardens and lawns and have healthier plants and less need for chemical treatments.

IPM Basics

IPM begins with preparing a site carefully and then focuses on choosing plants that are appropriate for the site and the local growing conditions. Stressed plants are always more inviting to insect and disease attack. Another key strategy is ongoing monitoring of plants to spot problems before they get out-of-hand. This means you *must* spend more time strolling through your garden, taking time to smell the roses, for example, and in the process look for the first signs of black spot or aphid damage. The earlier a problem is identified, the easier it is to control it with the least toxic means.

Then, when action calls for chemicals, IPM strategies recommend beginning with the safest, most effective controls available and using them only where needed and by following label instructions exactly. By practicing IPM strategies in your garden, you'll not only save money on chemicals, you'll be rewarded with more beautiful plants and a more beautiful planet.

Advice for Vegetable Gardeners

With thanks to the garden experts at Schultz Company, here are some examples of how IPM works. Instead of using heavy-duty chemicals, try starting with milder ones. Schultz recommends the following.

- Garden Safe Fungicide3
- Garden Safe Insecticidal Soap
- Garden Safe insect sprays that contain pyrethrin and canola oil

Tips for Insect Control

Once you have seen the problem and identified the pest or cause, try these steps as they apply to your situation for insect control:

- Prune out insect-infested areas of plants; this includes tent caterpillars, fall webworms, and similar pests
- Cover susceptible crops with a row cover and nylon screen or otherwise protect them from insects
- When appropriate, use insect traps; they're available at garden centers and in garden departments
- Hand-pick insects and destroy them (This works fine when a Japanese beetle outbreak is not severe.)

Don't jump to conclusions when you see some bugs nibbling your plants. Think back. Did a similar problem happen in the past? Was it really serious? Often problems run their course and cause minimal damage. Thoughtful gardeners know that it pays to try the simplest, safest control first and observe the results for future reference.

Pesticide Pointers

As you consider what to do about pest control in your own gardens and landscapes, here are some key points to keep in mind. A pesticide is any substance or mixture used to kill insects or other pests. This definition includes chemical pesticides and biological pesticides. When you decide that a pesticide is necessary, read and follow the mixing and application directions listed on the container or in the brochure provided.

Always read and follow directions when using any type of pesticide, whether herbicide or insecticide. The directions are designed to enable you to use the product safely and achieve the results intended. Excess chemicals can be very harmful to plants and you also risk harming yourself.

Categories of Pesticides

For your reference, here are the categories of pesticides:

1. Biorational pesticides are either chemical forms of naturally occurring biological chemicals or agents such as bacteria or fungi that are parasitic on pests.
2. Insecticidal soaps are soap solutions that smother insects.
3. Horticultural oils are highly refined petroleum oils that kill insects by suffocation. Insects breathe through their exoskeleton, so if their pores are clogged, they die.
4. Botanical mineral pesticides are made from plants and can be more toxic than many of the synthetic chemical pesticides. Mineral pesticides such as copper dust and sulfur are commonly used to form a protective coating over plant parts.
5. Synthetic chemicals are made by humans. These chemicals that kill or protect against pests are of either natural or synthetic origin.

Pesticides can have an impact beyond their intended target. Nothing is absolutely safe. Some products are toxic even in minute quantities. Others of moderate toxicity can build up to higher levels in the environment. Insects are more likely to become resistant to pesticides when they are repeatedly exposed to them.

Always read and follow the directions exactly as they are given, no matter what type of pesticide you use. Then, use it with care, avoid spilling any on yourself, and always wash thoroughly after use.

Smart Pesticide Use

Smart gardeners time treatments to be most effective on the target pest but least disruptive to natural predators of those pests. Here are key tips for smart pesticide use:

- Identify the pests attacking your plants. Check with nearby veteran gardeners, garden center authorities, or county extension agents.
- Choose the right pesticide to control that pest. Some examples of less toxic materials are pyrethrins, insecticidal soaps, and horticultural oils. Buy the smallest quantity needed so you don't have half-full bottles lying around your property.
- Check the label that identifies the chemicals in the container and carefully read the mixing and use directions.
- Mix pesticides correctly. More isn't better. It is wasteful and can be damaging and dangerous to your plants and you.
- Be careful of spills. Clean up any immediately with litter, newspaper, or rags. Do not try to wash it away.
- Do not apply pesticides when it is windy or raining or in a place where it is likely to drift to a body of water.
- Dispose of leftover pesticide mixes safely. Do not pour any leftovers in storm drains or in a field or elsewhere.
- Store containers of remaining pesticides safely, away from children, and dispose of the empty container as noted on the label.
- Never, ever sniff a bottle that has pesticide in it. Some people are especially allergic to chemicals. Always remember that pesticides are poisons designed to kill insects.

ALERT!

Don't take chances with your health. The label is the law! Pesticide users should never use a pesticide in any way contrary to its labeling directions. The instructions are like a prescription, they tell how to mix and apply and list precautions that must be observed.

Use good common sense when you are mixing and using pesticides of any kind. The septic system and its leach field can be seriously damaged if you empty pesticide chemicals there or pour them down a toilet. Check with your local authorities. Many towns now offer arrangements to dispose of unwanted garden chemicals safely.

Biological Insect Control

Many very effective biological pest controls have become available during the past twenty years. These naturally occurring pathogens destroy specific insects without harming other creatures.

The biological control most commonly used in gardens is *Bacillus thuringiensis* (Bt). This bacterium kills many kinds of insect larvae by paralyzing the digestive system. Bt is sold as a dust or liquid under trade names such as Dipel and Thuricide. Milky spore *(Bacillus popillae)* is another example of a biological pest control. Once the bacterium becomes established in the soil, it can effectively control the Japanese beetle population in your yard for up to twenty years.

Chapter 9

Natural Gardening Know-How

Today, millions of Americans want to get back to natural foods, natural tastes, and natural gardening. According to natural gardeners, if we tune in to what kindly old Mother Nature teaches us, we can all live better lives. This chapter will give you an overview of organic gardening and offer suggestions for success.

What Is Organic Gardening?

Basically, organic gardeners don't use synthetic fertilizers or pesticides. However, organic gardening is much more than what you don't do. Natural, or organic, gardeners think of their plants as part of a whole system within nature that starts in the soil and includes the water supply, people, wildlife, and even insects. An organic gardener tries to garden in harmony with natural systems and works to replenish any resources that the garden consumes. At its base, organic gardening begins with improving the soil by regularly adding organic matter.

Everyone has access to the raw ingredients of organic matter. You produce them every day from your lawn, garden, and kitchen. Decaying plant materials, such as grass clippings, leaves, and kitchen vegetable scraps, are the building blocks of compost. By adding compost to your soil, you're well on the way to raising a beautiful, healthy garden organically. The other key to growing organically is to choose plants suited to the site and area that are able to grow without a lot of special attention.

FACT

Today, more people want to restrict the amount of fats, salt, additives, and chemicals in their foods. Natural foods are being widely promoted; just look in your local supermarket.

Natural Growing Methods

Organic gardening is a practical, productive, and wholesome approach to producing an abundant and flavorful food supply. To some, organic gardening means growing plants without any commercial pesticides or fertilizers. The purists rely on manure, bone meal, fish and seaweed fertilizers, and other basics. Other organic gardeners use pyrethrum, an insecticide made from South African flowers, and accept commercial nitrogen fertilizers that are produced from a solid form of the nitrogen in the air, for use with phosphates and potash. Today there is a wide range of opinions as to what organic gardening really is.

People still ask if they can effectively, realistically control destructive garden insects without using pesticides. The answer is yes, without the extensive use of insecticides, you actually have less of a battle against bugs and beetles than you might expect.

FACT

Organic gardening has its roots in the victory gardens of World War II. At that time, commercial fertilizers and pest control chemicals were needed on farms to produce enough crops to feed the military and the country during wartime. Home gardeners had to learn to improve soil with organic materials and control bugs without pesticides. So they developed natural gardening methods, which they passed on, and today, more gardeners use these methods than ever before.

Pest Control Options

Many gardeners become anxious when they see pests on their plants. It is natural to react when you see damaged plants. However, good organic gardeners don't overreact. They focus on the central principle of organic gardening: growing plants in harmony with nature. Even those pests that eat your plants are a crucial part of that natural system. When you see them, be sure to take the time to see what they're really doing. Are they destroying the plant or just nibbling a bit? Healthy plants outgrow minor damage. Remember that insects mostly attack stressed, unhealthy, weak plants. Perhaps you should focus instead on fertilizer and soil improvement to build up your plants' health so they can resist insect attack?

ESSENTIAL

For reliable organic gardening information and bushels of details on how to grow naturally, visit the *Organic Gardening* magazine Web site at ✍ *www.organicgardening.com*. It contains a wealth of knowledge from leading experts.

Pest Control Products

To control harmful insects without harsh pesticides, you have a good choice of materials. These days you can find natural pest controls at garden centers, and many more are available from suppliers who advertise in organic gardening magazines.

Oil-Away suffocates insects and their eggs on beans, beets, cukes, squash, peppers, and tomatoes. Organic Spray/Dust is a four-in-one product that combines the benefits of sulfur, rotenone, pyrethrum, and copper to control diseases and many insects. Eco-Oil insecticide spray is useful on fruit trees all season long. Many other products are also available at chain-store garden departments and local garden centers.

To stop an acute pest invasion, you can choose from several natural products that affect specific insects and won't harm humans, pets, or wildlife. Among the best of those products is *Bacillus thuringiensis* (Bt), a naturally occurring bacterium that you can apply to your plants to disrupt the digestion of caterpillars and other leaf-eaters. Be sure to identify the pest positively before you buy this product. Each strain of Bt affects specific kinds of insects. Check the product label or call experts.

The leading mail-order firm for organic gardening pest control products, fertilizers, and a wide range of other aids is Gardens Alive at *www.gardensalive.com*. Their popular Stay Organic Garden Club has an extensive membership and is a great resource for natural gardening questions. (See Appendix C for their mailing address.)

Preventive Measures

The best defense against insect attack is to institute preventive measures. Fertilize your soil so it feeds your plant properly. Don't let them get too wet, too dry, or too shaded. Most important, encourage the pest insects' natural predators to hunt in your garden. Beneficial insects are amazingly helpful in controlling the bad bugs. Birds, frogs, and lizards also control pests by eating them.

Protective Barriers and Traps

Barriers such as row covers of netting and plant collars can effectively protect crops from pests. Sticky Tanglefoot compounds and pheromone lures are another way to minimize your pest problems without harming other living things in your garden. Reemay row covers and other barriers, along with traps available at your local garden center and in mail-order catalogs, are an organic gardener's alternative to chemicals.

ESSENTIAL

Always carry a zippered plastic bag with you as you wander around the garden. That way you will have a handy container to hold bugs that you pick off plants, the good old-fashioned way—by hand. Then simply crush them inside the bag.

Companion Plants Thwart Pests

Veteran natural gardeners realize that certain plant combinations have unusual powers for helping each other grow. Scientific research has confirmed that some combinations have real benefits. Hands-on experience has demonstrated how to match certain plants for their mutual benefit. Here are some special combinations and what they offer you for better gardening.

Cabbage and dill—Dill seems to be a useful companion for cabbage family plants, such as broccoli, Brussels sprouts, and cabbage, because dill attracts tiny beneficial wasps that control imported cabbageworms and similar pests.

Cabbages and tomatoes—Gardeners report tomatoes repel some moth larvae that would otherwise eat cabbage leaves.

Chives and roses—Pungent chive with its attractive purple blooms also seems to repel some rose pests. Chive in other garden areas also seems to have some bug-chasing advantages.

Corn and beans—Organic gardeners have said that beans attract beneficial insects that prey on corn pests such as leafhoppers, fall armyworms, and leaf beetles.

Cucumbers and nasturtiums—Veteran organic gardeners report that nasturtiums repel cucumber beetles. They are also host plants for beneficial insects that feed on cucumber pests.

Garlic and roses—Garlic repels rose pests.

There are many other combinations that you can look up in the *Rodale Organic Gardening Encyclopedia.* This book should be on the shelf of anyone who wants to become a successful and prolific organic gardener. The Rodales have been pioneers in the organic gardening movement since the World War II victory garden days.

Beneficial Bugs

Beneficial insects are another natural gardening tool. They help us by eating insect pests that devour or damage flowers, vegetables, trees, and shrubs. Happily, they are part of the natural balance of our ecosystem and are readily available by mail. Good bugs eat bad bugs. That's a fact. It is nature's way of balancing the environment. Scientists call this natural balance of good insects against bad insects *biological control.*

FACT

Kids get a kick out of watching bugs. You can get a lot done by putting the two together. Put the following beneficial bugs to work and watch kids really dig into gardening.

Each insect species has its own population range. If one species increases above that range, the insects that feed on that species will increase their own populations accordingly because there is much more food available. When the pest population has been brought down to a normal natural range, the amount of food available for the good insects to eat is reduced. As a result, the good insect, or predatory, population reduces itself naturally—through starvation or dispersion in search of better eating grounds. In this curious way, nature always works to achieve a balance.

You can take advantage of this natural phenomenon and put environmentally friendly allies to work for you controlling the nasties in your gardens and home landscapes. Here are some of your best beneficial insects and a bit about what they do for you.

Praying Mantis

The praying mantis gets its name from the form of its peculiar front legs, which are designed for seizing and holding prey. One segment of the leg, the femur, has a groove that is armed on both sides by a row of spines. The next segment is the tibia. This part snaps into the groove like the blade of a pocketknife.

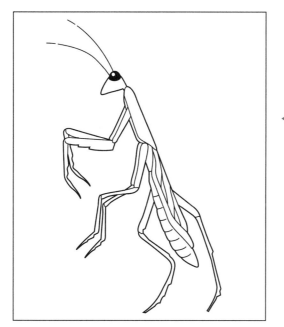

◀ Praying mantis

The mantis sits motionless with these powerful legs raised together in front of its body. To some, it seems to have a prayerful attitude. Probably prey-full is a better description. Mantises are the tigers of the insect world. They feed on almost any insect of a size they can overcome. They are also cannibals, feeding on any insect alive and moving, including other mantises.

After mating in the fall, females deposit their eggs in a frothy secretion that hardens and protects eggs from predators and severe winter climates.

The egg cases are attached to vegetation and may contain 100 to 400 eggs. The average is 200. At least ten to fifteen hot days in spring are required for hatching. When baby mantises hatch, they crawl from between tiny flaps in the case and may hang from silken threads in a living chain.

Mantises are well camouflaged and can range from brownish to green to blend in with foliage and bark. To harness their insect-eating appetites, you can hang cases you collect from shrubs and plants or buy them from mail-order suppliers. Run a needle and thread through the outer surface of the case and tie the thread to a branch.

You can also hatch them indoors in a large glass jar with a screen top, but you must watch them carefully. As soon as they begin to hatch, scoop up the young and distribute them around your garden so they can begin their useful insect-eating work.

FACT

Praying mantises fascinate kids and their classmates. Consider sending a mass of frothy eggs to school to hatch there. But you must get them home the day they hatch because they need to start eating right away and their food is the nasty pests in your garden.

Lovely Ladybugs

The common ladybug is the most abundant of about 370 species that occur in North America. It is an efficient and important insect predator because it feeds on tiny, soft-bodied insects, as well as the eggs and small larvae of many other harmful insects, including moths. The ladybug's favorite food is aphids, those juice-sucking nasties that can cripple young plants. They also consume scale insects, thrips, mealybugs, leafhoppers, leafworms, earworms, corn borers, and bean beetles. When ladybugs first hatch in spring, they begin feeding on aphids and other tiny insects. One larva, which looks like a black six-legged alligator with orange spots, will eat about 400 aphids during its larval period.

After three or four weeks, larvae attach themselves to a leaf or twig and enter the pupal state. In another week, the pupal skin splits and a hungry young ladybug emerges. They begin feeding on harmful insects immediately. As an adult, one ladybug may eat 5,000 aphids. Within a few weeks, each ladybug will lay up to 1,500 tiny yellow eggs in clusters of 10 to 50.

Ladybugs are available from biological insect control firms and mail-order seed companies. They are shipped as mature bugs and should be released immediately on arrival. However, if they don't like their new environment because there aren't enough insects to eat, they may fly away in search of a better food supply.

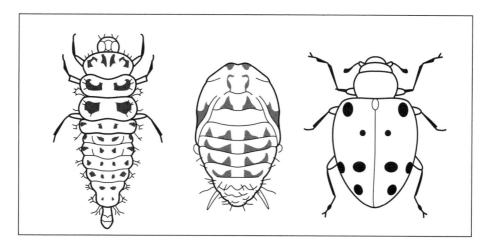

▲ Ladybug in stages of growth

It is best to release ladybugs in the evening because they will not fly at night and need a settling down period after being handled. Sprinkle the release area with water to give them a drink when you turn them loose. When releasing large quantities, gently scatter or spread them out so each bug can find food immediately. Ladybugs are another valuable insect ally for natural pest control around your home and garden.

Green Lacewings

The green lacewing is a beautiful, yet fragile, light green insect with lustrous golden eyes. Adults are ¼ to ¾ inches long. They feed on honeydew, nectar, and pollen. Adults place their eggs on foliage at the ends of short filaments as a means of protection, especially from each other. In a few days, lacewing larvae, also called aphid lions, emerge from the eggs. Larvae are excellent predators with a voracious appetite for a wide variety of aphids, mealybugs, cottony cushion scales, red spider mites, and thrips. They also eat the eggs of many harmful worms.

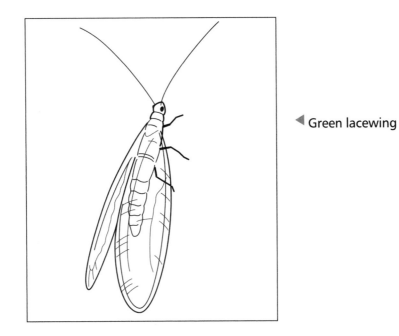

◀ Green lacewing

In two to three weeks, the larvae pupate by spinning a cocoon with silken thread. Adults emerge in about five days by cutting a hole in the cocoon. You can have several generations of lacewings in one season, depending on the climate. In warm summers, it is possible for a cycle to occur within a month.

Green lacewings are also available from biological control firms and mail-order seed companies that provide eggs. These eggs look like a mass of fibrous stalks with pale green eggs attached. Within a few days, they will turn gray and then hatch the following day, leaving a white eggshell.

The tiny larvae look like minute alligators, but they grow in several weeks to almost ½ inch in length. They should be released in your garden as soon as they arrive by mail. Lacewings are so active they will eat each other if they can't find a ready supply of harmful insects in the garden.

Hungry larvae will search almost 100 feet for their meals and can provide an effective, natural biological control in the gardens around your home. Put Mother Nature to work this year. These good bugs really are a natural benefit for all home gardeners.

FACT

Flower flies are attracted to flowers to feed on nectar and pollen. The larvae feed on aphids in tight places where other good bugs can't go, and they are especially helpful in early spring, before other beneficial insects are active. Flower flies also pollinate strawberries and raspberries, producing larger fruits and higher yields.

Other Beneficial Bugs

Here are few other insects that will prey on your destructive bugs.

Ground beetles are large, long-legged, shiny blue-black or brown beetles that hide under rocks and logs during the day. They feed on slugs, snails, cutworms, and root maggots. You can attract them by providing perennial ground covers, stones, or logs.

Parasitic wasps attack the eggs of insect enemies and are one of the most important insect groups that provide control of garden pests. You can attract them by growing pollen and nectar plants.

Pirate bugs, ambush bugs, and **assassin bugs** prey on many insects, including tomato hornworms, thrips, spider mites, many insects' eggs, leafhopper nymphs, corn earworms, and other small caterpillars. To encourage these helpful allies, consider planting buckwheat, corn, bunch grasses, shrubs, and other permanent plantings that provide them shelter.

Spiders feed on insects and are useful in preventing pest outbreaks. Spiders normally found in gardens do not move indoors and most are not poisonous. Permanent perennials provide shelter and increase spider populations in your gardens.

Tachinid flies look like houseflies, but they are very important enemies of cutworms, armyworms, tent caterpillars, cabbage loopers, gypsy moths, sawflies, Japanese beetles, squash bugs, and sowbugs. Grow pollen and nectar plants to attract them.

FACT

According to experts at *Organic Gardening* magazine, you can attract lacewings, ladybugs, syrphid flies, and other beneficial insects if you plant blazing star, candytuft, caraway, coreopsis, coriander, cosmos, scabiosa, sweet alyssum, tansy, and yarrow.

Trichogramma is a tiny, parasitic wasp. It stings and lays eggs on cabbageworms, hornworms, earworms, cabbage loopers, and many other moth pests whose eggs hatch into caterpillars.

Attracting the Good Bugs

Groundbreaking research over the past decade has revealed how to attract beneficial insects. Organic gardeners have been monitoring this research and compiling a list of plants that are both ornamental and effective in attracting and sheltering beneficial insects. Scientists are discovering that some flowers are much better sources of nectar and pollen to sustain beneficial insects than others. Their research is also revealing the best plants to grow for shelter to help good bugs thrive, which is good for them and great for your gardens! An added bonus is that many of the nectar-sipping, pest-eating insects that are attracted to flower pollen will also pollinate your fruit and vegetable crops and increase your yields.

Here are the top ornamental plants to use as adjacent plants to attract beneficial insects. All are easy to grow.

Anise hyssop is a perennial, summer-blooming plant with fuzzy purple or violet flower spikes on 2- to 3-foot-high plants with licorice-scented leaves. Nectar-rich flowers are attractive to butterflies and pest-eating insects.

Borage is an annual herb with bright blue clusters of edible flowers. Studies in Switzerland have shown borage to be attractive to good bugs including green lacewings.

Cornflowers or **bachelor's buttons** are useful because the leaves release nectar even when flowers are not blooming. Research in Germany has found that the nectar has a sugar content of 75 percent. This nectar is highly attractive to flower flies, ladybugs, lacewings, and beneficial wasps.

Fennel flowers attract beneficial nectar-feeding insects. Fennel is also a host plant for caterpillars of the anise swallowtail butterfly, a treat to see in gardens.

Golden marguerite is a long-blooming perennial that produces bright yellow 2-inch daisies that are attractive to ladybugs, lacewings, tachinid flies, and tiny wasps. This perennial thrives in poorer soils, growing 2 to 3 feet high and wide. Remove dead flowers to encourage it to rebloom.

Sweet alyssum is a low-growing annual that has lovely white blooms that are very fragrant. Various studies have indicated that sweet alyssum is highly attractive to aphid-eating insects.

Avoiding Disease

New, improved fruit trees, berries, and vegetable varieties are now available that have built-in genetic resistance to common plant diseases. If you can't find disease-resistant varieties locally, don't worry. Mail-order nurseries and seed firms have tuned in to the growing popularity of organic gardening. They now identify varieties that have genetic resistance to diseases. Carefully check the listings and select those that help you avoid diseases and the use of unwanted chemicals and still beat bugs. Be sure to put those plants in the conditions they require because a stressed plant is more susceptible to disease.

Many fungal diseases are encouraged by constant moisture and too little air circulating around plants. Avoid watering in the evening when moisture may stay on plant leaves and encourage fungus, mold, or rusts to grow.

Try these steps for plant disease control:

- Use disease-resistant hybrids and cultivars
- Rotate annual crops

- Allow enough space between plants and prune them
- Time watering so foliage dries by nightfall
- Remove and destroy diseased plants and plant parts
- Keep your garden clean of plant debris that may harbor disease organisms or insects

Plan your garden with enough room to accommodate full-grown plants; water evaporates more slowly and air doesn't circulate well among crowded plants. Also, water your garden beds deeply and then allow the top level of soil to dry out before watering again. If diseases do appear, remove the afflicted leaves from your garden as soon as possible.

ESSENTIAL

It is important to recognize that disease-resistant plants aren't just for organic gardeners. Plant breeders have been creating exceptional new varieties of vegetables and fruits that have excellent taste and high yields and are worth growing in your garden.

Sprinkler hoses are useful and newer drip irrigation systems are inexpensive and worthwhile. Timers enable you to set the amount of water to go into beds or garden areas and the water gets delivered while you're at work.

Natural Fertilizers

Garden centers offer a variety of processed and dried manures for easy use. Organic gardening firms also produce a range of natural fertilizers. For example, Vegetables Alive works wonders to boost productivity on salad greens, beans, melons, squash, and other garden vegetables. You can also try Tomatoes Alive, Sea Rich foliar spray, and Harvest Alive, made from plants, animal manures, and liquified seaweed nutrients.

Chapter 10

E Best Bet Vegetable Varieties

There's no doubt that fresh eating is the best eating. Prove it to yourself. Pluck a ripe ear of corn from the stalk, pop it into a pot of boiling water, and judge for yourself. Pick a ripe, red tomato and compare it with one from the supermarket. Any gardener with taste buds will verify that homegrown can't be beat.

Tasteful Fun

Vegetable gardeners are often asked why they grow food when they can buy it at supermarkets. Some say for exercise. Most explain that homegrown food just naturally tastes better than store-bought food. Others like the fact that you get to pick vegetables at peak ripeness when they are filled with vitamins and minerals. And some simply have fun growing their own veggies.

Picking your own fresh vegetables and fruits just outside your back door is tasteful fun. Homegrown food also provides a diversity of colors, shapes, and sizes. You can grow bite-size peppers for dips and salads or grape-size tomatoes that burst with flavor. Tomatoes, melons, lettuce, eggplants, Swiss chard, and even sweet corn are now available in a rainbow of colors. There are yellow watermelons, striped beets, purple beans, pink eggplants, purple asparagus, and red sweet corn available to grow as colorful meals. You won't find many of these exotics on grocery store shelves!

Kids can grow unusual vegetables in all shapes, colors, and sizes. For example, children can have fun growing white pumpkins, orange watermelons, UFO-shaped summer squash, blue potatoes, and even golden beets. You might just get them to eat the vegetables they've grown themselves.

To millions of Americans, gardening is one of the tastiest hobbies. In fact, gardening is America's number one family hobby and—pun intended—it is growing bigger! Look around your neighborhood and town. If you like what others have done with their gardens, think about what you can do with yours. You can have one of the better gardens and enjoy tastier eating by making use of the information you'll find here.

FACT

Some people think that all new varieties are hybrids, but many new flowers and vegetables introduced each year are open pollinated (i.e., OP varieties). An open-pollinated plant has one parent plant, while a hybrid plant comes from the seed that results from the cross-pollination of two different species of inbred parent plants.

All-America Selections

All-America Selections are truly the best in America. The secrets are in the seeds. Millions of dollars are spent developing and testing new, improved flowers and vegetables. Proof of performance of new varieties is demonstrated in 235 test and display gardens coast-to-coast, in all soils and climates. Those that are judged the best varieties become All-America Selections.

It's an incredible story of careful breeding, testing, and proving the best new flowers and vegetables for America's gardeners. Since 1933 there have been 573 winners named. All-America Selections trials are held at more than fifty-seven officially designated test gardens across the United States and Canada.

Trial rows of new varieties are grown for side-by-side comparison with the most similar established variety. To be judged a winner, the new variety must be adapted to a wide range of soils, climates, and cultural practices around the entire country. In evaluating vegetables, judges look for convenient size and improved flavor plus resistance to insect pests and adverse weather such as droughts. Home gardeners trying to avoid using pesticides have benefited greatly from the disease- and insect-resistance programs that have produced specialized varieties.

FACT

Some of the world's most experienced and knowledgeable authorities in flowers and vegetables plant and observe new variety seeds. All judges are volunteers with vast experience and expertise.

You can see for yourself these new varieties at All-America Display Gardens. Check the list included in Appendix B. You can obtain the location of the test and display gardens in your area by sending a stamped, self-addressed envelope to All-America Selections, 1311 Butterfield Road, Suite 310, Downers Grove, IL 60515.

On the Lookout for Location

Take a hard look at your land. Is your garden located in the best possible place? Location can be a major factor in success. Focus on the following key questions.

- Is the soil in the spot you've chosen clay, silt, loam, or a mixture? No matter what it is, you can improve it—but it is smarter to pick a site that already has rich organic soil and is well drained.
- Does the ground slope or have gullies? A flat area makes gardening easier and avoids erosion.
- Is there ample sunlight each day? Choose a site that gets at least six hours of sunlight daily. Avoid gardening close to tall trees that shade plants and compete for nutrients and water.
- What are water considerations? Water is vital to all plant life. Having ample water during the growing season is essential, especially when crops are ripening.
- Is your garden convenient? All other factors being equal, it is smart to pick a spot that is nearby (i.e., close to or just outside the kitchen door).
- What are the spring and fall frost dates? In northern areas, you'll need to look for short-season crops and extend your season by starting seedlings indoors.
- What food does your family prefer? Smart gardeners choose vegetables their family likes and will eat, especially the children.

Plan Your Garden Plot

You have a choice of three types of gardens: a conventional row crop garden, a raised bed garden, and a container garden. Most people prefer a row garden with marked borders where they can grow vegetables and herbs. These gardens are easy to plot on paper, organize, and plant. Basic row gardens are good for large crops such as corn, beans, and potatoes.

ESSENTIAL

Sometimes working backward from an expected harvest date makes planning easier. Count off the days on your calendar from planting to harvest. Then check your vacation dates to make sure you'll be home to enjoy the peak harvest time from your garden. Or, reschedule the planting dates.

Raised bed gardens are gaining popularity nationwide, especially among senior gardeners. You can make garden frames of wood or stone or merely add topsoil as raised growing areas. Gardeners who have tried raised beds report better drainage, faster soil warm-up, and easier care. By focusing on higher plant density and providing the necessary nutrients for a smaller space, raised-bed gardeners say that such beds produce more food for less work than conventional row cropping.

Container gardens are sprouting everywhere as well. They're on porches, balconies, patios, and even rooftops. Chapter 17 focuses on this fast-growing trend favored by millions of avid green thumb gardeners who have no backyard space but still want to grow veggies and flowers.

Plot It on Paper First

Plot your growing success on graph paper. Keep garden catalogs and this book handy for reference. Make a list of all the veggies that you would like to enjoy. Measure and sketch your garden site to scale on graph paper.

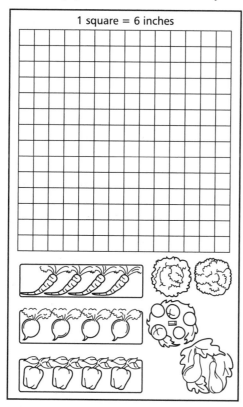

1 square = 6 inches

Clearly mark which crops will be seeded and which will be transplants. Then add notes of which seeds to start indoors so they'll be ready for outdoor transplanting at the frost-free spring planting time. You can use the seed catalogs to figure out the days to maturity for each crop.

Next, add estimated planting and harvest dates. If you want extended harvests, look for early-, mid-, and late-season maturity crops and also stagger the planting times. Be sure to plan as well for early cool-weather crops like broccoli and cabbage that can be planted in summer and again for a fall crop.

▲ Garden plot for planning your garden

Keep Records

Keeping records will help you map your growing success and help eliminate problems or plants that didn't thrive or perform as expected. You can also plot out pest control programs more effectively. Garden record keeping lets you learn from both mistakes and accomplishments. Set up your records in a way that makes sense to you. For example, you could record findings in table form:

How Much to Plant per Person	
Vegetable	**Fresh Use**
Broccoli	4 plants
Bush beans	15 feet of row
Corn	15 feet of row
Cucumbers	2 hills
Greens/Lettuce	10 feet
Peppers	3 plants
Pole beans	3 poles
Squash, summer	2 hills
Tomatoes	3 plants

ALERT!

Some disease and insect problems can attack the same crops every year if they are replanted in the same location. Crop rotation helps break the pest cycle by giving different crops a chance to use different nutrients in the soil and by giving some soil areas a chance to rest from crops that are big nutrient feeders.

Crossing Borders

Vegetables need not be restricted to vegetable gardens. You can expand your garden food growing anywhere you wish. A hot new trend in home gardening treats vegetables as decorative plants and mingles them in flowerbeds and borders. In recent years, vegetable breeders have focused on the ornamental qualities of vegetables, especially the colors of food crops. Today many vegetables look as good as they taste. For years, gardeners kept their vegetable plots separate from their flower gardens. This separation allowed them to use pesticides only on the veggies and kept the less-attractive food plots away from decorative gardens. Modern gardeners have new visions.

Today's gardeners have redefined what is ornamental including foliage, fruit, and seedpods. Since 1980, the typical backyard food garden has shrunk from about 800 square feet to about 200 square feet. Therefore, combining veggies, fruits, and ornamentals in limited space is practical. Container gardening has become popular, and with it, gardeners are blending veggies and flowers in planters on windowsills, porches, and balconies, thus producing food as well as beauty. Gardeners have also rediscovered herbs, which are beautiful, flavorful, and compatible in both the veggie patch and ornamental bed.

Designer Greens

Every few years new gardening ideas and delights land in America from gardens overseas. Mesclun is a case in point and worth attention. It is a fast-growing new trend nationwide and with good reason. The idea of planting and harvesting mesclun—many types of salad greens mixed together—originated in the Provençal region of France and has been enthusiastically adopted in this country. Fancy restaurants feature mesclun on their menus, and some grocery stores sell it for a whopping $8.99 a pound! These assortments of greens are appreciated for the sophisticated mixture of flavors, textures, and colors, wholesome taste, and ease of preparation. "Designer greens" are the rage for health-conscious Americans because these leafy mixes known as mesclun are not only low in calories and high in nutrition but also very tasty.

Mesclun Advantages

Mesclun yields for a long period, it does not need cooking, and it is nicely nutritious and delicious. Commercially packaged seed assortments typically feature plants with a variety of colors, flavors, and textures such as peppery mustard greens, chicory, butterhead lettuce, arugula, romaine, endive, cress, chervil, and perhaps parsley. Gardeners can make their own custom mesclun by mixing the seeds of several types of lettuces and other greens to suit their family's tastes.

Piquant and milder mixes are the two main divisions of mesclun. The National Garden Bureau recommends planting piquant and milder mescluns in separate wide rows and then harvesting them separately and mixing them in proportions to suit the occasion, meal, and personal taste.

FACT

Even edible flowers or the petals of bachelor's buttons, calendulas, chive blossoms, marigolds, nasturtiums, and violets may be part of a mesclun mix. Mesclun seeds are blended to many tastes and appropriately called by such names as spring salad, stir-fry greens, Nicoise, piquant mix, Provençal, garnish mix, and so forth. Rarely are seed packets simply labeled mesclun.

Let Lettuce Be a Base

Lettuce is often a base for mesclun. There are four types of lettuce: looseleaf, cos or romaine, butterhead, and crisphead. The easiest to grow are the looseleaf varieties, which are the backbone of most mescluns. An old variety that is quite heat resistant for summer growing is Oakleaf. Prizehead is a reddish-green variety known best for its crisp sweetness. Black Seeded Simpson is a fast-growing green leaf lettuce particularly suited to spring and fall crops.

Growing Mesclun from Seed

Mesclun, like lettuce and its other leafy components, will grow best in soil that is rich, loamy, and of good loose structure. Soils should be well drained and with a pH that is slightly acid to neutral. Salad greens prefer a pH of 6.0 to 6.5. Although some mesclun mixes include greens that are tolerant of heat, most are crops of cool mild weather and will grow in sun to partial shade. When growing mesclun during hot weather, choose a site that is shaded from hot afternoon sun for best results.

The lettuces and other leafy greens are shallow rooted. So work an inch or so of fine organic fertilizer or compost into the top few inches of garden soil before planting them. Mesclun also grows well in containers, making the leafy blends ideal for patio or terrace plantings in tubs and other planters.

Mesclun Care Tips

Mesclun is one of the easiest crops to grow. You can sow seeds and begin to harvest baby leaves in one to five weeks, depending on the season and the temperature of the air and soil. If you plant mesclun every ten days to two weeks, you'll have it for salads and stir-fry dishes all season long.

Seeds will germinate in cool weather, even as low as 40°F. Plant mesclun seed about one to two weeks before the last frost date. Check with your local Master Gardeners or extension agents to see what that date is in your region. Keep the mesclun bed moist but not soggy.

For rows, make a furrow ¼ inch deep, sow the seed, and then cover the furrow. If you sow areas, simply scatter the seeds and cover them with about ¼ inch of fine soil or compost. Keep seeded areas moist for good germination.

ESSENTIAL

Mesclun is at its crispy peak when picked early in the morning before the sun is strong. Use scissors to harvest mesclun greens, beginning when they are only a couple of inches high. This will encourage continued growth. Since some greens grow more quickly than others, the exact proportions of mesclun salads will vary from harvest to harvest.

Get Carried Away with Corn

Corn is as American as apple pie. When you learn how to grow some of the new super sugar sweet corn, you might just become your neighborhood's favorite gardener.

As gardeners, we are most interested in *Zea mays regosa,* the fancy scientific name for sweet corn. But, you can also grow popcorn, the specific type of corn that explodes when heated. Genetic dwarf or midget corn is a unique type with mature ears at 4 to 6 inches in length. The decorative broomcorn is grown for the long fibrous tassels that can be dried for arrangements. You may also want to grow some decorative multicolored flint or Indian corn for fun.

There are hundreds of sweet corn varieties from which to choose. It is worth trying different ones to see which you like best. In recent years, sweet corn has become much sweeter, thanks to plant breeders.

FACT

You have a choice of growing normal sugary *(su)*, sugary enhanced *(se)*, and supersweet *(sh2)*. These types refer to the sugar content and sweet flavor in the kernels when mature. Note the codes so you can order the ones you want when shopping in mail-order catalogs.

Tips for Growing Great Corn

There are just a few simple rules to follow to grow a bumper crop of sweet corn. Select a site on the north side of your garden. Corn plants are tall; so if you plant them on the east or west side, they will cast shadows on the other garden plants and decrease plant production.

There are two basic ways to plant sweet corn: in blocks or in hills. If space is not a problem, plant rows of corn in blocks of a minimum four rows, 2½ to 3 feet apart, as long as your garden space. For adequate pollination, sow all corn seed at the same planting. For small plantings of sweet corn, you may want to try sowing in hills. Hills are groups of four to five seeds sown in a circle, with 2 inches between each seed. Space the hills 2 to 3 feet apart; when the seedlings are established, thin each hill to two to three plants. Many gardeners choose to plant sweet corn varieties in successive sowings to extend the harvest.

When watering, irrigate the soil rather than the whole plant to ensure proper pollination. Sweet corn is wind pollinated; the pollen drifts from the tassel to the silk. If the tassels and pollen are wet with water, the pollen won't leave the tassel or will be washed down to the soil, hampering any chances for pollination. It is critical to water sweet corn during the kernel-filling state, which is just before the appearance of the silk and a couple of weeks after the silks turn brown. During a drought, irrigation every ten to fourteen days will sustain the plants.

Sweet corn matures in nine to fifteen weeks, depending on the variety. For optimum growth and production, keep the sweet corn rows or hills weeded. Hoeing is recommended until the stalks stand 12 to 15 inches tall. As they grow taller, avoid deep disturbances around and between the corn stalks because it may damage the shallow root system. Sweet corn is a heavy feeder and will quickly deplete soil nutrients. Additional fertilizer or compost is needed when stalks are 8 inches tall and again when the tassels appear.

ALERT!

Many gardeners find that raccoons, deer, and other wildlife prefer corn to other garden vegetables. To protect the young ears of corn from raccoons, Jim Schuster, at the University of Illinois Extension Service, suggests sprinkling stalks and leaves with baby powder. Reapply after each rain to deter the raccoons. To deter both deer and raccoons, dangle a bar of Dial soap 6 inches off the ground among the stalks.

When to Pick Corn

Most varieties of sweet corn are ready to eat two and a half to three weeks after pollination. If the husk fits tight to the cob, the corn is ready; if there seems to be looseness or softness, allow the kernels to fill out for another day or so.

If the ear seems to be mature, but you still feel uncertain, carefully pull back part of the husk to expose the kernels. Kernels should be full and plump to the tip of the ear. For normal sugary sweet corn, pop one of the kernels with your thumbnail. If milky juice spurts out, harvest it. If the juice is clear, wait another day. This thumbnail rule for milky juice does not apply to the high sugar types. Both supersweet *(sh2)* and sugary enhanced *(se)* types are mature when the kernel juice is clear. To remove the ear, pull down and twist.

The Tastiest Tomatoes

Tomatoes are America's favorite vegetable. Since the W. Atlee Burpee seed company introduced the first F1 hybrid tomato in 1949, thousands of hybrid tomatoes have been bred and introduced. The most significant breeding accomplishments have been the multiple disease tolerances bred into tomatoes. These tomatoes tolerate diseases such as fusarium wilt or root knot nematodes that would kill other tomato plants. As a result, there is less need for fungicides or pesticides to kill insects that spread diseases.

Classifying Tomatoes

There are three ways to classify tomatoes: fruit shape, earliness to mature, and color. The five major fruit shapes, from the smallest to the largest, are cherry, plum, pear, standard, and beefsteak. Cherry tomatoes are produced in clusters like grapes but have a tendency to crack if not picked regularly. The plum and pear tomatoes weigh between 2 to 6 ounces. Normally, they have meaty interiors, thick fruit walls, and less gel than others. The standard tomatoes are round to a globe shape and weigh 4 to 8 ounces. The beefsteak can be 2 pounds or more, depending on the variety. Tomatoes are quite diverse and many gardeners enjoy growing several types.

Check Maturity Dates

Tomatoes can be early, mid-season, or late. Early tomatoes will ripen from fifty-five to sixty-five days after transplanting, mid-season in sixty-six to eighty days, and late types require more than eighty days.

There are basically two types of plant growth for tomatoes: determinate and indeterminate. Indeterminate growth means varieties grow, blossom, and produce tomatoes throughout the growing season until killed by frost. The continuous growth produces many main stems, all of which are capable of flowering and producing fruit. Because of the abundant lush growth, pruning indeterminate plants is highly recommended. To support the plant growth and keep tomatoes off garden soil, you should use a wire hoop or a stake for support. Indeterminate plants may be pruned to force larger tomatoes. Without pruning, plants produce smaller tomatoes but more of them. To prune, pinch out the shoots that develop in the U between the main stem and a branch.

Determinate tomato plants reach a predetermined height or number of fruit clusters and don't grow beyond it. The plants flower, set fruit, and ripen in a short time so the main harvest is concentrated into a few weeks for gardeners who wish to can or preserve the fresh tomato harvest.

Sowing Tomatoes Right

Tomato seed should be sown indoors six to twelve weeks before the last expected spring frost date. Most seeds will germinate in five to twelve days. Use a prepared, sterile germination mix as the growing medium and place it in containers with drainage. Water thoroughly and allow them to drain. Sow seeds and cover them lightly with the mix. Mist the top of the medium and cover it with newspaper or plastic to prevent drying out. Keep in a warm place and check every day for germination. When the seeds have sprouted, remove the cover and place the container in a sunny location. Keep seedlings warm and watered regularly.

After a week or two, transplant the young plants into individual 2-inch peat pots filled with a soil-less growing medium. Tomatoes perform best in rich loam with lots of organic matter. Add compost and other organic materials to your soil to improve nutrients, texture, and moisture-holding capacity. Break large clods of soil into small pieces. Rake the garden bed so that it is flat and level.

Tomatoes are one of the easiest garden plants to grow. They need as much direct sunlight as possible to produce the highest yield. Wait until the air and soil have warmed before transplanting tomatoes. Native to the tropics, tomatoes require warm, 70°F temperatures for good growth.

Planting Options

There are several ways to plant a tomato. The traditional method is to dig a hole in the soil and place the plant in it. For you northern gardeners, if your plants are tall and leggy, don't worry, just dig a deeper hole and bury the plant to the first leaf stem. The buried stem will grow roots, which helps develop a deep root system. Deep-hole planting is not recommended for southern gardeners due to fungal rot that attacks the young stems.

Some people prefer the trench method of planting. Dig a long shallow hole and lay the tomato plant horizontally into the trench. Pinch leaves off the stem. Allow the top 2 to 3 inches of stem to lead out of the trench. Push soil on top of the trench and push a pillow of soil under the top stem. The stem will grow up toward the sun. If it doesn't rain for a week, be sure to water tomato plants as long as they are setting fruit. Established tomato plants need about an inch of precipitation per week from rain or irrigation.

Feed Tomatoes Properly

Tomatoes need phosphorus, nitrogen, potash, and minor elements. There are many types of fertilizer. The easiest to use is a timed-release fertilizer at the time of planting. Always follow directions on the label of the fertilizer you buy. Be sure to select a fertilizer that contains more phosphorus *(P)* than nitrogen *(N)* or potassium *(K)* because phosphorus promotes flowering and fruit setting.

Pick Perfect Tomatoes

To achieve the full tomato flavor, allow the fruit to fully ripen on the plant. Wait until it is deep red, or whatever final color the tomato is. Once harvested, no additional sugars will go into the fruit. To harvest, gently hold the tomato and twist it, so that the stem separates from the vine.

ESSENTIAL

Put a tuna fish can in your garden near tomatoes. That will show you if the rain has delivered an inch of water for the week. And, it lets you gauge an inch of water when you sprinkle the garden.

Store tomatoes at room temperature. It is unnecessary to place a ripe tomato in the refrigerator. Tomatoes will store on a kitchen counter for several days. At the end of the season when frost is predicted, all green tomatoes can be harvested and placed on a windowsill for future use. Most will gradually turn red and have some degree of tomato flavor. Placing unripe tomatoes in a closed paper bag will hasten the ripening process.

Avoid Disease and Pest Problems

Tomatoes can get diseases unless you only grow new disease-resistant types. It pays to grow only tomatoes that have that built-in genetic protection. The codes *V, F, N,* or *TMV* mean the plant is genetically tolerant of the following diseases or virus:

Verticillium wilt *(V)* is caused by a soilborne fungus. Symptoms include wilting of older leaf tips, yellowing and browning of leaves in a V-shaped pattern, and leaf drop beginning with the older foliage. As the fungus moves throughout the plant, all leaves will curl upward and the stunted plant will not respond to water or fertilizer.

Fusarium wilt *(F)* is also a soilborne fungal disease. This infection commonly occurs when the soil is above 75°F. Light sandy soils and soils with low pH are most susceptible. Symptoms include yellowing, curling, and dying leaves. Infected plants are stunted and fruits will be small or deformed.

Nematodes *(N)* are microscopic worms living in the soil. Some nematodes are good; some are bad. Bad root knot nematodes cause plants to wilt or portions of plants to die.

Tobacco mosaic virus *(TMV)* is one of the most widespread viruses affecting tomatoes. Weeds harbor the virus, and insects feed on the weeds, transmitting the virus to the plant. The virus source is tobacco. This virus turns leaves dark or light green, possibly even a mottled yellow.

There is no cure for these four diseases or viruses. If you suspect one of these problems may be infecting your plants, they should be destroyed. Do not place diseased plants into your compost. The easiest way to insure you do not have problems with these diseases is to grow tomatoes with disease or virus tolerances.

Late Planting Yields Fall Crops

You can extend your vegetable growing season and get maximum use of your garden space through late summer and early fall by succession plantings. During late summer, newly seeded crops will make rapid growth and mature before extremely cold weather sets in. During fall, days are shorter and temperatures cooler. These conditions, plus favorable soil moisture, provide an excellent growing environment for some vegetables, especially those that "go to seed" during the long, hot days of summer. Here are some excellent late-planting crops to consider:

- **Endive:** Full Heart Batavian, Green
- **Leaf lettuce:** Salad Bowl, Slobolt, Oakleaf
- **Radish:** Cherry Belle, Red Boy, White Icicle
- **Snap beans:** Tendercrop, Provider, Tendergreen
- **Spinach:** Long Standing Bloomsdale, Virginia Savoy
- **Turnip:** Just Right Hybrid, Purple Top White Globe
- **Winter radish:** Round Black Spanish

You can also have success with late summer–planted broccoli for fall harvest and parsnips, which you can leave in the ground and pull all winter. For easier digging, add warm water around those you want to pull out when the ground is frozen.

Chapter 11

(E) International Vegetable Favorites

America's food tastes are changing dramatically. Today ethnic cooking is very popular. In the process, American gardeners have been looking for exotic vegetables to grow for exciting eating adventures, and seed companies have responded. You can now enjoy some of the world's tastiest vegetables picked fresh from your own gardens.

Tasty Wonders of the World

New waves of immigrants have made their homes in the United States in the past decades. You can see the diversity in schools, communities, and in supermarkets, too. For a long time, much of the "face" of the United States reflected the look of Europe; among the largest immigrant groups were Irish, French, German, Polish, Italian, and Scandinavian.

Immigrants Bring Flavor

During the past few decades, however, immigration patterns have changed. Many immigrants have come from Asian countries such as Japan and Vietnam, with many more arriving from Mexico and Central and South America. These newest Americans brought their favorite foods with them and introduced them to their new communities. Many people liked the taste of Asian and Mexican foods. Seed firms saw the demand and responded. Stir-fry cooking rolled across America. Tex-Mex meals became popular. The National Garden Bureau took note of this appealing new phenomenon and responded accordingly.

Year of the Asian Vegetables

To give American gardeners new tastes, the National Garden Bureau celebrated Asian culture and its contributions to North American gardens and ethnic cuisine. They declared 1999 the "Year of Asian Vegetables" and promoted some of the best tastes they could find. There were five popular Asian vegetables featured in the Year of Asian Vegetables. Two require warm summer weather to produce well—Asian eggplant and asparagus (yard-long) bean. The other three vegetables are considered transitional crops; that means they are grown best under spring or fall conditions. These include daikon, pak choi (bok choi), and snow peas. All five vegetables are flavorful, easily grown from seeds or plants, and offer gardeners the opportunity to explore Asian cuisine.

Thanks are due to several expert gardeners who graciously provided tips and growing advice: Kate Jerome, Yukie Benech of American Takii, and Joe Kojima of Sakata Seed America, which the National Garden Bureau harvested and shared for your growing adventures.

Asian Eggplant

Eggplants have been grown in China and India since the fifth century. In the twelfth century, Arabs introduced eggplants into Spain. Supposedly they became popular as an aphrodisiac, which was part of eggplant folklore. Eggplants eventually became popular in England and Italy in the sixteenth century only as ornamental plants; according to historic reports, eggplants were believed to cause madness if consumed. Today you don't need to be mad to eat eggplants. They have become popular worldwide, and there are hundreds of cultivars available.

FACT

Asian eggplants have smaller fruits on smaller plants than traditional Italian and American types. Different types may have glossy black, white, lavender, pink, purple, or green fruit. Asian eggplants are typically long and slender, usually about 2 inches in diameter and up to 9 inches long.

Eggplant Requirements

Choose a site in full sun. Eggplants will thrive as long as the soil is well drained. This is so important that if you have heavy clay–type soil, eggplants should be grown in raised beds. Eggplants also require rich soil with high potassium levels. Adding large amounts of organic matter will help make the soil rich and moisture-retentive. Eggplants need warm soil to grow well.

FACT

Eggplants have long been a favorite food in Greece and other Mediterranean countries. According to nutrition experts, eggplants are also one of the most nutritious foods. As Asian eggplants make news in garden and cooking columns nationwide, this vegetable is finally attracting the attention it deserves.

Be patient. They take a long time to reach maturity. In northern areas, it is best to start eggplants from seed indoors or to purchase bedding plants. Start seeds indoors ten to twelve weeks before the last frost is expected. Plant them outdoors after hardening them off and only after all danger of frost is past.

Transplanting Tips

Transplant eggplants 18 to 24 inches apart in rows 30 to 36 inches apart. In intensive or raised bed gardens, give eggplants 24 inches of growing room in all directions. Eggplants do best in hot weather. They are heavy feeders, so in addition to providing rich soil, feed them with composted manure or a balanced fertilizer when the plants are half grown. Eggplants can tolerate dry conditions but naturally will produce more if well watered during dry spells. Mulching helps preserve soil moisture.

When your plants begin to bloom, cut off the first few flowers. This forces the plants to set more fruit. Oriental eggplant experts recommend staking and pruning Asian eggplants as you would tomatoes. Be aware of flea beetle damage or yellowing bottom leaves that often indicate verticillium wilt. One good way to control flea beetles is by growing plants under row covers until they bloom. If you suspect verticillium wilt, immediately remove the entire plant and destroy it. This action helps prevent the disease from infecting other plants. Another key point: Don't grow eggplants where you've grown any other nightshade plant for three years. That includes tomatoes, of course.

Harvest and Storage

Harvest usually begins in mid to late summer, about seventy to ninety days after seeding. It is best to pick fruits when they are about 6 inches long and their skin is glossy and firm. Use shears or a knife to cut fruits to avoid damaging the plant. If the skin isn't glossy, the fruit is past its prime and will taste bitter. Discard fruits that aren't firm.

Eggplants do not store or freeze well. They are best eaten as soon as possible after picking but can be refrigerated for a few days. A better idea is to cook them with your favorite recipe and then freeze the food. Check your favorite cookbooks for directions.

Asian eggplants are milder and more delicate in flavor than American and Italian types. Gourmets believe they have a more "eggplant" flavor. Because they have especially tender skin, usually there is no need to peel them. Eggplant aficionados declare that these are flavorful grilled, fried, roasted, pickled, or stir-fried. Long Asian eggplants cook very well in a microwave. Test the timing and you'll get a feel for perfection.

Asparagus Beans

The asparagus or yard-long bean originated in southern Asia. It has been grown extensively in Europe and most recently has gained popularity in the United States. These unique beans grow on twining, delicate stems with a strong root system. Plants bloom in midsummer. Once pollinated, these flowers are followed by tiny dark green beans. They can grow to a foot long in a few days. If left unpicked, the beans can grow up to 3 feet long and are a surprising sight.

FACT

Although asparagus beans resemble pole snap beans, asparagus beans are more closely related to southern cowpeas. Asparagus bean, *Vigna unguiculata* subsp. *sesquipedalis,* goes by other names. It is called dow gauk in China, sasage in Japan, and Chinese long bean or yard-long bean in Europe and the United States.

Treat Your Asparagus Beans Right

Asparagus beans thrive in garden soil that is loose and friable. Rich garden soil heavy in nitrogen causes abundant leaf growth but few beans. These are true legumes, which means they enrich their soil by trapping atmospheric nitrogen in nodules on their roots. With the help of nitrogen-fixing bacteria, the plant makes its own food.

To grow asparagus beans most productively, pick a sunny site and loosen the soil to a depth of 8 to 10 inches in preparation for sowing because these plants set deep roots. In the spring, mix in compost or composted manure to boost soil fertility. As climbing beans, they must be grown on a trellis or wire support system. Whichever method you use, make it at least 7 feet high to accommodate these lengthy vines.

Planting and Growing

Asparagus beans thrive in heat and wither in cold, so sow the seeds after all danger of frost has passed and the soil has warmed. Usual timing is to sow them about two weeks after sowing green beans. To move the schedule ahead, you can put down a black plastic mulch to warm the soil earlier.

If you're using a tripod system, plant three or four seeds to each pole. If you're using a row trellis, plant the seeds 3 to 4 inches apart in rows 8 inches apart. Plant the seeds 2 inches deep in good soil or an inch deep in heavy soil. If you have a very long growing season, consider making one or two more successive sowings at two- to three-week intervals. In northern climates, a single sowing in late spring often produces until frost. Asparagus beans germinate in seven to ten days. They will begin producing abundantly once the weather heats up.

ALERT!

Asparagus beans easily tolerate hot weather and even some drought. However, to keep the beans producing, water them during dry spells. It is unnecessary to fertilize asparagus beans unless you have nutrient-poor soil.

Pick, and Pick Some More

You should have mature beans about two months after planting seeds. The vines should continue bearing throughout the summer and into the fall. For the best taste, pick the beans when they are about half the diameter of a pencil; this should be before the seeds have filled out inside and when the pods snap when bent. Continuous picking keeps plants producing. Plants will stop producing, however, if beans are left to ripen. These beans will keep several days in the refrigerator but are best eaten when first picked. You can also blanch and freeze them.

FACT

Asparagus beans get their name because they have a taste similar to asparagus. They have a denser texture than snap beans and a more intense bean flavor. Gourmets say that their texture and flavor hold up well when stir-fried or steamed. If you allow beans to mature, they can be shelled and cooked like southern peas.

Daikon Radishes

There are written references and archaeological remains of winter radishes in ancient China. Today, these radishes go by the name *daikon,* which is the Japanese name for the radish that is so popular in Asian cuisine. Daikons are long and narrow and usually white, green, or creamy yellow. Typical eating size ranges from 2 to 3 inches in diameter and from 6 to 15 inches long. There are round types, too.

Planting a Root Crop

Daikons are a root crop and must have enriched soil for good development. If they grow slowly, they become woody and strong-flavored. Loose, deep, friable soil allows their long roots to develop well. Plant them in full sun for best success. Remember that these particular veggies are a cool-season crop to be harvested in spring or fall.

If you look around, you may find heat-tolerant varieties that will grow during summer. In northern gardens, sow in early spring or late summer. In southern gardens, sow about two months before the last frost so the roots will be ready for harvest in late spring. Plant the seeds ¼ to ½ inch deep in rows 12 to 24 inches apart and thin seedlings to 10 to 12 inches apart.

Key Daikon-Growing Tips

Thinning these radish plants to the correct spacing is very important to the development of healthy, tasty roots. Keep the plants well watered to encourage tender roots. You should also fertilize four weeks after planting with a high-phosphate, high-potash fertilizer. Avoid high-nitrogen formulas that promote leaf development at the expense of roots.

Watch for root maggots, especially if you have grown carrots, cole crops, or radishes in the same area in years past. A sprinkling of wood ashes around the plants will help curb the damage, according to organic gardening authorities.

ALERT!

Store and Serve

Daikon roots are ready for harvest about fifty to sixty days after sowing. You can leave them in the ground after they mature, but the longer they stay, the more pithy and woody they may become. You are well advised to harvest all of the plants as they mature and store them for use. Dig carefully with a spading fork to avoid damaging the roots, especially if you plan to store the plants. They will hold well for several months in a refrigerator or in a root cellar or a cool basement in damp sand. If you don't have good storage conditions or space, you can blanch and freeze them.

Flavors vary from mild to pungent. All types of daikon are crisp and similar to turnips. Peel and slice them raw to serve with dips or in salads. Or, you can boil or steam them and serve them like cooked turnips. Another option is grating them into a stir-fry meal. Daikon greens are tasty when picked young. Try them sautéed like turnip greens. Check seed catalogs and try several types to compare the flavors you like best.

Pak Choi or Bok Choi (Chinese Cabbages)

Pak choi is native to eastern Asia where it has been grown for thousands of years. According to historic records, the Celts brought the vegetable to the British Isles. These Chinese cabbages became popular in Europe in the late 1800s and in the United States around 1900. The plants are grown for their thick white tender stalks that are the petioles and the main veins of the leaves. Typical leaves are dark glossy green with white veins. You can also grow a miniature green variety with green tender stems.

Brassica rapa (*Chinensis* group)—more correctly called celery cabbage, Chinese celery, and Chinese mustard cabbage—is more closely related to mustard than cabbage. Further identification from records tells us that the Cantonese name is *bok choy* or *pak choi* and the Mandarin name is *pe-tsai* or *pei tsai*. The name means "white vegetable" in Chinese. Pak choi is a member of the mustard family, Brassicaceae, to which cabbage, mustard, broccoli, kohlrabi, and turnips belong. Try that knowledge on your guests as you stir-fry their dinner.

Peak Performance

Pak choi performs best in full sun in a somewhat cool spot. It needs rich, loose soil that is very well drained to prevent crown rot. Incorporate lots of well-rotted manure or other organic matter into the planting bed to help retain moisture. Plant pak choi in very early spring and again in mid to late summer for the fall garden.

In cool climates, sow seeds ¼ to ½ inch deep directly in the garden after danger of frost has passed. Sow seeds 3 to 4 inches apart. Thin seedlings to 8 to 12 inches apart.

Plant your Chinese cabbage in rows 2 to 2½ feet apart, or space them a foot apart in raised beds. For fall planting, sow seeds directly in the ground about 3 to 4 inches apart. Thin to 8 to 12 inches once the seedlings develop.

In areas with hot summers, you should start your plants indoors six to eight weeks before the last frost. Plant them in individual pots to avoid damaging their tender roots when transplanting them outdoors, which should be two to three weeks before the frost-free date.

Watch for Pests

Pak choi is a heavy feeder, which means it is important to fertilize with composted manure or a balanced fertilizer four weeks after setting out transplants. Watch for and take precautions against cabbageworms, cabbage root maggots, and flea beetles. These delicious plants can be grown under row covers to keep pests out or sprayed regularly with *Bacillus thuringiensis* to prevent worm damage. Some organic gardeners report having luck repelling flea beetles by alternating rows of pak choi with garlic and green onions. Or, use sprays if you wish.

Harvestable Heads

Pak choi greens can be picked as early as thirty days after sowing, but it takes about fifty to sixty days to produce harvestable heads. For real taste treats, pick outer leaves while they are tender early in season. As the weather heats up, use the tender inner leaves. You can also cut the whole head. At maturity, they may run 3 to 4 pounds. Pak choi is a short-season vegetable so it tends to bolt quickly.

Pak choi keeps several weeks in the refrigerator or for a week or so in a cool cellar. Stalks are not fibrous, even though the plant is sometimes called celery cabbage. Actually they are tender and tastiest when cooked lightly as in a stir-fry. Pak choi is a favored basic ingredient in many Chinese recipes. You can shred the stalks and add them to coleslaw with other types of cabbage. Leaves can be cooked like other greens and the thinned seedlings are a real spring treat when lightly sautéed. Pak choi can be blanched and frozen to add to soups and stews.

FACT

Breeders are developing types of pak choi that take much longer to bolt, but pak choi is a cool-season vegetable, so it just naturally sends up a flowering stalk as soon as the weather gets warm. A flower stalk usually indicates that the stalks and leaves are getting tough.

Chinese Snow Peas

Snow peas actually originated in the Mediterranean. Most people don't realize that they were grown widely in England and Europe during the nineteenth century. They were called English sugar peas or *mangetout* in France. The Chinese incorporated these peas in their cuisine, and they have been known as Chinese snow peas ever since.

Typically, snow peas have light green pods that follow purple or white sweetly scented flowers. The aroma isn't as strong as sweet pea flowers but is pleasant in the vegetable garden. Some varieties climb with twining tendrils to 4 or 5 feet. They save garden space. Dwarf types grow to 2 or 3 feet. Snow peas are true legumes, classified as *Pisum sativum* var. *macrocarpon*.

Preparing for Peas

Snow peas need soil that is rich in phosphorus and potassium. If your soil is somewhat acidic, add wood ash or ground limestone. To provide the best nutrient level, add a fertilizer high in phosphate and potash. There is no need for extra nitrogen since the plants are true legumes and fix atmospheric nitrogen on their roots. Snow peas are another veggie that performs best in soil with ample amounts of organic matter. Plant them in a full-sun site. It also pays to rotate peas to other areas each year to avoid blights and root-rot organisms that may be in the soil.

ALERT!

All snow peas need some sort of trellising, even the dwarf varieties. They have fairly weak root systems, so peas without support don't produce as well as those on a sturdy support. A lightweight trellis of netting or string is sufficient as long as it is securely anchored. Some gardeners use shrubby branches to make a natural trellis. A hoop of green-coated wire is also useful.

Planting Tips

In areas with hot summers, snow peas should be grown as an early spring or fall crop. In areas with mild winters, you can grow them as a winter and early spring crop. Make successive sowings every ten days from March through May for harvest through early July. Some gardeners soak pea seeds for twenty-four hours or sprout them before planting to give them a head start in the cold ground.

Plant peas when the soil temperature reaches 45°F and the soil is dry enough to till. Plant the seeds 1 to 2 inches deep in prepared soil, 2 to 3 inches apart in rows 18 to 24 inches apart. Be sure to put your trellising system in place when you sow the seeds to avoid disturbing the tender roots later.

Keep snow peas well watered during dry periods and cultivate lightly between the rows to remove weeds. Don't cultivate too near the peas, because their roots are extremely sensitive. It helps to apply mulch as the weather warms in order to keep soil cool. As soon as the pea plants have finished bearing, turn them under rather than pulling them, which will provide the soil with nitrogen for future crops.

ALERT!

Watch for fusarium and root-rot diseases. Fusarium wilt, a vascular disease, can usually be avoided by rotating your crops. Another veteran gardener's tip is to avoid root rot by not planting your peas too early.

Pick and Eat

Snow peas are ready to harvest fifty to sixty days from sowing. Pick them when the tiny peas are just beginning to swell inside their pods. That is usually five to seven days after flowering. Harvest as long as the peas are very small, usually daily to keep your plants producing more peas. If the peas are not picked regularly, your plants will stop producing. They also stop producing as soon as the weather gets hot.

Eat or freeze your snow peas as quickly as possible after picking. They can be kept in the refrigerator up to two weeks but tend to lose their intense sweetness. The sweet, crisp, tender pods are eaten whole, either raw or lightly steamed or sautéed.

FACT

The pods lack the papery inner membrane of regular peas, which is why they are so tender. The tender shoots are called *dow miu* and the leaf buds are considered a delicacy in China. You may wish to try these other assets of snow peas yourself.

Hot Pepper Perfections

As Tex-Mex food has grown in popularity from its origins in Mexico and the American Southwest, peppers have become a major crop in gardens nationwide. There is much debate about which peppers are the tastiest and which provide the most authentic flavor and degree of hotness.

In fact, specialty and ethnic peppers from Eastern Europe and Asia also compete with hot peppers that trace their ancestry "South of the border, down Mexico way."

A Variety of Peppers

Hungarian Hot Wax is an enticing yellow pepper. Italia is a Corno di Toro long Italian type, in the shape of a bull's horn and well suited for pasta sauces and stir-fry meals. Habañero is a fiery-hot little orange pepper and Caribbean red Habañero is another ultra-hot. Thai Dragon is an early-maturing fiery red Thai hot pepper. Serrano del Sol is a large, high yielding serrano type. Space doesn't allow listing more, but seed catalogs have hundreds of varieties.

National seed firms also offer a wide range of salsa vegetables. Many seed companies promote a marvelous selection of mild to super-hot peppers. Some newer varieties are ideal for landscaping because of the profusion of bright red and yellow peppers that look like bright ornaments or blooms on the plants.

FACT

Plants get their names in interesting ways. For example, Antohi Romanian pepper is named for a touring acrobat from Romania who defected to the United States in 1991. He had visited his family and brought the seeds of this delicious heirloom pepper to the United States. It now bears his name.

Planting Picky Peppers

Peppers can be a bit difficult, so you should pay attention to their needs. They need a sunny site with enriched soil that has adequate amounts of composted humus. Be sure the earth has warmed up well and any danger of late frost is past. Starting seeds indoors is a good idea to give you a jump on spring and the extra weeks needed for some varieties of peppers.

Once transplanted outdoors, or sown directly from seeds in warm ground, thin seedlings as directed on the seed package for the varieties you grow. Add mulch around them to smother weeds and fertilize them with liquid fertilizer during the season.

Different peppers need somewhat different cultivation, so read the specific directions on the seed package and also in the catalogs. With all the new varieties coming to America, you have a wide choice for tastier eating. Try a variety of peppers and taste-test them on friends, too. That way you'll share the new growing and eating adventures available from around the world, whether you like life very, very hot or not.

Pick peppers when they are ripe and ready. You can cook, stir-fry, make salsa, or even dry these peppers for future use. Give them a premier place in your international garden plans this year.

ESSENTIAL

Check maturity dates, especially if you garden in northern areas. Some peppers begin bearing early and others take longer. Pick early-bearers, start them indoors on your windowsill, and you'll have many weeks of fine dining and peppery pleasures.

Popular International Veggies

Mail-order seed firms have been wandering the world looking for more international food favorites and popular ethnic vegetables. As American plant suppliers find them, they are quick to test, evaluate, and add the best to their catalogs. You'll find a list of dozens of mail-order firms that provide free catalogs in Appendix C. Request a few. Look up the international veggies and try some this year and some others next year. Bit by bit, you'll become a well-read and well-fed gourmet gardener. E

Chapter 12

Enjoy Blooming Beauty

Flowers provide a magnificent bounty of blooming beauty. You can focus on bulb gardens, add other perennials, and include a wide variety of annuals, too. Glorious gardens are yours to enjoy. This chapter is a primer about the blooming beauty you can enjoy and bouquets of flowers you can pick from your home gardens.

Experimenting with Flowers

Today there are thousands of different varieties of flowers in dozens of flower families to brighten your garden. You can plant perennials that reappear every year. Or you can focus on appealing annuals for sparkle. More gardeners are exploring new flower horizons with exotic flowers and new varieties that are being introduced by plant hybridizers each year.

QUESTION?

What is an annual?
Basically, an annual completes its growth in a single growing season and then dies. It starts from seed, sets its roots, grows a stem or stalk and leaves, and produces flowers and seed, all in one growing season.

Colors Can Brighten Your Life

It's a fact. Colors affect people's emotions. Advertisers know that bright colors such as red and yellow excite and give people a warm feeling. That's why they are often called hot or warm colors. Blue, lavender, green, pink, and peach are considered cooler and calmer.

For your home entrance, you may want to create a feeling of warmth and excitement. You can do that by using stronger, more exciting colors such as yellow marigolds and scarlet zinnias. Or, bright red roses!

For your backyard garden, you may want to create a more relaxing mood by choosing cooler or softer colors such as blue violas and pansies. Cool colors work well for a meditation garden or a thoughtful area for quiet reflection.

Dramatic color combinations can give your gardens a distinctive welcoming look. Instead of something as ordinary as red and white, consider orange and blue, which are direct complements on the color wheel, or light pink and green.

Blend Colors Creatively

There are fashionable color trends today for garden and home, according to the National Garden Bureau. In a recent survey, they asked color expert Ken Charbonnau, director of color marketing at Benjamin Moore Paint Company, for his insights on color trends. His professional thoughts as a color expert deserve quoting exactly.

"The biggest thing affecting color over the last five years has been the economy," said Charbonnau. "People want more value for their money, so we are seeing a return to more classic colors and color combinations. Colors will be less trendy and more long-lasting.

"Purple and blue-violet have become popular, but in small doses. Purple and blue-violet bring out the rest of the palette." An avid gardener himself, Charbonnau noted that purples and blues tend to fade away in the garden. They need lots of sun to highlight them, and they must be planted in masses to be seen, or combined with white or yellow to really show off. Home gardeners can bring little doses of purple to their gardens with petunias and a wide choice of other annuals.

Bridging Colors

Next on Charbonnau's list of important colors was coral. In his yard, he has masses of coral and peach-colored flowers against a weathered gray fence. "People are just amazed when they see it," the color specialist exclaimed. "We are also seeing color being used to link new things with things from the past," he said, calling them *bridging* colors. "For example, people tend to think of *Salvia splendens* as coming only in red. Well, have I got news for them—it comes in twelve decorator colors today." Salvia, a long-time favorite, is now fresh and new.

Magenta and Yellow Are Taking Over

Magenta is another important color these days. What was pink is now moving into magenta. It is replacing the rose and mauve colors, which are declining in popularity. Today gardeners seem focused on brighter, happier colors, a National Garden Bureau report notes.

Charbonnau also indicates that yellow is returning to the color palette after a long absence, pointing to combinations such as yellow and white and periwinkle, or yellow and white and purple, noting the use of purple in small doses to bring out the other colors. Gold and yellow-greens are also returning.

Quick Tips on Color

For the past several years, the National Garden Bureau has focused on color in the garden. Here are a variety of useful tips about color that you can use in many different ways.

1. When planning a garden, envision it as a three-dimensional painting. Let the flowers for your beds and borders serve as colors on an artist's palette. Some colors will dominate; others will give depth and dimension. Picture your garden panorama the way you want it to look at its blooming peak.
2. To brighten shady areas, use light-colored annuals. Try white, light pinks, or blues. Dark colors tend to get "lost" in shady areas.
3. Consider how plant colors will blend or contrast with their surroundings. For example, dark red flowers get lost against a brick wall or redwood fence, so use white or pink flowers there. Against a light-colored background, consider a more dramatic color scheme such as dark blue or magenta.
4. Repeated theme colors can unify different garden areas. For example, a row of yellow marigolds or same color petunias can tie different garden areas together.
5. For pleasing variations and a dramatic effect, try using the same colors but in different plant types. If white and blue are your favorite colors, plant different types of bluish flowers such as lavender, blue petunias, and blue salvia. If you like sparkling white, consider white geraniums, white impatiens, or white petunias to carry the color theme but with different flower shapes, form, and foliage.
6. Each area of your garden should have a focal point. If there isn't a focal point such as a pool of water or statuary, use color to create one. Plant a mass of one color in the center of a bed and surround it with flowers or plants that contrast in color, texture, or height. Let your imagination fly.
7. If there is something unsightly in your garden that you can't get rid of and really can't hide, such as a utility pole, plant a colorful focal point away from the object to draw attention from the eyesore.

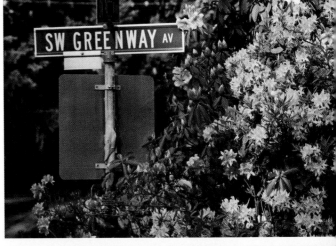

Take Advantage of Annuals

Annuals offer both diversity and versatility. There is an incredible array of sizes, shapes, growing habits, and colors to choose from. Depending on your needs, you can pick annuals that are tall, medium, short, or even climbing like morning glories. Newer hybrids are dwarf in plant growth with large blooms that do well in containers. Most annuals prefer full sun. Others have special virtues such as a delightful fragrance like stock and nicotiana. A few, such as coleus and dusty miller, feature handsome foliage.

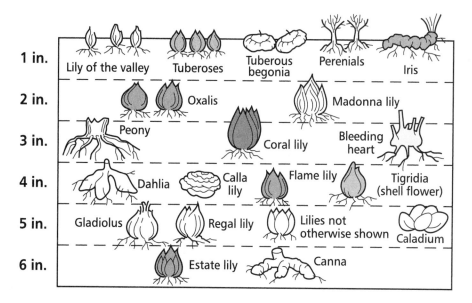

▲ Depth guide to seed planting

Start Annuals from Seed

Aside from the lower cost of a packet of seeds compared to prestarted seedlings, the other major reason for starting annuals from seed is a much wider choice of varieties. Even the best garden centers don't carry the full selection of worthwhile garden annuals; most sell the popular bedding plants. Part of the reason is economics. Garden centers like to sell six-packs of plants that are already in bloom because their customers like to see what they're getting. They also have instant gardens when they buy flats of blooming plants.

You have a choice of starting annuals indoors or seeding them directly in the outdoor garden. As you browse through catalogs, select those annuals that appeal to you and check on their growing needs and suitability for your gardens.

Hardy and Semi-Hardy Annuals

These types of annuals can be sown directly in the garden as early in the spring as the soil has warmed up and can be worked. To get a jump on spring, sow them indoors in pots or flats eight to ten weeks before the last spring frost date. Then transplant them to the garden when the danger of a late frost has passed.

Semi-hardy annuals can be planted outdoors after the threat of frost is past. If you wish to gain growing time, plant seeds indoors six to eight weeks before the last spring frost date.

Tender Annual Considerations

You can sow seeds of tender annuals directly in the garden after all danger of frost is past. Get to know when that is for your locality. Garden center owners are reliable advisers. For an earlier start, sow seed indoors in pots or flats six to eight weeks before the last spring frost date for your area. Again, check with local authorities or the county extension agent for that information. Tender annuals include ageratum, celosia, cosmos, foxglove, marigolds, morning glories, petunias, and zinnias.

FACT

You can take advantage of the prolific nature of some annuals that self-sow at the end of their blooming period when they set and drop seeds that produce brand-new plants the following year. These prolific annuals include ageratum, larkspur, and petunia, among others.

Growing Tender Perennials as Annuals

A tender perennial can be defined as one that won't survive the winter in your climate. Many gardeners treat these plants as annuals for one season and let them die in the fall. Tender perennials that are commonly grown as annuals include hyssop, some flowering sages, and verbenas. Other flowering plants grow from tender bulbs such as cannas, dahlias, and gladioli. Gardeners often plant them as annual flowers for cutting gardens or in mixed ornamental borders.

These tender perennials won't survive the winter outdoors in most of North America. However, because of their beauty and profusion, many gardeners like to grow them and then simply dig up the bulbs at the end of the growing season and store them indoors for replanting the following year.

Care of Annuals Outdoors

Most annuals prefer well-drained soil with a pH between 6.3 and 6.7. They also like organic matter. To get the best results, dig or till in peat moss or compost to help build up the soil's organic matter and allow the plants' roots to spread quickly and get a firm roothold. Space your seedlings as recommended on the seed packet so they don't crowd each other. Remember, all plants need room to mature.

Fertilize transplants at planting time with an organic or slow-release fertilizer. Read and follow directions for the fertilizer you purchase. If you can't plant the seedlings immediately, be sure to keep them in a shady area and water them regularly. Try to get them planted within a few days.

Most annuals flower all season long until cold temperatures or frost kills them. To get the most out of them during their blooming time, try these annual beauty tricks.

- **Deadhead.** Simply pinch off old flowers as they fade. By deadheading, the plant will continue to set flowers and not produce seed.
- **Fertilize at planting time with a slow-release fertilizer.** You shouldn't have to fertilize annuals again during the season. Overfertilizing, especially too much nitrogen, can lead to lush foliage growth.

- **Avoid overhead watering, especially in the evening.** That can harm some types of flowers, especially petunias, and contribute to a buildup of botrytis fungus. A soaker hose or drip irrigation system puts water at the soil level, not on foliage.

ALERT!

Beware of potbound plants. Plants in pots or flats often become potbound with bunches of roots at the bottom of the tray. Carefully break the root mass apart to encourage roots to spread quickly into the surrounding soil.

Consider Climbing Flowers

You can gain dramatic effects with climbing annuals, especially with containers such as window boxes and hanging baskets. They provide an old-fashioned look and are useful on fences, trellises, or other supports. Morning glories, moonflowers, and cardinal climbers are some of the great climbers.

Brighten Up Shady Spots

Areas along walls or shaded by nearby trees may need some help. To brighten them up, think creatively as you consult local garden center specialists and garden catalogs. Coleus and impatiens are good selections.

ESSENTIAL

When winter winds wail, dig out your garden catalogs and locate flowers that thrive in shady spots. Then give them a try in your garden or in containers. The advantage of containers is that when you entertain, you can move the color around to change your outdoor living areas.

Impatiens are particularly beautiful when planted in filtered shade. You can grow them in the ground or in portable containers. Half barrels work well. You can roll them around to dress up patios for parties. Coleus are another excellent choice for brightening shady areas. They are favored for their variegated leaves in yellow, red, and multicolors that add a sparkle themselves. The flowers are of less significance.

Use Cuttings for More Annuals

When your garden has shown you its glory by late summer, you can take cuttings from annuals such as coleus, geraniums, and impatiens and pot them up for winter bloom indoors or for replanting outdoors next spring. Here's how:

1. Clip off all flowers or buds so the plant will focus its energy on developing new roots on the stem cutting.
2. Select cuttings from growing tips or side shoots that are 2 to 6 inches long. Strip off all bottom leaves where the stem will be inserted into the rooting medium. (To give yourself an edge, buy rooting hormones. Then dip the cut stem end into the rooting hormone powder and plant it. This hormone is designed to encourage rapid root growth.)
3. Next, insert the cutting into potting soil and water well. It is a good idea to cover your pot with a clear plastic bag to create a moist, humid greenhouse atmosphere. (Keep this important fact in mind: Don't use a soil-less growing medium for cuttings. They need a potting soil mixture to set roots right.)
4. Check for roots in one to three weeks. To test, gently tug on the cutting. If it holds firmly to the mixture, roots have formed.
5. The next step is to repot new plants in 4- to 6-inch containers. Keep them out of direct sunlight for three to five days as they adjust. Then place your plants in a sunny location.

Benefit from Hybrid Vigor

Annuals have many advantages. New hybrids have more. They are created by plant breeders to grow better and faster and provide better results, often including larger and more profuse blooms. You can try some and if they aren't to your liking, try others next year. Try them for brightly colored flowers and foliage in beds and borders, especially to brighten up shrubbery areas. Use bold splashes of colorful plants in groups for dramatic effect.

For example, many new petunia colors have been introduced over the years. It is worth some space to see how these new, improved, more prolifically blooming petunias can benefit your landscape.

Perfect Perennials

Perennials are perfect for many gardeners. Once planted, they arise each year to reward you with their glorious blossoms. Just as many annuals treat you to several weeks of blooms, some perennials also have extended flowering periods. Here are some favorite perennial flowers.

Perennials That Bloom Eight to Twelve Weeks

- *Achillea*, also called the common yarrow
- *Anthemis tinctoria*, commonly called golden marguerite
- *Chrysanthemum parthenium*, known also as feverfew or *matricaria*
- *Gaillardia grandiflora*, the blanket flower
- *Phlox paniculata*, the old-fashioned favorite garden phlox
- *Rudbeckia*, AKA black-eyed Susan or coneflower

Lasting Favorite Perennials

Perennials should be the base for your flower garden. Once you prepare the soil well and plant them, they will reappear every year to give you decades of delight. Here you'll find a list of top favorites collected for this book from a poll of long-time gardeners. With thanks also to the National Garden Bureau and friends at leading nurseries, treat yourself to perennial loveliness with these favorites. For more information about those that appeal to you, look them up in mail-order catalogs. In the maturity size, the first number is height and the second refers to width.

- **Bouncing Bet** (*Saponaria officinalis L.*) produce clusters of pink, red, or white 3-inch flowers in summer and autumn. It matures at 24 by 20 inches.
- **Creeping phlox** (*Phlox stolonifera*) comes in several colors; it is shade tolerant and produces spring blooms. It matures at 1 by 1 foot.

- **Daffodils** (*Narcissus L.*) are available in many highly fragrant varieties in the poeticus, triandrus, jonquilla, and tazetta groups. They mature at 1 by 1 foot in clumps.
- **Daylilies** (*Hemerocallis L.*) are a delight with the many new varieties being introduced. Here are a few of the most widely available and fragrant ones: Barbara Mitchell, Forty Carats, Fragrant Light, Kathy Rood, and Top Honors. Daylilies mature at 2 by 2 feet in clumps.
- **Fall phlox** (*Phlox paniculata*) is an old-time favorite that deserves space in every garden for its long and fragrant summer blooming. Phlox matures at 3 by 4 feet.
- **Lavender** (*Lavandula L.*) can have purple, pink, or white flower spikes in summer. The newer varieties are hardy and fragrant. Lavender matures at 2 by 2 feet.
- **Lilies** (*Lilium L.*) are available in many hybrid trumpet and oriental varieties with splendid, dramatic colors. There are strongly fragrant varieties, such as the giant white Casa Blanca. Other richly scented varieties are Goldband lily, Regal lily, and Madonna lily. Lilies may grow 3- to 6-feet tall; plant several bulbs for truly dramatic displays.
- **Lily of the valley** (*Convallaria L.*) are perfect for shady areas. This marvelous, low-spreading ground cover has white or pink spring flowers. It likes part shade or sun, matures at 9 inches, and spreads as a ground cover. It can be invasive if the conditions are right.
- **Pinks** (*Dianthus L.*) prefer well-drained soil and full sun, and the spreading plants bloom spring to summer. Pinks mature at 6 by 6 inches and up to 8 by 24 inches.
- **Plantain Lilly** (*Hosta Tratt.*) can have a strong fragrance, in varieties such as Fragrant Bouquet and Guacamole. Hostas have trumpet-shaped white to pinkish flowers in summer. They are one of the better plants for blooming in part shade and for attracting hummingbirds. Hostas mature at 2 by 3 feet.

Enjoy Fragrant Flowers

Beauty is important with flowers. To many veteran gardeners, fragrance is equally important, especially for outdoor entertaining. It pays to plant fragrant flowers upwind so that the usual flow of air or breezes will carry their perfume to where you will be in the garden. By selecting various flowers, both annuals and perennials, you can be assured of the outdoor elegance of the most delightful aromas during the various blooming periods.

For some, the scent of lilacs is a favorite aroma. Others love roses. Here are some plants to consider that may be overlooked but deserve a sniff at garden centers to see whether they would be a fragrant addition to your gardens.

- **Garden heliotrope** (*Heliotropium arborescens L.*) has large violet or white flower heads with a vanilla or cherry pie scent, depending on how it smells to you. It matures at 12 by 12 inches.
- **Garden Mignonette** (*Reseda odorata L.*) has a strong vanilla/ raspberry fragrance from small yellowish flowers. It matures at 12 by 9 inches and attracts beneficial insects.
- **Night-scented (or evening) stock** (*Matthiola longipetala*) has small lilac-colored blossoms with a powerful lily-like perfume. It matures at 12 by 9 inches.
- **Petunia** (*Petunia Juss.*) varieties can have little fragrance, but some old-fashioned white or purple vining types have a strong lily-like aroma at dusk. Ask for fragrant petunias at garden centers or check catalogs. They are mature at 1 by 3 feet.
- **Stock** (*Matthiola incana*) has spicy clove-scented flower spikes that are excellent as cut flowers. It matures at 1 by 1 feet.
- **Sweet alyssum** (*Lobularia maritima*), true to its name, has honey-scented white flowers that are attractive to beneficial insects. This low-growing ground cover matures at 6 by 8 inches.
- **Sweet four-o'clock** (*Mirabilis longiflora L.*) has multicolored trumpet flowers on bushy 2-foot-high plants. The flowers have an orange-blossom scent. It grows 2 by 3 feet.
- **Wallflowers** (*Erysimum asperum,* biennial and *E. perovskianum*) have sweet-smelling short spikes of yellow or copper-colored flowers. They mature at 12 by 10 inches.

Plant Cutting Gardens

Everyone loves to give and receive flowers. For gardeners, the ultimate pleasure is to be able to cut flowers from their own garden to bring indoors and to give away to friends and family. One problem is that picking flowers from the garden reduces the floral show in the yard. The perfect solution is to have a separate area specifically as a cutting garden. Then you can see your flowers and pick them too!

Fill your cutting garden with plants that produce the flowers and foliage you love. Use it as an area to experiment with new plants and colors. Place it where it is not on public display and indulge your fancy. Consider making your cutting garden part of your vegetable garden (i.e., a production garden created to be harvested).

Cutting gardens often look beautiful at the peak of the season, but because they are not intended for display, a purely utilitarian layout makes the most sense. Once they are established, they are easier to maintain and require much less attention than ornamental beds do. Plant cutting gardens in widely spaced rows you can easily move through and between while planting, thinning, fertilizing, deadheading, and, of course, harvesting.

Choose a site that receives generous sun and prepare soil so it drains well. Create one or more beds of whatever size and shape fit into sunny spots along the back property boundary, in a neglected corner, or behind the garage.

Maintaining a Cutting Garden

Mix a granular, slow-acting fertilizer into the soil at the beginning of the season to provide consistent, balanced nutrition to the plants over many weeks. Periodic doses of dilute liquid fertilizer sprayed on plant foliage will boost the energy of profusely blooming plants.

For easier maintenance, it is best to cluster plants with similar requirements for sun, water, and drainage. Plant tall types together where they won't shade smaller ones. Spread a 2- or 3-inch layer of organic mulch around plants in the cutting garden as soon as they are a few inches tall. Mulch will discourage weeds, keep the soil moist longer, and contribute some nutrients to the soil as it decomposes in the heat of summer.

Plants for a Cutting Garden

Lots of different kinds of flowering plants are suitable for a cutting garden. Long-stemmed annuals or perennials are most useful. Typically, colorful annual flowers dominate most cutting gardens because they are such prolific bloomers. Cutting their blossoms encourages them to produce more. All kinds of daisies are popular and combine well with other flowers.

Long-blooming perennials have a place in the cutting garden as well as in the more formal flower border. For example, coral-bells and fringed bleeding hearts will produce flowers all season, especially if they are picked regularly. Purple coneflowers and black-eyed Susans produce bold, bristly seed heads that are useful for floral crafts.

ALERT!

Be sure to group species of plants for efficient use of space and easy harvest. To get maximum production, plant annuals in succession; that is, group early-season, mid-season, and late-season bloomers together. As you pick one group, you can till that area and plant a fall-blooming flower crop.

Add Extra Income

Many gardeners have enjoyed their cutting gardens and realized that they also offer a potential for supplemental income. Cutting gardens and roadside stands are cropping up all around the country. People today can't seem to resist stopping to buy a bouquet of flowers for the office or their family. Once you've had success with your own cutting garden, and if you have room, consider expanding it. A few gardeners interviewed for this book have greatly expanded their gardens. They now provide flowers every week to local restaurants, sometimes as a cash crop and other times in trade for dining out. You may want to ask around town and see if there is a market for cut flowers. The barter system is alive and well!

Suggested List of Cut Flowers

Here's a list of suggested annuals and perennials as a beginning. Most are easy to grow and especially productive. You can add many others as you develop your own cutting garden.

Try these annuals for your cutting garden:

- Ageratum
- Bachelor's button
- Bells of Ireland
- Celosia
- Cleome, also called spider flower
- Cosmos
- Helichrysum, or strawflower
- Matthiola, or stock
- Snapdragon
- Zinnia

Try these perennials for your cutting garden:

- Achillea, or yarrow
- Aster
- Chrysanthemum, such as Shasta daisy
- Coreopsis
- Echinacea, or purple coneflower
- Lavender
- Phlox
- Rudbeckia, or black-eyed Susan

Bulb Flowers for Your Cutting Garden

When it comes to a cutting garden, think about flowers from bulbs, too. Most are perennials and once planted give you ample blooms every year.

Here is a list of some of the best candidates for the cutting garden from the Netherlands Flower Bulb Information Center in Brooklyn, New York.

- **Allium:** Particularly the tall purple puff-ball flowers of *A. giganteum* and *A. aflatunense*
- **Dahlias:** A multitude of shapes and colors, all magnificent performers
- **Ranunculus** or **Persian buttercup:** Has 2- to 5-inch flowers packed with petals, in every color except blue or green

Here are some fine flowers that have fragrance plus the bonus of a long vase life, too.

- **Anemone de Caen:** Poppy-like flowers in white, blues, or red
- **Asiatic lilies:** Early-summer bloomers
- **Calla, Zantedeschia:** Sheath-shaped flowers of flawless beauty in white and pastel shades
- **Galtonia,** or **summer hyacinth:** Bell-shaped flowers atop 2- to 3-foot stems; blooms when gladioli do for use together in arrangements
- **Gladiolus:** A flower made for cutting, with tall stately stalks covered with huge florets in every color imaginable
- **Iris:** All kinds, especially the Dutch iris or xiphium species in white, blue, yellow, bronze, purple, or bi-color
- **Oriental lilies:** Usually late-summer bloomers

QUESTION?

What makes a great cut flower?
Great cut flowers are those with sturdy stems, interesting flower shapes, colors that don't fade, and abundant long-lasting blossoms. That tells you that many of the best are bulb flowers.

Chapter 13

Landscape Basics for Beauty and Benefits

You can upscale your landscaping with colorful shrubs, flowers, and trees to make your home more beautiful. In the process, you can also increase the value of your home 8 to 10 percent. This chapter will offer suggestions and advice to help you create a landscape that you can be proud of.

Put Your Money in the Ground

Good landscaping can let you enjoy great growing while reaping financial rewards. Attractive landscaping can bring a recovery value of 100 to 200 percent of its cost at selling time. Realtors also report that an appealing landscape can speed the sale of a home by five to six weeks. Attractive landscaping can increase the market value of a home up to 10 percent, according to recent real estate surveys. In addition, landscaping with trees and shrubs can help you save energy, reduce air pollution, and create a more attractive living environment.

Boost Property Values

Landscape research has demonstrated that homes in neighborhoods with overall excellent landscaping sell for about 7 to 9 percent more than similar homes in other neighborhoods with poorer landscaping. All things being equal, such as the condition and quality of the kitchen and bathrooms, improving the quality of a home's landscaping can boost resale prices 8 to 10 percent. Other research by state college horticulturists and realtors proves that homeowners who upgrade their landscape quality from "good" to "excellent" realize 4 to 5 percent in increased resale prices in neighborhoods where other homes have excellent landscaping.

Consult Local Info Sources

To prove to yourself how better landscaping can be a worthwhile investment, check with local realtors and landscape contractors. Also, do some long-range thinking about what you want to have as landscaping and as an outdoor living environment. Consider how your house looks from a distance, as well as when you approach your front door as guests and visitors do.

To improve the overall appearance, plant attractive shrubs along the front; flowering shrubs offer spring and summer beauty. Also consider planting multipurpose trees that have blooms in spring and colorful fruits or berries in the fall to frame your house and showcase your gardens. Local landscapers can suggest attractive plants to enhance the overview of your property; from experience, they know which plants grow best in your area.

To achieve a landscape you can be proud of, consider the advice of professional landscapers. They suggest driving past your home, or viewing it from the most prominent angle, and making notes about what features can be improved.

Some easy improvements might include:

- Creating a colorful, welcoming entryway
- Planting a kitchen garden of herbs and cutting flowers
- Planning a backyard entertainment area of fragrant flowers
- Planting some specimen shrubs or trees with eye appeal

Reduce Energy Bills

It's a proven fact that trees and shrubs can help you keep cool. Cities can be 5° to 10°F warmer than suburbs. Known as the urban heat island effect, this difference is caused by heat-absorbing surfaces such as roads, buildings, driveways, and of course homes. According to scientists, as much as 8 percent of summer electricity demand is for air-conditioning, which is used to compensate for the heat island situation.

The Environmental Protection Agency is sponsoring a five-year tree planting, called the Cool Communities demonstration project. By planting trees, you can achieve substantial heat reductions, from the shade provided and from the cooling effect as they give off moisture. Evaporation from one large tree produces an estimated cooling effect of more than a million BTUs in its lifetime. That's equal to ten room-size air conditioners running twenty hours a day.

Trees also save energy in winter, reducing fuel bills. According to energy researchers, coniferous (evergreen) trees are excellent along the north and west sides of a home. Because they keep needles year-round, they act as a windbreak to shelter the house from chilling winter winds. To help stop cold air infiltration, you also can plant evergreen shrubs such as yews and junipers around the foundations of your home.

Deciduous trees, those that shed their leaves in the fall, are best planted on the south and west sides of your home; in other words, those areas that receive the most heat from the sun. Planted there, deciduous trees shade the house in summer and thus help lower cooling bills. Then, when leaves drop in the fall, the sun can shine through the leafless branches to warm the house.

Keep Bonus Values in Mind

Naturally, most people set out to improve their home landscaping because they want to have more attractive homes and outdoor living areas. However, as you begin to improve and add to your landscape, keep these other bonus values in mind. You'll be able to plan for and achieve many additional benefits that will add up nicely in appealing plants and property value. The nicest part is you can begin small, add to your landscape as time and budget allow, and let the plants and trees grow naturally in beauty and value year after year. With these thoughts in mind, take another look at your home and use the ideas, tips, and advice you'll find in this chapter.

Use Trees to Meet Your Needs

Trees should be your first investment in any landscaping plan, especially if you purchase a new home that really needs a landscaping lift. Your best bet is to plant fast-growing multipurpose trees that provide blooms in the spring and fruits, berries, or vibrant foliage in the fall. Avoid buying trees that have weak secondary branches growing from the trunk. These braches are likely to break off during ice, snow, or windstorms.

Here's a smart move: In the fall, visit your nursery and pick the trees with the brightest colors. The brilliance of a tree's foliage as a sapling will be retained throughout its life. You may see twenty maples, but one will be a standout.

Leave Room When Planting

When planting, leave 18 to 24 inches between the sapling and the grass, and mulch around the trees. This will help you avoid scarring the trunk when you mow the lawn since you won't be tempted to mow so close to the tree.

It helps to stake saplings on both sides for their first two years to prevent winds from knocking them down. Trees grow in size and landscape value.

▲ Digging the hole larger than the rootball gives roots room to spread.

List of Top Trees

Although it is true that trees provide landscape beauty all growing season, it pays to think year-round and to focus on the beauty of fall foliage. Here are some key color pointers.

- Aspen, beech, birch, gingko, and poplar trees turn yellow.
- Black oak, hickory, hornbeam, horse chestnut, and white oak trees provide orange and brown colors.
- Dogwood leaves turn crimson.
- Honey locusts have thin, airy foliage that provides light shade and yellow fall foliage.

- Norway maples are hardy, excellent shade trees that turn bright yellow in the fall.
- Red maples bear reddish blossoms in spring and scarlet leaves in the fall.
- Red oaks are the fastest growing oaks with a deep red fall color.
- Sassafras turns orange to scarlet, and sweet gum turns scarlet to burgundy.
- Sugar maples have bright red, orange, and yellow foliage and a tall, symmetrical shape.

Specimen Plants Are Appealing

Some plants have a "wow" appeal. Use them for specimen tree plantings or groupings. Consider autumn olive, dogwood, mountain ash, and ornamental crabapple of all types. Ornamental crabapples bear white, pink, or reddish blooms and bright berry crops in fall. Hawthorn is a favorite for hardiness, blooms, and fall berries.

Trees Reduce Street Noise

In addition to beauty, trees have another benefit worth your attention. They break up street and traffic sounds to reduce noise pollution, a definite advantage when buyers come to inspect your home, especially when the backyard is a quiet, restful area.

Stand Out with Shrubs

To give your home roadside appeal, plant blooming shrubs in front. Choose shrubs that have flowers in the spring and colorful fruits, berries, or foliage in the fall. Some examples are flowering perennials such as azalea, burning bush, mountain laurel, and rhododendron. Shrubs with fall berries include American crabapple, bayberry, bittersweet, and holly. Ask local nurseries to suggest plants that grow best in your area. Good plants may cost $20 to $50 each or more, but they grow in value.

Don't buy plants with torn bark or insect infestation on branches, buds, or at the ends of branches. Smart veteran landscapers suggest you avoid buying at discount chain stores, which often have less expertise in plant care and sell plants that aren't as hardy as those you'd buy at a local nursery.

Attract Garden Songsters

Many gardeners enjoy bird watching. So do many homebuyers. If you choose plants that attract songbirds and provide wildlife habitats, you get to enjoy them and they'll be around to delight buyers when you plan to sell your home. Among the best plants to attract birds are aromatic sumac, bayberry, bittersweet, and firethorn. Others that look great and offer abundant food include American cranberry, barberry, holly, and Virginia creeper. You can also add property borders of honeysuckle, multiflora roses, and even blackberries, which also will hide unattractive areas.

Develop Garden Plans

Experienced gardeners have no problem deciding when to plant their peas and corn or how deep to put their crocus and tulip bulbs. But when it comes to designing a garden, even the most seasoned gardeners can worry. Old-time gardeners admit they can spend weeks deciding the perfect spot for a new shrub or many months sketching plans for a new perennial garden. Many worry that their gardens won't measure up to what they see on neighbors' land.

Perhaps many gardeners believe that landscape design should be the work of experts such as landscape architects, landscape designers, or landscape contractors. This is not necessarily so. In fact, some of the most beautiful gardens in the world were not designed by experts. The gardens of Thomas Jefferson, which you can visit in person or via the Internet, are the result of an attentive eye and a sensitive hand.

Some gardeners would never consider planting anything without having a comprehensive design. Others do their landscape planning spontaneously when they come home with some new plants. You can decide which way you want to go to grow. If you prefer to follow your own intuition, dig in and grow that way. However, if you feel you need professional advice, you can find landscape designers everywhere. It pays to ask their credentials and see some of the gardens they have designed.

It pays to match plants to the growing conditions you have. One way to do that is to check with the U.S. Department of Agriculture or National Arboretum. There you will find worthwhile details about horticultural zones and plants that grow in them. You can also get the same information from local landscape contractors or nurseries.

Try Expressing Yourself

It is wise to remember that there is no ultimate garden design for any property. In fact, there are as many different designs as there are gardeners. Have faith in yourself, your vision, and your growing ability. Express yourself. Experiment. You can also make changes once you see how plants look after a year or two of growth.

Drawing Your Garden

Most veteran homeowners interviewed for this book believe a good landscape should begin with a thoughtful site plan. That's nothing more than a bird's-eye view of your home grounds. Drawing your garden on paper makes it much easier to identify and put into scale elements such as traffic patterns, structures and existing trees, beds, and so on. A professional designer will prepare a site plan precisely to scale.

However, you can also draw your own basic design. Here are some tips:

- Sketch in all major features—trees, shrubs, fences, outbuildings, paths, driveways, and your home
- Mark where utilities run, overhead and underground (Before digging, always check with utilities and your town. In many states it's the law.)
- Add the priority plants you prefer, from trees and shrubs to garden beds and borders

That covers the basics. You can sketch in more details, but with the basics you have a good starting point.

Should I hire a professional, and if so, what do I really want them to do?
It isn't necessary to contract for a full-scale site plan. Most designers will be willing to focus on a particular area such as your entryway or other priority project and then do more when and as you wish.

The Basic Points of Garden Design

Here are some basic design principles that can help you work out your own landscape designs more easily than you expected. Naturally, if you have the budget and want to hire a designer and then a landscape contractor to do the planting, by all means do so. However, most homeowners seem to like to do their own planting and gardening. Once you have decided to sketch some basic plans, you're well on your way to growing more attractive home plantscapes. Here are some key points to consider.

Give Your Garden Style

Every garden has its own style or personality. Let yours express you. Do you want a formal or informal look? Consider your site, the style of your home, and your own preferences. A formal home should probably have a more formal garden. A rambling house would seem to need an open, naturalized landscape. Let your mind set the style you wish to have.

The next step is to think about flow; that is, there should be a logical progression from one area to the next in your landscape. Paths are one way to connect areas. So are masses of similar plants or color. Think in terms of focal points as well, much as an artist does. Perhaps a focal point could be a dramatic bed, specimen shrubs or trees, or a sculpture.

Create a Sense of Balance

Rhythm is another design element to keep in mind. Think of rhythm as repetition of colors, flowers, and plants. Repeating displays of certain plants or colors will establish a rhythm and help guide the eye to focal points. Your garden also should have a sense of balance. Humans seem attracted to symmetry, which is the balancing of features in art, buildings, and gardens.

Symmetry can be pleasing, but if it is overdone, it can look stiff. Great formal gardens have won wide praise. However, people today tend to be more relaxed and seem to prefer a more natural look. Again, you must decide how you want your garden to look. Keep in mind that nature is subtle. You should strive for a feeling of both symmetry and spontaneity in your designs.

Shapes, Sizes, and Textures

Trees, shrubs, and plants are available in a wide variety of shapes, sizes, and textures. Look around the gardens that appeal to you. Make written or mental notes of plants that have special appeal. Note how round plants can provide a background for shorter branching types, or tall flowers like delphinium and snapdragons can be backdrops for shorter marigolds and petunias.

ALERT!

Scale is another key point and refers to proportions—basically how the sizes and shapes of things relate to each other. Expert landscapers point out that most scale problems are due to skimpiness. They urge gardeners to think big and bold. You can always cut back the size of flower beds or prune shrubs if they look too dominant.

Plants also have texture. Compare the glossy leaves of holly, magnolia, and roses with the suede-like foliage of lamb's ears, heliotrope, and coleus. Note how the fat leaves of a sedum are so different from the needle-like foliage of rosemary or the multicolored leaves of a blue-green hosta. Flowers also have texture differences. For example, compare velvety roses with cosmos or airy Queen Anne's lace. It pays to study living flowers in other gardens so you can imagine how they will look in your own unique home landscape.

Color Can Be a Key

Many books have been written about using color in garden designs and in other ways as well, including interior home decorating. Here are some basic points to keep in mind as you examine colors and decide which will work best in your gardens, and which flowers to plant to have those colors.

Generally speaking, red, orange, and yellow are "hot" colors that jump out at you. They are lively and stimulating. Package designers use these colors so their product catches your eye on the supermarket shelf. These colors give the impression that they are closer to the eye than they actually are. However, if you plant too many hot-colored flowers and don't balance them with cool-colored flowers, your garden could be too glaring. It pays to remember that other important design element, balance. Green, blue, and violet are "cool" colors. They tend to be soothing and calming. These flower colors can create a more restful feeling, which makes them a good choice for meditation areas in your garden.

Consider Garden Décor

Gardens shouldn't just be plants. For centuries, some of the great gardens large and small have benefited from décor with trellises, furniture, sculpture, and decorative planters. You too may find that furnishings and decorative features will be useful. For one thing, they provide a place to sit while dining and entertaining. For another, sculptures, fountains, and other elements serve as focal points amid your blooming plants and festive foliage.

Many gardens can benefit from fences of various types. They fence out unwelcome views, support climbing vines and other plants, and can be artful property dividers. For gardeners who enjoy a tuneful landscape, it pays to encourage birds to visit and also make their homes around the property.

Rustic wooden birdhouses and split-rail fencing give a casual, country feeling to a landscape scene. A bubbling fountain that fills a birdbath provides the soothing sounds of water and also gives birds a place to wash and drink. Birdhouses also have their place. There's something almost magical about birds that flit in and out of birdhouses, especially when they're raising their young.

ESSENTIAL

As you plan your total landscape look, consider how fences, bird feeders, fountains, urns, and sculptures can fit in. Look at how these elements will fit harmoniously with the style you are trying to achieve and any other decorative nonplant items in your garden.

Garden Design Books and Software

If you want more help in designing your landscape, there are dozens of books available in the library. You also can find many basic garden plan books for landscape ideas. Be aware that most ready-made plans are theme-oriented to specific types of gardens. Many plans include a site plan, planting list, and drawings that show what the garden will look like when grown. You can vary the designs, pick up a few ideas, and transplant them into your land.

Computer stores and departments also have a variety of garden planning software. These include pictures of plants so you can draw designs, put in the plants to see how they look, and rearrange them, too. You also have the option of seeing how plants look at maturity, to make sure they don't outgrow your home or garden. Garden designing can be as simple or expansive as you wish to make it.

Making the Most of Your Landscape

Your focus as you plan, improve, and upgrade present landscaping should rightfully be to create a more beautiful outdoor living area. By using the ideas and tips in the following sections, you will be able to make the most of your landscaping efforts, as well as boost your property value.

Focus on Your Entryway

The entryway is what guests see as they come to visit. Appealing shrubs and flowers say welcome. For spring beauty, plant crocus, daffodils, hyacinths, tulips, and lilies that give you color and beauty from earliest spring through summer. Add other perennial flowers. Once planted, perennials bloom every year with minimal care.

To extend the blooming season, check mail-order catalogs that give blooming dates so you can have blooms from different flowers all season long. Multipurpose trees and shrubs also yield rewards. In addition to the beauty you'll enjoy, flowering shrubs and trees with colorful fall foliage add appeal to a home at resale time.

Enjoy the Fragrance

You can easily add fragrance to outdoor living areas with sweet-smelling shrubs and flowers. To get the most from them, plant them upwind so that usual prevailing breezes blow their pleasing scents where you spend time outdoors. Some of the most fragrant include lilacs, lily of the valley, old-time roses, sweet clematis, syringa, and viburnum. From seeds, smell-good flowers include carnations, lavender, mignonette, nicotiana, pinks, and violas. Fragrant biennials (plants that bloom best during the second year) include dame's rocket, English wallflower, and sweet William.

Think Tastefully

Think tastefully, too, when you plan landscapes. Just a few bushes or rows of blueberries and raspberries or strawberry beds are attractive. You get to eat those treats every year. When it is time to sell, treating potential homebuyers to delicious berries tempts them to buy a home with productive gardens already in place.

Plant More Colorful Landscapes

As fall foliage glows, visit your local nursery. That's the time to identify the most colorful autumn accents for your landscape. You'll discover a wide range of deciduous shrubs and trees that delight the eye with colorful leaves or bright fall berries for birds. Look closely at trees of the same variety. Select the most colorful for your home grounds. The list on pages 165–166 will give you a few ideas.

Foliage brilliance changes each year. Brilliance is improved by ideal weather conditions including cool nights and warm sunny days. Intensity of light will intensify reds and purples. If fall days are overcast, you'll probably see more oranges and yellows in foliage.

FACT

Frost has almost nothing to do with autumn colors. In the fall, cells at the base of a leaf stem begin to harden. Photosynthesis slows and stops. The green chlorophyll that colors summer leaves green vanishes. Actually, the green masked the other colors within the leaves all summer. In the fall, they are revealed and turn leaves those glorious colors that people love.

Many shrubs as well as trees offer multiseason beauty. They provide blooms in the spring and yellow, gold, scarlet, or red foliage for weeks of autumn beauty before leaves fall. Take a drive around your area and state. Look for the best fall displays and plan to adopt some of the ideas and plants to improve your own home grounds.

ESSENTIAL

Washington hawthorn has dense, shiny foliage and white flowers each spring. By fall, orange leaves are complemented with small red fruit that birds enjoy. Hopa crabapple grows only 20 feet tall, has rose flowers in spring, and small red fruits in autumn. Both are excellent specimens for home grounds.

Plan Focal Point Gardens

Interior decorators know that rooms of a house benefit from a focal point. You can use the same concept, an eye-catching focal point, as you upgrade your landscape design. Look at your garden through the eyes of a decorator. Is there one area where your eye is drawn first? One or more trees can anchor a landscape and give it a feeling of permanence and stability.

Pruning Pointers and Advice

One of the classic oversights among gardeners is that many don't seem to like to prune their plants. That's too bad, because pruning is a good way to keep plants in line and to stimulate growth. You can shape plants, trim them to attractive forms, and also remove winter and storm damage. As you look at your shrubs and trees, use this list to help them all grow better.

1. Look behind the shrubs along your house. If they are overgrown, they can be keeping moisture next to your home wall, which can cause mildew, and damage paint and siding. Prune shrubs so they don't create a damp area or rub against painted house walls.
2. Remove storm-damaged branches as soon as possible. If big limbs are involved, it is best to hire a specialist to remove them (and stumps) safely.
3. Prune shrubs whenever they seem to overgrow their size and shape. This keeps them in bounds and more attractive.
4. Cut back forsythia, lilacs, and other blooming shrubs so they don't overgrow an area.
5. Keep privet and other hedges in line with annual pruning.
6. Remove any diseased wood or branches from your shrubs.
7. Use a sharp saw to cut broken limbs flush to the trunk of a tree.
8. To encourage bushier shrubs, prune out in-growing branches.
9. Remove spent blooms of lilacs and similar plants so new buds form properly.

Natural Landscape Elements

Many gardeners are frustrated because they have difficult areas that won't allow for the cultivated plants they want. You can improve poor soils, drain wetlands, or otherwise remake the land for better plant growth. However, too often that requires far more work than most people want to invest. Sometimes, growing naturally is a better path to take.

The most obvious place to begin turning your lawn into a natural landscape is where grass doesn't thrive: the shaded areas under trees, wet sections of the yard, steep banks, rocky outcroppings, and roadside areas. These places can be good candidates for alternative or natural plantings.

Experimental Beginnings

It is best to start small. Here are some key points to keep in mind:

- Research the problem and read up on possible solutions
- Ask nearby gardeners who share your soil type, area, and climate for suggestions
- Plan for a natural look rather than a formal one
- Choose a few plant varieties and bunch them together to see how that looks
- Consider using ground covers such as periwinkle, vetch, ground roses, or ivies
- Think about paving the area, broadcasting thick mulch, or making parking or play places
- Grow wildflowers that tolerate the light and soil conditions

Good Ground Covers

Ground covers typically form a ground-hugging mass and protect soil from erosion as they spread. When they're mature, they keep weeds and other unwanted plants from gaining a foothold. It may take patience and effort to establish ground covers, but they certainly have their values.

If you have shaded areas, try planting periwinkle, or vinca minor, under your trees. Ferns, lily of the valley, and pachysandra also thrive in shady spots. To give some spring color, you can try crocus and daffodils, which will bloom before tree leaves form.

If you have sunny, dry problem areas, daylilies are one of the easiest, fastest-spreading perennial ground covers you can grow. Creeping thyme as well as creeping juniper, euonymus, and creeping phlox also grow into carpets in sunny spots. E

Chapter 14

E Landscape Fruitfully

Growing fruit isn't as difficult as you might believe. Fruit trees are versatile. They fit well into outdoor landscapes providing shade, appealing shapes, and tasty fruit. This year, plan to landscape more fruitfully. Just a tree or two for starters will undoubtedly whet your appetite to grow a fruitful landscape in the years ahead.

Small in Stature, Big on Fruit

Nothing really beats sun-ripened fruit, plucked at its juiciest from a tree in your own backyard. With loving care, home fruit trees will reward you tastefully, year after blooming year. Using fruit trees as part of your landscaping will provide special pleasures. Besides having decorative value, they reward you with tastier and healthier eating. You get to enjoy beautiful blooms in the spring and then fresh fruit picked at the peak of ripeness each fall.

FACT

Two key mail-order nurseries specialize in fruit trees and berry bushes. They are Miller Nurseries in New York and Stark Bro's Nurseries in Missouri. You can order their fruitful catalogs on the Internet at ✑ *www.millernurseries.com* and ✑ *www.starkbros.com,* respectively.

To enjoy naturally fresh flavors, begin to landscape fruitfully this year. You have a choice of standard, semi-dwarf, or even dwarf fruit trees. These smaller trees fit nicely into limited space and bear full-size fruit. Many tasty varieties of fruit can't be found in supermarkets because some varieties don't ship or store well. But, you can grow the tastiest varieties in your own mini-orchard.

As you plan your fruitful landscape, pick a spot; trees need eight hours of sun each day to thrive and produce the sweetest natural sugars in the fruit. To ensure tastier living all summer long, select varieties that ripen early, mid-, and late season. Local nurseries can advise you which are best.

Apples Are Appealing

You have a wide choice of apples. Northern Spy, Duchess of Oldenberg, Cox Orange Pippen, Braeburn, Idared, Yellow Transparent, Lodi, Arkansas Black, and even exotic apples like Winter Banana are available from mail-order nurseries.

Focus on varieties that will bear in early summer, late summer, early fall, and later for good eating all season. Whatever fruit you prefer, remember that plant breeders have developed productive varieties that are resistant to common diseases. Focus on these to save time and reduce the need for sprays. For early eating, Lodi, Summer Rambo, and Grimes Golden are good. These varieties are attacked less by insects and disease than varieties that ripen later. Prima ripens midseason with a dark red color on a yellow background. Macoun also ripens midseason—a red-striped apple with crisp white flesh.

Normally, apples prefer cooler parts of the country, though some apples do well in warm areas. So if you like apples but live in warmer parts of the United States, take heart. Tropical Beauty was discovered in South Africa and has proved successful in warm areas, including Florida and Hawaii. It produces medium-size, carmine red fruit and has a mild flavor.

ALERT!

When you are shopping for apple varieties, be sure to check the catalog listings to be certain that the variety you want will tolerate the winter in your area. This is even more important with peaches. All catalogs give the horticultural zones in which each plant will thrive.

Here's a suggested list of the best apples around for most parts of America.

Empire has the sweetness of the Delicious type combined with the flavor of McIntosh. It ripens in mid-September, is highly productive, and resists problems.

Granny Smith is a superb apple that resists cedar rust and diseases. It ripens in early November, has a tart flavor, and stays fresh in cold storage for several months.

Grimes Gold is a hardy, disease-resistant variety that's tasty fresh and makes great applesauce. Yellow in color, it ripens in mid- to late September.

Jonafree is an improved, bright red apple that resists diseases. Great for desserts and pies, and especially hardy, it ripens in mid-September.

Liberty is an extra disease-resistant McIntosh type with huge crops that are ready to harvest in late September.

Redfree is bright red and is resistant to apple scab and other problems. It has a sweet, pleasant flavor, stores well in the refrigerator, and ripens in early August.

Winesap is a dependable bearer of old-time apples, bearing young and regularly. This all-purpose apple ripens in mid-October to early November.

Dig in and plant some appealing apples. They'll reward you tastefully for years to come.

Check catalogs or call the nurseries for their recommendations of varieties that will grow well where you live. Then try apples that aren't offered at your supermarket. Unique and different apples can become the best part of your home plantscape.

Charming Cherries

Sweet or sour, cherries have their very own charm. Modern breeding has produced many improved varieties. Cherry trees grow to medium height, between the size of standard peach and apple trees. They bloom earlier than most fruits. Cherries prefer growing conditions that are suitable for peaches with full sun, good drainage, sandy loam, and protection from prevailing winds. Their graceful shape, bountiful spring blossoms, and fruitful yield make them useful landscape additions.

Sweet cherry trees grow larger with upright growth and are tastier for eating fresh, but they have one disadvantage: You must grow two compatible varieties so they cross-pollinate and set fruit crops.

Sour cherry varieties are self-pollinating. They make better tarts and pies but are preferred by birds. Birds, it seems, like tart fruit rather than sweet fruit. Plastic netting solves that problem easily.

There are several delicious cherry choices available. Emperor Francis is among the best sweet cherries with large dark fruit that resists cracking. Trees are vigorous and productive, bearing yellow-skinned cherries early. Napoleon is a high-quality yellow cherry, while Stella is a large, dark red type.

Among the best sour cherries for pie, jam, or tarts are Montmorency, Meteor, North Star, and Mesobi. All are relatively cold tolerant. Rich-flavored Black Tartarian, Kansas Sweet, and Windor are good varieties as well.

Peaches Are Peachy

Peaches have gained wide popularity since the early Spanish explorers brought them over. Today, vastly improved, disease-resistant trees make them tasty favorites. Thanks to new varieties, you can even grow hardy peach varieties in northern areas.

Brighton, Candor, Collins, Garnet Beauty, and Harbinger are delicious, early-maturing types. Prairie Dawn, Reliance, Redhaven, and Raritan Rose bear later. For mid-season, you can pick Eden, Glohaven, Trigem, or Vanity. If you live in cold areas, plant only those varieties known for their cold weather hardiness.

Site Selection Is Important

Although peach trees can survive cold, their fruit buds are tenderer than other fruit trees. Proper site selection is vital. Peaches love sun. Choose a spot with well-drained soil that gets full sun. Avoid frost pockets or areas punished by strong prevailing winds. The best site is a protected, sheltered, sunny area warmed by day and shielded from extreme winds or frosty night air.

ALERT!

Many varieties of peaches are available, but some can't tolerate cold winters. To avoid disappointment, always check the horticultural zones in catalogs.

The Peach Alternative

Some people just can't stand the fuzzy feel of peaches. If that includes you, then think about the mouth-watering goodness of nectarines. They grow in the same type soils, climates, and conditions as peaches. If you live in colder, northern areas, select the varieties that are noted and recommended for their winter hardiness.

Pears Will Surprise You

Pears are not as widely grown in home landscapes as they deserve to be. That's a pity because they are so delicious and many different flavor varieties are available. Pears are also troubled less by common diseases or insects than other fruits. Once established, pears require less pruning and care to produce abundant harvests.

ESSENTIAL

Unlike other tree fruits, pears should be picked before they ripen on the tree and be allowed to ripen in your kitchen. To enjoy the best pears, pick them about a week before they are fully mature. Otherwise, they tend to get mushy.

Pears offer markedly different flavors and a range of texture, size, and shape. When you select varieties, remember that some are self-pollinating and others are not. Usually you need two varieties so they can cross-pollinate to ensure adequate fruit set. Be sure you check which variety you're purchasing. Here are some of the best and most productive varieties:

Bartlett is a superior pear for fresh use. Trees bear large, golden yellow pears early and abundantly.

Bosc ripens late. These large pears with a dark yellow undercolor and a fine russet veil have white, aromatic, tender flesh.

Clapps Favorite has pale lemon yellow fruit with a bright pink cheek.

Comice is a premium pear, the kind you see in fruit gift baskets—long, golden, and blushed with red.

Kieffer is a winter pear for all areas.

Magness bears late on spreading trees. Fruit is oval, medium size with a soft, very juicy, sweet taste.

Moonglow bears early. Trees are vigorous, upright, and have large juicy fruits for eating fresh or cooking.

Seckel matures late on vigorous trees. They are productive, yielding small, smooth fruit with white to slightly yellow flesh that is aromatic and spicy.

Plums Are Plum Dandy

Plums are another fruit often overlooked by gardeners. They make colorful blooming accents to landscapes each spring and offer a wide choice of tasty fruits by summer and early fall. Even better, plums can be grown more easily in more parts of America than most other fruit trees.

There is a great selection of species and varieties to choose from. Some plums can tolerate extreme cold, while others prefer warmer climates. Their small tree size lets you enjoy plums both as decorative landscape accents and for their abundant fruits.

There are five basic plum groups, descended from European plum families:

1. The Prune group provides plums that can be picked and dried with the pit intact.
2. Green Gage plums have round fruit with sweet, juicy yellow, green, or reddish flesh.
3. Yellow Egg plums are mainly commercial canning types.
4. Imperatrice plums include most of the blue-colored ones that bear heavily, yielding medium-size, oval fruit with a firm flesh.
5. Lombard-type plums are reddish, smaller, and somewhat lower in quality.

American and Japanese plums are also available now. (The Japanese plum is more attractive in blooming habit.) Then there are European plums that have the best flavor and offer the widest choice of varieties. The following are some popular favorite plum types:

Abundance is a heavy yielder of large, cherry-red fruits. It does well in warmer climates.

Burbank has bright reddish-purple fruits and matures late.

French Damson is vigorous, productive, and yields large plums, good for preserves.

Green Gage is a favorite with medium, yellow-green fruit mottled with red; it's ideal for dessert.

Leaton Gage bears quality plums on vigorous trees.

Montfort is an old French blue plum with dark purple, juicy fruit.

Mount Royal is good for desserts or jams and survives even icy Canadian winters.

You Deserve Nuts

Once established and nursed through their traditionally slow start, nut trees are about as carefree as a tree can be. There's little pruning needed and nearly no other care. Pecans are commercial crops in southern states. Almonds and English walnuts are crops in California. However, by choosing the right types and varieties, you can grow nut trees in almost any state. In addition to being good shade trees, nut trees reward you each fall with a rich harvest.

Nut trees are larger than most fruit trees and will require lots of room to spread. They also have long taproots that grow deep into the ground. You must dig deeper and better when planting to get nut trees started right. Here's a list of some favored nuts that deserve consideration for multipurpose landscape trees:

Butternut trees yield rich, buttery-flavored nuts. They may reach 40 to 60 feet and prefer rich soil.

Chinese chestnuts appreciate well-drained soil. Space them 20 feet apart.

They grow rapidly, resembling standard apple trees in size and shape, and bear earlier than most nut trees.

Hazelnuts, also called filberts, are another hardy landscape addition. Nuts are produced on vigorous shrubs that mature at 6 feet tall. They have red and yellow foliage in fall after the summer nut harvest. Hazelnuts prefer well-drained, rich soil, and should be spaced 15 feet apart.

Hickory trees are native to the United States. These tall, pyramid-shaped trees prefer rich, well-drained soil. They prefer heavy mulching for best performance and mature at 50 feet tall.

Pecans are large, spreading trees that prefer southern climates. They mature at 40 to 60 feet and prefer deep soil with a steady moisture supply. Some hardier varieties are now available for northern climates, so check with your local or mail-order nursery.

Walnuts are nicely rounded trees that grow 50 feet tall. They like rich loam to set strong roots. The new varieties are nicely thin shelled.

Most nut trees will require a companion for pollination. Check catalogs so you can plan for two where cross-pollination by another variety of the same tree is required to get the needed nut production.

Tree Planting Pointers

Fruit trees do best when they receive full sun, have a well-drained, loamy soil, and are sheltered from strong prevailing winds. Since trees are permanent parts of your home landscape, dig deeply to prepare the soil well for proper planting. See page 188 for a guide to fruit tree planting. If you have poor soil, add well-rotted manure, peat moss, and composted humus to improve growing conditions. Mix a bucket of compost or composted manure with each bucket of soil for a good fertile mix to give trees the best possible start.

Dig Deeply for Best Results

Some trees are sold balled and burlapped; others are sold in containers. Mail-order trees usually arrive bare-rooted, wrapped in moist moss. Plant them immediately. Make the hole twice as large as the rootball. Spread the bare roots well. Pour a bucket of water into the hole. Place the rootball or the container or burlap-wrapped trees carefully into the hole and fill halfway with soil mixture. Tamp it down and give it about a half bucket of water. Then, fill the hole with the remaining soil, tamp down to remove air pockets, and add another half bucket of water.

Leave a saucer-shaped depression around each tree to catch rain or irrigation water. Some experienced gardeners suggest adding mulch over a circle of weed-preventing mesh to stop all weeds and also to prevent mowing too closely and damaging the trunk.

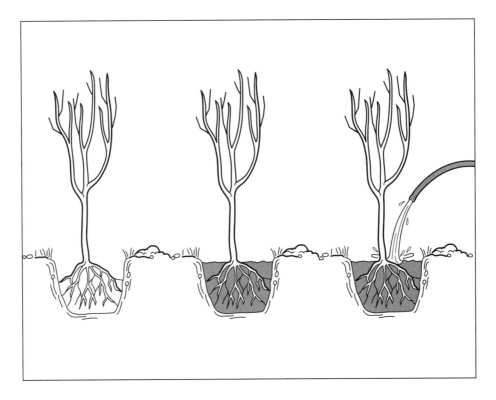

▲ Planting a bare-root tree

Mulch, Prune, Water

Mulch around each tree with leaves, compost, peat moss, or grass clippings to smother weeds and help the soil hold moisture. Prune off any broken branches. Water weekly, at least an inch of water, so your tree can send out new feeding roots and set a firm roothold in its new home.

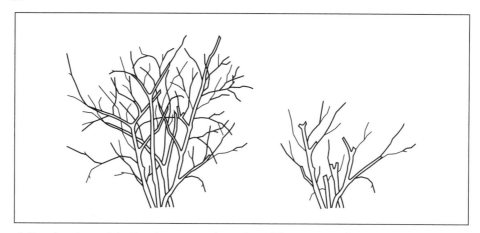

▲ Pruning trees to stimulate growth and avoid overgrowth

Take the time to plant well, and your trees will get the strong, sturdy start they need. Once established, they'll reward you fruitfully, year after year, with tasty eating from your home mini-orchards or specimen tree plantings.

Pest Control

Because there have been so many changes in modern pesticides and in the rules and regulations about applying chemical sprays in different states, it is not possible to give a pest control guide that will apply to all parts of the country. Your best bet is to consult your local garden centers. Their owners and experts should know the latest on what spray materials can be used and how best to apply them. Always focus on new fruit tree varieties that offer disease-resistance. Apples are more susceptible to insects and diseases than most fruits. Pears usually have fewer problems.

Fruit Tree Spacing Guide and Bearing Age

Fruit Trees	Planting Distance	Mature Height	Years after Planting
Apples (s/d)	12 x 12 feet	12 to 15 feet	2 years
Apples (s)	35 x 35 feet	20 to 25 feet	3 to 10 years
Apricots (d)	10 x 10 feet	8 to 10 feet	2 years
Apricots (s)	20 x 20 feet	15 feet	3 years
Cherry, sour (d)	10 x 10 feet	8 feet	2 years
Cherry, sour (s)	20 x 20 feet	20 feet	3 years
Cherry, sweet (s)	25 x 25 feet	30 feet	3 to 4 years
Peach/Nectarine (d)	10 x 10 feet	8 to 10 feet	2 years
Peach/Nectarine (s)	20 x 20 feet	20 feet	3 years
Pears (s/d)	12 x 12 feet	12 to 15 feet	2 years
Pears (s)	20 x 20 feet	25 to 30 feet	3 to 4 years
Plums (d)	10 x 10 feet	8 to 10 feet	2 years
Plums (s)	20 x 20 feet	20 feet	3 years

s = standard size; s/d = semi-dwarf size; d = dwarf size

Chapter 15

E Berry Tasty Gardens

Dig in today and you can enjoy delicious berried treasures from your own backyard for years to come. Berries are an easy-to-grow, rewarding part of a home garden. This chapter will introduce you to the variety of berries available and show you just how simple it is to grow these tasteful treats at home.

Plant Berried Treasures

It's easier than you think to grow the sweetest strawberries, most bountiful blueberries, reddest ripest raspberries, and mouthwatering blackberries, year after tasteful year. Just a few bushes of berries, or rows of strawberries, can yield several quarts of fruit.

Begin with a few bushes or plants. These plants will be permanent parts of your home landscape, so you must prepare the soil deeply; dig or till 10 inches deep. If you have heavy clay soil or sandy soil, add compost or composted manure and peat moss. For bushes, make the holes twice as large as the bare rootball or the size of the container-grown plants.

Pour a half-gallon of water into each hole. Carefully place the plants in the hole to avoid disturbing the roots. Fill the hole halfway with soil, tamp it down, and water again. Then add the remaining soil, tamp it well, and water. Leave a saucer-shaped depression around each berry plant to catch the rain or irrigation.

Mulch your bushes with compost, grass clippings, rotted leaves, or peat moss. All fruit plants need ample moisture and nutrients, especially as they set fruit. Follow the directions on the package of fertilizer. Too much fertilizer can be as bad as too little.

ESSENTIAL

As you plan your garden, remember that berry plants and bushes need a good growing year to set their roots and prepare to give you years of tasty harvests. Most will set only a few berries the first year and many more the next. Be patient, that's the nature of berry plants. By the third year and beyond, you'll be amazed what prolific crops you have.

Super Strawberries

Think mouthwatering strawberry shortcake, jam, and strawberry-rhubarb pie. You can enjoy them all with plump, sun-ripened strawberries picked from your own yard. Strawberries are the most productive berry. They can be grown in any fertile, well-drained soil with ample sun. They like slopes but avoid planting them in low areas where frost may settle to nip the spring blooms and kill the fruit set.

Key Planting Pointers

You can edge a walk, interplant them with flowers, or even grow them in tubs and barrels on your porch or patio. Space strawberries 12 inches apart in garden rows or beds. Be careful that the crowns, the point where the roots grow down and the leaves sprout up, are right at the soil surface.

▲ Plant strawberries with the crown at the soil surface.

Spread the roots well, and keep them moist while planting. When the plants take root, they will send out runners the first year and the parent plants may yield a few berries. They'll bear larger crops the second and third year. After that, cut them back or remove older plants.

Renovate the Beds Periodically

Strawberries need periodic renovation. Fortunately, the older plants send out runners to establish young, healthy plants for future tasty crops. Keep the beds well mulched to stop weeds, retain soil moisture, and act as a cushion for a clean berry crop. Remember that all fruit plants need ample moisture and nutrients to perform well, especially as they set fruit. Plan to add an inch of water each week, a bit more during dry periods to ensure plump, ripe fruit.

Stretch Harvest Seasons

Planting several varieties lets you pick berries very early, in midseason, and at late harvest. You may even grow ever-bearing varieties that begin with small crops in the spring and continue producing luscious strawberries right up to the first frost. Be the envy of your neighborhood; grow and enjoy tasty strawberries all season long.

Some of the newest varieties begin early and keep producing plump, tasty strawberries until the first killing frost. In fact, two new types now in most catalogs keep greenish leaves under the snow and are ready to set blooms and fruit as soon as spring arrives. That's good news for strawberry lovers in all northern areas.

Blueberry Treats

You can enjoy the best blueberry pie, muffins, and pancakes with blueberries picked from bushes in your own backyard. Many prolific varieties are available today. Blueberries give you more fruit for less effort than other berry bushes. They also serve well as ornamental shrubs, producing bell-shaped flowers every spring and clusters of berries each summer.

FACT

By choosing early- to late-ripening varieties, you can stretch your tastier living season over several months. Some varieties are best for fresh use, others for pies and preserves, while others are conveniently multipurpose.

Know Their Growing Needs

Blueberries have special requirements. They prefer loose, well aerated, and somewhat acid soil (about 4.8 to 5.0 pH for best results). You can provide what blueberries need by adding acid fertilizer and mulching with acid-inducing oak and maple leaves, pine needles, rotted manure, and leaf mulch. Blueberries have a fine, hairlike root filament system, so you should prepare the soil a year in advance if possible. Turn under compost, manure, peat moss, and oak and maple leaves to produce a light, fluffy, acid soil condition.

Nitrogen is the main fertilizer element blueberries need. A garden fertilizer such as 10-10-10 spread on the soil or on top of mulch helps nourish the plants. Because these plants have shallow roots, don't cultivate them. Weed, or better yet, apply mulch to smother any weeds and retain soil moisture.

Order Two-Year Stock

Buy two-year-old blueberry stock because it has better root development for a more successful adjustment to your home grounds. Here are a few varieties to consider:

- **Earli-blue**—A vigorous, upright plant that produces clusters of large, firm berries
- **Blue Ray**—A vigorous, somewhat spreading bush with smaller, tight clusters of firm, light blue berries
- **Colville**—Productive with medium berries
- **Blue Crop and Berkeley**—Midseason varieties

Be patient the first two years as your blueberries set their roots. By the second and third year, you'll be amazed at the blue bounty they'll provide for years to come. Check mail-order catalogs for the newest varieties. Plant breeders are developing more abundant bearing varieties that can be added to your blueberry patch.

Really Ripe Raspberries

Raspberry tarts, raspberry jam, and raspberry pie are all yours from the rich, ripe raspberries you can grow productively in your garden. You can grow them in beds, berry patches, or along property lines. They thrive in almost any type of soil, so you can grow them in areas not suited for more selective crops.

Raspberry Growth

Red raspberries have upright growth and form thickets by sending out underground runners that produce new plants to fill in the rows. They prefer full sun. Plant the rooted raspberry canes by opening the soil or digging a hole, spreading the roots, and firming the soil over them. Space the red varieties 3 to 4 feet apart in rows 6 to 8 feet apart. Remove the old dead canes and top back the tall ones each year to force new side branches that bear the berries on second-year canes.

FACT

Think red, black, and purple when you consider raspberries. All three types provide their own distinctive and delicious flavors and are easily grown in most gardens.

Ever-bearing Raspberries Are Prolific

Old-time varieties may bear early, mid-, or late season. Improved new varieties offer two crops a year: one in spring, another in fall. Some begin bearing fruit in late spring and continue right up to frost. Depending on what you want for flavor, check into the new ever-bearing varieties. They give you raspberries for your cereal for months on end. Among the best reds, Heritage is vigorous and ever bearing. The plants are winter hardy and produce moderate summer crops, followed by a prolific fall crop of medium-size berries.

Plant breeders have created many disease-resistant, highly productive new varieties. The following are a few examples.

- **August Red**—Begins producing in July and yields to September
- **Citadel and Comet**—Later varieties
- **Heritage**—A small late June crop but a big yield of bountiful berries from September to frost
- **Hilton**—One of the largest with long, conical, firm berries ripening in midseason
- **Latham, Sunrise, and Southland**—Earlier varieties
- **Taylor**—Tall and hardy with firm, sweet berries

ALERT!

Raspberries have shallow roots, so if you cultivate rather than mulch for weed control, do it lightly to avoid damaging roots.

Blackberry Bounty

If you want to enjoy one of the tastiest fruit berries and have a handsome hedge that grows even in poor soil, think blackberries. Modern blackberries are not the tart wild ones you may remember from childhood. Today's blackberries are large and luscious, and plant breeders have produced thumb-size berries on thornless bushes. Chestern Thornfree and Triple Crown Thornless, for example, are tasty and you don't get stuck when picking them. However, blackberry bushes with thorns also serve another purpose—as property borders they keep out wandering cats and dogs.

The Dependable Fruit

Few fruits for home gardens are as dependable as blackberries. They prefer most temperature climates and once established, can produce crops for fifteen to twenty years. They do best in sandy loam since roots may penetrate 2 to 3 feet deep.

Darrow is one of the most productive varieties but has lots of thorns. Chester Thornfree is an introduction from the U.S. Department of Agriculture and is a rarity in nature. These bushes need staking to hold them upright. Other varieties are sturdier. Illini is hardy and tests reveal it withstood temperatures 20°F below zero when grown at the University of Illinois. Give blackberries shelter from the wind, such as a house, garage, or fence, if possible. As with all fruits, avoid low areas where frost settles.

Planting Points

Prepare the soil thoroughly 8 to 12 inches deep. Set plants 3 feet apart. Once established, these berries will spread by underground stalks to become dense rows. Although blackberries do well in poor soils, the addition of organic matter and manure boosts their development and greatly increases their productivity. Pruning by cutting off tall tops and side branches keeps the bushes under control. Blackberries are best picked when the berries turn black. Try a few as they darken and you'll soon get a "feel" for when to pick them at their flavorful peak.

Berry Culture

Gardening fruitfully is easier than once thought. You can have the mouthwatering goodness of berry tasty treats, from blackberries and blueberries to raspberries and strawberries. Here's a basic list for the planting and care of berries.

1. Plant berry bushes in deep, well-drained, crumbly soil; strawberries prefer a lighter sandy soil.
2. Younger plants usually transplant the best.
3. Plant berries early in the spring when the soil has warmed. Dig in deeply because berries are perennials and that permanent site should be well and thoroughly prepared.
4. Dig the hole large enough so the bare roots can spread properly.
5. Pick a sunny site; avoid low areas where frost settles.
6. Choose proven old favorites but test newer, improved varieties, too. Plant breeders have worked wonders in the past few decades. Everbearing raspberries and strawberries are one of their many wonders.

7. Be patient with bush berries. Most need to set roots well and won't bear much until the second or even the third year.

8. Pruning is a key to bountiful berry yields. It stimulates the growth of shoots, branches, and canes, resulting in new fruiting wood. Make pruning cuts to an outside bud so new branches grow out, not into the center.

9. Nitrogen is the key element for berries, but a balanced fertilizing plan is important for fruit set and development. Check garden centers for the recommended fertilizers.

10. Water plants regularly, especially as the fruit sets and begins to ripen. The plants need ample moisture so the natural sugar content rises as the berries ripen.

11. Follow safe and sane pest control. New disease-resistant varieties are helpful. Consult local garden center authorities about the best, approved pesticides for bug control since there may be special rules about garden chemical uses in your area.

12. Practice peak of perfection picking. Get to know your berries, and you'll soon learn when each is ready for picking. The timing may change each year because of weather and water conditions.

Chapter 16

Spice Up Your Life with Herbs

Herbs are easy to grow. They are hardy and don't require much care. They're also nice to look at and smell. Even better, herbs let you spice up your life, enjoy tastier food, and eat more naturally without excess salt or other additives. Add it all up and herbs deserve a place in your garden.

Grow a Tastier Life

Many herbs bear beautiful blossoms. Others add fragrance to gardens and rooms. But the best thing about herbs is their flavor. Even a small pinch of one herb or a leaf of another can make meals come alive with super new taste. You can sprinkle herbs on salads or add them to soup. You can blend them with vegetables or into gravy or sauces. You can also use them to season meat. Some herbs, like parsley and mint, add beauty and enhance flavor.

You can grow herbs in a garden of your own, either outdoors or indoors. They respond to simple, basic cultivation methods, and you can enjoy them year-round, unlike most other food plants that are harvested once a year. When your herbs mature, you can snip off a piece any time you want some special flavoring.

FACT

Annual herbs grow for just one season. Perennial herbs keep sending up new growth every year. Biennials are planted in one season and bloom the following season. Many gardeners prefer to grow perennials, but annuals and biennials offer distinctive tastes that are also worth trying.

Indoor Herb Gardens

If you decide to start an indoor herb garden, there are three basic things you will need: pots, pebbles and gravel, and trays or pans. You probably have some of these around your house now. If not, all are available at your local garden center and at most chain stores.

You probably have all kinds of pots already. You can use basic clay pots or more decorative ones. If the pots once held houseplants, be sure to wash them well to get rid of any old fungus or disease organisms.

Next you'll need pebbles or gravel. Put a base of ½ inch of small stones or gravel in the bottom of each pot before you fill it with soil mix. For pots that are 8 inches or more in diameter, use an inch of gravel. This provides vital drainage so excess water doesn't rot the roots.

To protect windowsills or furniture, use trays or saucers to hold your pots. Spread a layer of gravel in the tray and set the pots with the herbs on top of the gravel. That gives a neat look. You then can let water trickle out of the pots and into the tray where it will be hidden by the gravel but still provides useful humidity around the plants.

ALERT!

If the window you select gets intense sun or heat at times, be sure to keep the pots back from the glass panes so your plants won't get sunburned. Never put plants on top of a hot radiator.

A good place for most herbs indoors is in a window that faces south. If your south-facing windows are shaded by tall trees or buildings, however, east-facing windows provide a good spot for most herbs.

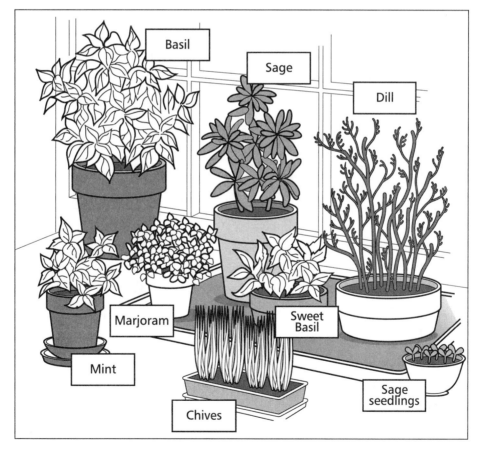

▲ Place potted herbs on a windowsill.

Outdoor Herb Gardens

Pick a sunny location for those herbs that thrive in sun. Select a more shaded spot for those that like only partial sun. Later in this chapter, you'll find the specific growing needs for each of the ten most popular herbs. Sun-loving herbs should get five to eight hours or more of sun each day. Those that prefer partial shade still need three to five hours of sun daily. It is important to match the plant's needs to the growing location for sun or shade. You can then vary the amount of water they need.

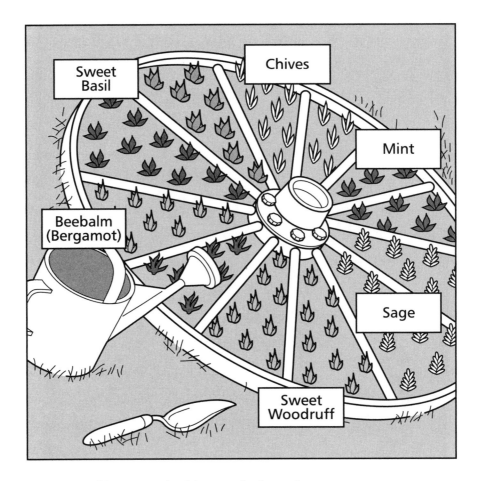

▲ Using an old wagon wheel for your herb garden

One of the nice things about growing herbs outdoors is that there are many ways to plant them. Some herb lovers prefer to plant herbs combined with vegetables in a "kitchen garden" just outside the kitchen door. That way they can easily pick veggies and herbs for mealtime. You can place them right in the ground in beds or rows as part of an outdoor garden that includes other plants. You can plant them as a border around a flower bed or even in a rock garden or along a path.

Some people enjoy planting herbs in special designs. One popular design is a wagon wheel arrangement. You can make that design easily. Tie a string on two pointed sticks. Firmly place one stick in the center of what will be the wheel. Then use the other stick to mark a circle. Next, divide the circle into pie pieces for different herbs.

Herb Planter Gardens

If you don't have a backyard or enough space for a regular garden, you can still grow herbs in pots or planters on your patio, balcony, or porch. There are many types, styles, and sizes of containers to use. Some are made of redwood in box or tub shapes. You can also use large wooden half barrels or lined metal tubs.

You can sink individual pots directly in the ground. They look nice that way and blend into the garden. When frost threatens tender annual herbs, you can simply dig up the pots and bring them indoors.

The advantage of growing herbs in pots or planters is that you have portable herbs. You can place them anywhere you like as long as they get the sun or shade they need. You can take potted herbs along to parties or meals at friends' homes and simply pass the pot around so guests can clip off the freshest herbs for their meals.

Double-potting is a handy idea. Place a smaller pot inside a larger, more decorative pot. Fill the space between with sphagnum or peat moss. Water drains out of the inner pot so roots don't get waterlogged. Clay pots work well as inner pots because the porous clay lets excess water escape.

Planting and Care Tips

You can obtain a variety of soil mixes at garden centers and chain stores. Check the labels to find out which will be best for potted herbs. Usually a basic mix that is not too fine or too coarse works well. Most veteran gardeners recommend a soil-less mix that is a combination of peat moss, sand, and vermiculite with perlite added to some blends.

Herbs tend to send down deep roots when they can, especially perennial herbs. Therefore, it is important to pick the right garden spot and prepare the soil deeply and well.

Deep spading or rototilling to 10 to 14 inches is the first step. Dig down to the full depth of a garden spade. As you turn the clumps over and break them up, add composted humus. This addition of organic matter will improve the soil structure for better root penetration and drainage.

Many gardeners like to use peat moss to improve soil; this is an inexpensive and worthwhile practice. Peat moss helps improve drainage by retaining water for plant roots in sandy soil and also opening up heavier clay soils.

Once your garden is well spaded or tilled and ready, the next question is whether to use seeds, seedlings, or cuttings. Gardeners have debated this question for decades. You can start seeds indoors on windowsills or in cups and pots or even on heated trays. Using seedlings or cuttings produces plants faster, but you may want to purchase mature plants.

ALERT!

Never cover seeds too deeply. If the seed packet says to only cover with a pinch or two of sand or soil mix, do as the seed supplier says. They are the experts with years of experience and want to give you the best directions to ensure your success.

Seed Starting

Starting herbs from seeds is fairly easy, costs less, and enables you to grow many plants for your own garden or to trade with others. Some herbs require lots of patience. They are really slow to sprout and develop. Read about each herb's special habits to know what to expect and when. Some herb seeds are very small, so be sure to follow the seed packet directions.

Planting Seeds

In general, herbs take longer to sprout than most vegetables or flowers. While you are waiting, keep soil moist, not wet. Eventually the first stems and leaves will begin to push through. Shortly after the initial leaves appear, the first true leaves will form. Sprinkle seeds with water regularly so you don't disturb seedlings as they set their tiny roots.

Shopping for Seedlings

You may not find a wide variety of herbs in local chain stores, but you have other options. More major mail-order seed and plant firms now offer started herb seedlings.

Another good source is your local herb garden. They often offer started seedlings in peat pots, trays, and even larger plants with stronger and better-developed root systems. Shop around. Many people grow herbs today. Often these local specialists will provide bushels of worthwhile herb-growing tips, lore, and harvest and use tips.

ALERT!

If seedlings are in a tray or other container, moisten the soil mix and carefully remove each seedling for planting. Take your time and keep as much soil mixture as possible around the seedling to prevent transplant shock.

Planting Seedlings

Make holes with a dibble or dig them with a trowel. The holes should be large enough for the entire rootball and deep enough so that the rootball is about ½ inch lower than the rim of the hole.

▲Planting rooted seedlings

Place the seedling in the hole, and gently firm the soil around it. Add another ¼ inch of soil or potting mix and moisten it. Finally, put a light layer of composted humus or peat moss around the seedling and water it. Water the seedlings daily to keep the soil moist as they send their roots into the ground in search of water and nutrients.

ESSENTIAL

Veteran gardeners agree that you "hedge your bets" by having an extra seedling in the pot. Just in case things aren't quite right, chances are at least one seedling will set roots well.

Cuttings Are Useful

Some herbs are best started by taking cuttings from parent plants. To make a cutting, snip off several inches of stem from the top of a mature plant. Then snip off the lower leaves of the piece you cut off. That should give you about six top leaves and the tender growing tip. You can start cuttings in two ways. One way is to put the stems in a glass of water.

Once you see tiny new rootlets begin to form, watch daily. When they look like roots, carefully transfer the cuttings to potting soil. Firm them gently into the soil as you would with a seedling and keep them moist. They will take root and begin growing into new herb plants.

◀ Root cuttings in water

Another way to start cuttings is to place them immediately into a potting mix. Keep the soil moist. Check them every day; extra moisture is needed since the stems are not in water. New rootlets will firm and gain a good roothold. Soon stems will develop side shoots and begin the natural process of becoming full-grown plants.

Both systems work well. Try them both at the same time to hedge your bets and let the plant cuttings decide which way they want to become new plants.

ALERT!

If your tap water is heavily treated with chlorine and other chemicals such as fluoride, it is best to buy bottled distilled water for root cuttings.

Transplanting Herbs

Some herbs spread naturally by sending out underground runners that develop new stems and root systems. To make a new plant, simply dig down around the stem of the new plants. Carefully cut its roots away from the parent plant. Then, dig that young plant up and move it to its new location. Mint and chives are two herbs that can be easily divided and transplanted.

America's Ten Favorite Herbs

As herbs have popular once again, many gardeners have begun growing a wide range of them. Some are exotic and appeal to gardeners with gourmet cooking skills and flavoring tastes. Some good, down-to-earth herbs have been popular for years and still are. Here you'll learn about the ten most popular herbs, according to gardener surveys.

1. Basil
2. Chives
3. Dill
4. Mint
5. Oregano
6. Parsley
7. Rosemary
8. Sage
9. Sweet marjoram
10. Thyme

Bravo for Basil

There are many types of basil. The most common is sweet basil because it has fragrant leaves for flavoring. It is an annual low-growing plant that won't get through winter but can be kept for months on a kitchen windowsill.

Basil grows 1 to 2 feet tall but stays small when grown in a pot. Somewhat pointed leaves have a sharp, spicy flavor similar to cloves. Sweet basil has shiny green leaves 1 to 2 inches long. In summer, white flowers appear on spikes at the end of the stems. Pinching leaves and sprigs will delay flowering and plants will become bushier.

How to Grow Basil

Once the ground has warmed, sow basil seeds $1/8$ to $1/4$ inch deep, about 1 inch apart. Allow 18 inches between rows. When seedlings are several inches high, thin them to 8 inches apart. Pinch top shoots for bushier plants. Water once a week outdoors. Indoors, use a 6-inch pot for four to six seeds. Basil grows best in a south or east window. Keep soil moist so leaves are plump and succulent.

How to Use and Store Basil

Basil gives foods a distinctive clove-like or nutty flavor. You can use fresh or dried leaves. It is fine on cheese dishes, with fish, in stews and egg dishes and is most often used with tomato dishes or with spaghetti and Italian foods.

Hang a spray of basil to dry in a cool dry room. When thoroughly dry, remove the leaves, crumble them, and store them in an airtight glass jar to preserve their unique aroma and flavor. You can also strip leaves off stems and freeze them whole to seal in their flavor. With basil you have a choice: fresh, frozen, or dried.

Charming Chives

Chives are hardy perennial herbs that can stand temperatures 25°F below freezing if you add mulch over them in the winter. Chives are easily identified by their round, hollow, stem-like leaves that look like a bunch of baby onions. They grow in grass-like clumps and have a mild onion flavor. Pink-purple flowers resemble clover blossoms and plants may grow 12 to 24 inches tall. Their profusion of purple blooms makes them an attractive part of any garden.

How to Grow Chives

In the spring, sow seeds in moist, outdoor soil $1/8$ inch deep, 2 inches apart. Keep rows 18 inches apart. Thin chives so each bunch has 6 to 8 inches of growing room in a row. Or, use them as clumps in your perennial beds.

To grow chives indoors, put four to six seeds in a 6-inch pot with good potting mixture and space them evenly. Keep the pot near a southern or eastern window. With sufficient sun, chives will grow inside all throughout the year. Chives grow well in fairly rich soil, with full sun and moist growing conditions. Water them at least once a week so they are juicy indoors; misting with a spray of water twice a week helps them thrive. If you grow chives outdoors, divide a clump and plant them in a pot before winter for indoor growing use.

Whenever you want some chives for salads, soups, or with sour cream on baked potatoes, just snip off the tops with scissors. Don't cut chives lower than 4 inches or you will weaken the plant.

Delightful Dill

Dill is an annual that must be planted from seeds each year. Both its seeds and leaves are useful, as well as having a sharp but delicious flavor. When dill produces seeds in late summer or fall, be watchful. They're tiny and very valuable for making tasty dill pickles from your cucumber crop.

Dill is a tall plant with finely divided leaves and flowers. The feathery light green leaves add an almost fernlike look to gardens. Flowers are greenish yellow and form an umbrella-shaped cluster, called an umbel, 3 to 6 inches across. Outdoors, dill grows 3 to 4 feet tall. As an indoor potted plant, it grows 12 to 15 inches high but still yields lots of leaves and seeds.

How to Grow Dill

When frost danger has passed, plant three to five dill seeds per inch, $\frac{1}{8}$ inch deep in outdoor garden soil. Space rows 24 inches apart in sunny locations. When sprouts are a few inches tall, thin dill seedlings to 5 inches apart.

When seeds are forming, check the plants daily, and be ready to hervest quickly. As seeds ripen, shake the heads to release seeds on a white cotton sheet. Rub them with your fingers to remove the outer chaff. Store seeds in one container, leaves in another.

Indoors, use an 8-inch pot that is 10 to 12 inches deep because dill has a long taproot. Plant six to eight seeds 1 inch apart and thin them leaving the two strongest plants. Keep dill in a sunny window. Because dill is very slow to sprout and slow growing at first, keep soil moist and free of weeds in an outdoor garden. Water every other week outdoors and every week indoors.

How to Use and Store Dill

To dry dill, cut the best leaves and place them on a clean cotton sheet in a warm, dry spot. Leave them there for a few days. After dill is thoroughly dry, crumble it and put in an airtight glass container.

▲ Dry and store your dill. If you prefer to hang bunches of dill to dry, do it over a white sheet so that you can see seeds when they drop and collect them easily.

Marvelous Mint

There are many types of mint. The most popular are peppermint and spearmint. Mints are perennials that thrive in soggy places. Mint tends to spread and can be invasive.

Mint grows 2 to 3 feet high and bears lovely small lavender or purple flowers. All mints are easy to recognize by their unusual square stems. To determine which is which, simply crush a few leaves and sniff. There's no mistaking that fresh, minty aroma. Peppermint leaves are 2 to 3 inches long, dark green, and toothed. Spearmint has smaller dark green leaves with a crinkly feeling.

How to Grow Mint

Mint is probably the easiest herb to grow outdoors. In fact, its roots spread so rapidly it is advisable to grow mint in pots, even outdoors, so it doesn't invade other plant areas. You can start mint from seeds, from seedlings, or cuttings or transplant it.

To plant mint indoors, dig up a small part of a parent plant or set three to four seedlings in a pot. Keep mint on a western or northern window since it prefers shadier sites. Be aware, mint likes lots of moisture. Water at least once a week during droughts or if indoors.

Don't pick mint leaves until new plants are 10 to 12 inches tall. If you pick too soon you will weaken the plant.

Mint leaves and sprigs are fun and tasty to chew in cool lemonade or iced tea and also make a fine hot tea with a touch of honey. Crushed mint leaves with a little vinegar and water makes for one of life's palate-pleasing pleasures on lamb or in stews. Unlike most herbs, mint is best used fresh.

Original Oregano

Oregano is a very hardy plant that grows 18 to 30 inches tall and is related to sweet marjoram. The most common oregano variety has rounded leaves with blunt tips. Dark green leaves may be an inch or so long. Small pinkish to purple blossoms appear in summer. After several years, oregano plants become woody. They spread by underground runners or stems, so you can easily take young plants to start in new areas as you thin out older growth. As a houseplant, pinching produces a more attractive, shorter, bushier plant with tastier leaves.

▲ Dry and store oregano in sealed glass containers or in freezer bags for instant flavor.

How to Grow Oregano

Sow oregano seeds outdoors in early spring or late summer, one seed every 3 to 4 inches, ¹/₈ to ¼ inch deep. Cover lightly with soil and space rows 18 inches apart. Seeds take three to four weeks to sprout. After seedlings sprout, thin them to 18 inches apart. You also can take cuttings from the tender tops of fully grown plants and root them.

Indoors, oregano grows best in a southern or eastern window. Plant four to six seeds evenly in a 6-inch pot. When seedlings are 2 to 3 inches tall, thin them to leave the strongest two plants.

Oregano enjoys full sun. Water every week. For the sweetest, sharpest flavor, supply only enough water to keep the soil moist and the leaves juicy and tender.

How to Use and Store Oregano

Oregano leaves and flower tops are used fresh or dried as flavoring for all kinds of salads, soups, and stews. Hang a bunch to dry in a cool area. Remove the leaves when they are dry enough to crumble. You may also want to freeze fresh leaves. Take off the stems, put them in zippered plastic bags, and store them in the freezer. Then thaw what you want to put in soups, sauces, and stews.

Perfect Parsley

Parsley is a popular garnish to decorate plates or platters of food. It is tasty, rich in vitamin C, and one of the easiest herbs to grow. You can recognize parsley by its ruffled, crinkly look.

How to Grow Parsley

Parsley favors partly sunny to shaded areas. It can take some frost but won't survive winters outdoors in northern areas. Plant parsley seeds 2 inches apart, cover with ¼ inch soil, and space rows 18 inches apart. Parsley spreads in a low-growing bushy pattern. Thin plants about 10 inches apart in rows. Snip plants to use and they'll send up more leaves.

Indoors, parsley does best on western or northern windows with less sun. Plant four to six seeds in a 6-inch pot. Let them all sprout and clip what you want when they are a few inches tall. Keep cutting and parsley keeps growing. Parsley likes rich soil that is partly moist, so water it regularly. If you keep parsley growing year-round, fertilize the plants with liquid fertilizer according to directions on the brand you prefer.

Take a taste of parsley, especially to sweeten the breath. It is amazingly good at making your mouth feel, taste, and smell fresh again.

How to Use and Store Parsley

Parsley is most commonly used to decorate salads, soups, and many other dishes. It is also a wonderful flavoring for vegetables, meats, casseroles, soups, stews, and salads. A little goes a long way, so try various amounts. Parsley is best used fresh.

Rosemary Delights

Rosemary is a beautiful perennial with a piney fragrance that is hardy and does well even in poor and dry soils. This wonderful plants acts like a natural air-freshener that gives off a pine scent. Outdoors, the taller varieties can grow as decorative hedges or shrubs. After a few years, rosemary becomes woody and gnarled, which adds to its eye appeal.

Rosemary blooms are lavender blue in small clusters during spring and summer. Shiny, needlelike leaves sprout all around upright stalks and resemble needles of a spruce branch. This plant can grow 2 to 5 feet tall, depending on the variety you select. In pots or containers, outside or indoors, it stays more compact.

Don't waste money on room freshening. Put rosemary to work and you'll enjoy the soothing smell of the forest.

How to Grow Rosemary

Rosemary is best grown from seed. Plant the seeds outdoors in a sunny location as soon as the soil is soft. Spade deeply because they set deep roots. Sow seeds ⅛ to ¼ inch deep, 18 inches apart in rows. They'll sprout in two to three weeks. When seedlings are 2 to 3 inches high, thin them to 6 to 8 inches apart.

Indoors, plant four to six seeds in a 6-inch pot and place it in a sunny south or east window. When sprouts are 2 inches high, save only the two strongest. Inside or out, pinch off the top shoots every few weeks to have bushier plants. Because rosemary thrives in drier soil, water it just once each week until the plant is 4 inches tall. Too much water causes leaves to drop. Outside, you can fertilize it once a year. Indoors, fertilize it sparingly.

How to Use and Store Rosemary

Crushed and dried leaves are tangy in soups and gravies. Just a pinch per pot is enough. Try a fresh sprig to brush sauce on chicken, burgers, and ribs. To store, tie the stems together and hang them upside down in a dry room or lay them on a clean window screen. Keep them cool while drying, then remove the leaves and store them in sealed, wide-mouth glass jars.

A Salute to Sage

Sage is a distinctive herb with a pungent aroma and taste. This hardy perennial can take cold weather and come back each year as flavorful as ever. The fragrant, slightly bitter taste comes from its leaves, which rank it among one of the most popular herbs. Sage grows as a shrub about 2 feet tall. When fully grown, it has lavender or white flowers and oval leaves that may be 3 to 4 inches long, grayish green, and coarsely textured. Members of the sage family include a tricolor type, golden sage, purple sage, and others. It is a favorite for use in poultry sage and onion stuffing.

How to Grow Sage

Outdoors, sage prefers dry soil in full sun. Plant seeds ¼ inch deep; spacing them 2 to 3 inches apart in rows 24 to 36 inches apart. Seeds take three to four weeks to sprout. Thin the seedlings to 10 inches apart. As the plants blossom, cut back woody stems, and new branches will form to provide more leaves for use.

Indoors, sage grows best in sunny windows. Plant four to six seeds in a 6-inch pot. When they are 2 to 3 inches tall, thin them to the strongest two seedlings. Sage requires little water and does very well without much attention.

Sage leaves, fresh or dried, are a basic ingredient in stuffing, sausage, and meat flavoring, especially poultry and lamb. To store sage, cut it and hang it in sprays to dry, or strip the leaves from the stems and spread them on a clean window screen in a warm, dry room. Then crush the leaves and store them in airtight jars.

Sweet Marjoram

This tender, sweet-smelling herb thrives as a perennial in southern gardens but needs replanting in colder northern areas. Marjoram grows between 12 to 24 inches tall but stays smaller in pots. Leaves are oval and grow in opposite patterns on upward branching stalks.

How to Grow Sweet Marjoram

For outdoor use, plant seeds or cuttings in a sunny location. Place five to seven seeds per inch, $1/8$ inch deep in late spring in well-warmed soil. Allow an 18-inch space between rows. Seeds require several weeks to sprout, so have patience. Thin the seedlings so they stand 6 to 8 inches apart. Sweet marjoram is a slow starter, so early weed control is important. A 2-inch-deep mulch on soil smothers weeds and retains soil moisture.

For indoor use, plant tiny seeds evenly in a 6-inch pot. It grows best in south- or east-facing windows. Remove all but the two strongest seedlings when they are 2 to 3 inches tall.

When drying any herbs, it is important to have a dry, well-ventilated room so the moisture can evaporate from foliage quickly, whether you are hanging bunches or drying them on a clean screen.

How to Use and Store Marjoram

Pick sweet marjoram any time for use in salads or casseroles, or for making herbal tea. Use leaves to season meats, stews, and soups. Sweet marjoram grows well indoors to use fresh year-round. To dry, cut it and hang the branches in a dry, warm, well-ventilated room. When the leaves are crisp and dry, strip them from the stems and put them away, whole or chopped, in an airtight glass jar for later use.

Tempting Thyme

Thyme is a shrubby, low-growing (useful for beds and borders) fragrant perennial with a spreading habit that grows well in temperatures as low as 20°F below freezing. Thyme leaves grow along upright stalks in opposite patterns and flowers appear at the ends of the stalks as spikes.

There are many varieties of thyme: silver with green and silver leaves, lemon with lemony fragrance, and others you'll find in herb catalogs.

How to Grow Thyme

Outdoors, use seeds or cuttings. Thyme thrives in moderately dry, light soil with a sandy texture and prefers good sun. Plant seeds early in spring when the ground is warm $\frac{1}{8}$ to $\frac{1}{4}$ inch deep, 2 inches apart, and then thin to rows 18 inches apart. Seeds sprout in fifteen to twenty days.

Indoors, sprinkle tiny seeds in a circle in a 6-inch pot and place the pot in a south or east window. When they are 2 to 3 inches tall, thin them to the strongest few seedlings. Because thyme prefers drier growing conditions, water it only every few weeks. Thyme, like mint, has a tendency to spread, so prune it regularly to keep it in line.

Mulch thyme with humus, about 1 inch deep each spring. Bees are attracted to thyme and thyme honey has the fragrance of the herb.

To expand your herb knowledge, check out ✍ *www.wholeherb.com* and taste the treats in store.

How to Use and Store Thyme

Fresh or dried, thyme adds flavor to vegetable juices, soups, and gravies. Dried, it adds taste and aroma to fish and poultry as well as meats, and a tang to sauces too. Its flavor is strong, so use it sparingly.

Gather thyme leaves and stems on a dry day. Spread them on a clean screen or hang small bunches to dry. When they are dry, strip off the leaves and store them in airtight bottles. (E)

Chapter 17

E **Container Gardening for All**

There's an exciting, colorful, flavorful new look on porches, patios, balconies, and even rooftops across America these days. It's container gardening, the biggest new growing trend to take root in this country in many years. In this chapter, you'll find the successful container gardening secrets of veteran gardeners.

It's the Trendy Thing to Do

Container gardening is welcome news for those who thought they didn't have space for growing flowers or food. No matter where you live—apartment or condo—you can grow more productively than you ever thought possible. Millions are already doing so in containers of every description and in the most unlikely spots.

There are several reasons for this gardening phenomenon. Some people want to cut food costs. Others feel the need for flowers to brighten their surroundings. Still others just want to decorate more naturally with plants for more colorful, cheerful living environments.

Many types of containers are readily available. Soil-less soil provides an ideal growing medium. More profusely blooming flowers and high-yielding vegetables can be obtained from new hybrid compact plants. All these factors, combined with American ingenuity, triggered the container gardening boom.

Good Vegetables for Containers

Although you can grow most types of vegetables in pots, tubs, raised beds, and other planters, you'll be rewarded with top yields if you select the newer varieties specifically bred for container cultivation. Look for them on seed racks and in mail-order catalogs. Here's a brief list of the varieties garden friends have tried and recommended:

- **Beans**–Kentucky Wonder pole, Green Isle beans
- **Beets**–Ruby Queen, Detroit dark red beets
- **Cabbage**–Little Finger, Tastie hybrid, Meteor
- **Cucumbers**–Bushcrop, Superslice hybrid, Surecrop (Remember that cucumbers will climb on supports or wire hoops.)
- **Lettuce**–Great Lakes, Salad Bowl, Buttercrunch, Ruby with its attractive reddish leaves
- **Peppers**–Emerald Giant, Yolo Wonder, Hungarian Yellow wax, Long Red Cayenne
- **Radishes**–Early Scarlet Globe, Cherry Belle, Scarlet Knight

- **Squash**–Black zucchini, Daytona hybrid, Table King Bush
- **Swiss chard**–Rhubarb, Fordhook Giant
- **Tomatoes**–Patio hybrid, Tiny Tim, Better Boy, Americana

Remember that leafy vegetables thrive with less sun than fruiting or root vegetables.

Good Flowers for Containers

Container flower gardens have become the rage all across the United States. You too can enjoy the blazing, blooming beauty in pots, tubs, planters, and window boxes as millions of Europeans have for generations. Expert container gardeners say that the most important factor for success is the variety of flower that you plant. Some have built-in genetic capabilities to grow spectacularly in containers. To grow well, most flowers require full sunlight and adequate moisture and nutrients. You must be attentive to these needs in containers.

There are so many flowers available that your best bet is to look through mail-order catalogs and pick your pleasure. Pay attention to mature height and other special considerations, such as dwarf growing habit. Most catalogs today will identify flowers that are recommended for container cultivation.

Columbine, geraniums, smaller marigolds, all types of petunias (including the cascading type that are wonderful for hanging basket displays), and dwarf phlox are good choices. Remember that the restricted growing environment of a container will tend to keep plants smaller. Pruning is also an option to keep them looking nice.

Stick with compact dwarf types of flowers and vegetables. They have traits that have been bred in to enable them to perform most satisfactorily in containers. You'll find them featured at garden centers and in mail-order catalogs.

Pick the Right Containers

Your choice of containers is limited only by your imagination. You can use anything that holds soil mix and provides proper water drainage. You can grow plants in fancy decorator pots or recycle common containers that will assume new life from the plants within them.

At garden centers, look for a wide selection of clay and ceramic pots and tubs, plastic and fiberglass planters, trays, and hanging baskets. Wooden barrels, tubs, and trays of all descriptions offer even greater versatility.

You can adapt containers from flea markets, garage sales, or closets. Old pots, pans, and washtubs work well. So do kettles, metal and plastic cans, and laundry or bushel baskets.

QUESTION?

What are the best woods for planters?
Redwood, cedar, and cypress are preferred. They resist rotting and are handsome in their own right. If you use others, be sure to paint them with nontoxic preservatives. Local garden stores can guide you.

Some gardeners use flue or sewer tiles, or cinder blocks, or they stack bricks and wood to build bed-style containers. You can design your own container to fit your available space.

◀ Cinder blocks as growing containers

A Few Key Points to Keep in Mind

Here are key considerations to ensure the best plant growth from whatever containers you use. Be certain your containers provide adequate drainage. Plants hate soggy roots. It often kills them. More plants are killed by overwatering than anything else. That's true with houseplants, and people tend to overdo with container gardens as well. Even porous soil mix won't ensure against excess water. Be sure to drill holes in all containers that you buy or make. Since proper drainage is vital, place several inches of coarse gravel or clay pot shards in the bottom of containers.

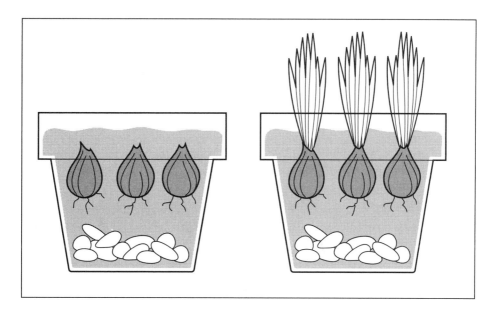

▲Using coarse gravel or clay pot pieces to ensure proper drainage

Use only porous soil mix that you can make from equal parts peat moss, vermiculite, and perlite. Your best bet is to buy bags of potting mix at garden centers.

Choose containers that are large enough for the plants you want to grow in them. Most flowers and smaller vegetables will grow well in containers that are 6 to 8 inches in diameter and 8 to 10 inches deep. Dwarf varieties require less space. Taller plants may need larger pots, tubs, or barrels. Match the container to the mature plant size.

Mix and Match

For greater productivity, consider doubling up your plants. For example, surround tomatoes with leaf lettuce and marigolds for color. Mix several types of flowers such as petunias or zinnias with vegetables such as peppers or chard to enjoy blooms along with tasty eating.

One high-rise gardener used an old bathtub surrounded by wood-trim fencing. It provided salads for many months. The warm roof "climate" of heat absorbed by the building warded off frosts. Another used cedar planks to build a pyramid planted in the corner of a balcony. Now commercially made plant towers are available in various sizes.

FACT

Old bathtubs are classic planters. The old-timers with cast-iron feet are popular, so you may want to shop around.

Use Soil-less Soil

One secret of success with container gardening is soil-less soil. Soil-less soil is a well-balanced blend of peat moss, vermiculite, and perlite with added plant nutrients. It is available under many different brand or trade names. Veteran container gardeners as well as beginners swear by the stuff. Their impressive results in pots, baskets, tubs, and assorted other planters are living, blooming proof that this growing medium works wonders. Actually, soil-less soil is not a secret new development. Professional growers have used it for years. They call it the ideal plant-growing medium.

What is news is the widespread availability of soil mixes. It makes good sense to use this proven planting mixture. Consider the advantages. Backyard gardeners must contend with bacteria, fungi, and insects. They must fight weeds and solve the problems of dry soils and soggy clay ground. You can avoid all those problems with a sterilized, scientifically blended planting mix. Most of today's mixes are based on the original Cornell University formula.

The basic Cornell formula included long-fibered Canadian peat, which is a partially decomposed sphagnum moss. Peat is loose and spongy so it absorbs great quantities of water without becoming soggy.

Water Absorption

The water-absorbing characteristic of soil-less soil combined with its natural porosity is important because it allows oxygen to reach the plant root and allows roots to roam freely, picking up the nutrients you add periodically with liquid fertilizer.

Horticultural vermiculite, another key ingredient, is heat-treated mica that is expanded to twenty times its original volume. Vermiculite retains moisture and attracts plant nutrients while ensuring good water drainage and oxygen flow to the plant's feeding roots. Perlite adds even greater fluffiness to these materials.

Store-Bought Soil Mixes

You'll find prepared soil mixes under a variety of trade names such as Jiffy Mix and Terra Lite. Nationwide chain stores now often sell their own "named" mixes. There isn't space here to give the names of Wal-Mart, Home Depot, or other chain brands of soil mix. If you shop at chains rather than local garden centers, ask to speak with the garden center authority. Explain your plans for container gardening and ask for the right ingredients, from containers themselves to soil-less soil mixes, liquid fertilizers, and perhaps also new easy-to-use wick watering systems.

Avoid using garden soil. It contains fungi, bacteria, and insects. Why give yourself a handicap when sterilized soil mixes are readily available and reasonably priced!

Mix Your Own

You can also mix your own soil-less soil material. Here's a basic formula. Mix one bushel of peat moss and one bushel of vermiculite. Add a gallon of perlite and stir well. Then add 8 ounces of 5-10-5 fertilizer and 10 ounces of ground limestone. Sprinkle with water to keep the dust down while mixing. Most gardeners prefer the convenience of prepackaged mixes.

Special Watering Considerations

Plants bloom and bear profusely in container gardens if you understand and satisfy their natural daily thirst. Container plants need more water than those in backyard gardens because of their restricted growing habitat. Their roots can't roam in search of moisture. They are also exposed to drying air on all sides, even the bottom. Sun and radiated heat from nearby walls increase evaporation. Check the container's soil daily. Be especially sure to check smaller containers because their soil dries out faster.

Container gardens need deep watering to ensure that moisture gets to all parts of the soil mix, which encourages deeper and better rooting for sturdier plants. Light sprinkling only promotes shallow surface rooting, which makes plants more susceptible to drought damage.

It pays to use containers that have built-in watering systems. For example, you can insert nylon or cord wicks from a water tray or pans up into the draining holes of your containers to pull water into the lower levels of soil where plant roots can get it. Newer containers have special watering systems built in. When shopping for containers, ask about these innovative new systems. Or, ask about the add-on watering methods now available for other types of conventional containers.

Try the toothpick test to check moisture. Stick a toothpick into the soil. If it comes out with particles attached, it has sufficient water. If it comes out dry, you need to water the soil mix.

Cloud cover, low temperatures, and recent rains can alter plant needs. Test the soil of your container daily. If it feels dry, water it thoroughly so your container plants flourish. Watch for their signals. In time, you'll learn to spot their signs and tune in to container plant needs.

Special Feeding Considerations

Plants need to eat so they can grow, and they need a balanced diet. In containers, their roots can't roam as widely as they can in outdoor gardens in search of nutrients. So it's up to you to provide nutritional needs. Nitrogen, phosphorus, and potassium are the big three that all plants require.

Nitrogen feeds vegetative growth. A soil deficient in nitrogen will produce stunted pale-green foliage. A nitrogen overdose produces fast-growing foliage with few vegetables and poor flowers. Too little phosphorus weakens roots, causing plants to lie flat rather than stand tall. Potassium deficiency produces strong-looking stalks that are actually weak and vegetables that ripen before maturity.

Types of Plant Food

Fortunately, many well-balanced plant foods are available today. Especially with water-soluble food, it is easy to keep plants thriving. Rapidgro, MiracleGro, Hyponex, and other brands can be purchased at garden stores and chain stores. Ask which ones are recommended for container growing, and which translate to potted plants, since most brands come in several formulations. Some fertilizers are best for flowers and others are intended for vegetables. Be sure that your fertilizer also contains trace elements that plants also need.

FACT

There are many good fertilizer formulas available for use with container gardens. Be sure to read and follow the directions to give your plants the proper nourishment.

You can use slow-release pelleted or prilled fertilizer mixed with the soil mix. Gardeners continue to debate whether water-soluble fertilizers or slow-release pelleted plant food is better. Try both types and see which works best for you. Just be sure the formulation provides sufficient food since porous planting mixes are devoid of most nutrients.

Feeding Guidelines

Here are some basic guidelines. When plants are about half-grown, begin weekly feedings of ½ tablespoon of 20-20-20 liquid fertilizer per gallon of water. At blooming or bearing age, use a full tablespoon per gallon of water weekly. This is just a guide. Each fertilizer formula has its own directions.

Watch your plants. Look for yellow or discolored leaves. Note drooping leaves. Yellowing or browning leaves may mean that more food should be applied. But be sure that you are not overwatering them and drowning the roots; that, too, will lead to yellow leaves.

In time you'll get the feel for feeding your container gardens. Different plants have different nutrient needs. Each container may need different applications based on the amount of soil mix and number of plants. Many fertilizers come with handy fliers that give tips and advice. Read and follow the directions.

ALERT!

Check under pots to be sure the plants aren't root-bound. If you see roots coming through the bottom holes, it is time to repot into a larger container. This is even truer with permanent houseplants.

Ask for Help

If you have doubts about feeding your container plants, there's help available at your local garden center and from specialists who provide your growing supplies. Ask your neighbors who have container gardens. Gardeners love to share their knowledge, especially when they can show you examples of their success. Growing together with neighbors can be very rewarding, especially when you're swapping different taste treats with others.

Get Creative with Container Gardening

Once you start playing with container plantings, you'll probably find many places for them. Place a big container in the middle of your garden. Try another amid ferns. Move pots around. Group pots on the front steps; add them to deck rails, along paths, in any odd spot. Put them on decks, under shrubs, just outside the garage door, by the mailbox. Try some old-fashioned window boxes for a truly classic European look!

Repetition Creates Balance

Gardening can be a bit like painting. Try creating appealing compositions with mixtures of color, form, scale, and texture that create balance with repetition and contrast. Pick plants that seem to blend together but don't quite match. You'll find that repetition of related colors ties "the big picture" together. Three to five colors work nicely as a base. Pick the colors that please you and grow to your heart's content.

Some veteran gardeners believe the best plantings, whether in containers or in landscaping, are those in which the plants actually intertwine, growing together or looping through one another or holding others upright.

Bring Life to Dull Areas

Another good design technique employs container plantings to soften the stark look of dull areas where no soil or garden area is available such as side yards or walkways, decks, along garage walls, or cement areas bound by chain link fences. It's easy to build your own garden in these barren areas. Line up window boxes or pots along a wall, for instance, placing them a few inches out so they aren't crowded. The containers can be all the same or a mix of types. Use low plants and climbing vines. Move them around to change the growing scene.

For a lush, cool leafy look, nothing beats caladium bulbs, which produce abundant leaves in various shades of green or green enlivened with pink dots or splotches, white or magenta borders, or other exotic colorations. Then for vertical display, add a backdrop of wooden or metal latticework that will support climbing vines such as moonflowers, sweet peas, or morning glories.

FACT

Two important notes: (1) All containers must have drainage holes, and (2) water container plantings regularly—even daily during heat waves. Container plants drink lots, and often.

Try Space-Age Containers

Learn about new fiberglass, resin, and synthetic containers now on the market. Many are patterned after rare old estate containers in handsome designs of pseudo-stone, molded cement, terra cotta, even cast iron. Dramatic containers are also available. Let your imagination run wild and plant dramatic plants, too.

Your choice of containers is as wide as your imagination and ingenuity. Search in flea markets, chain store garden departments, and local garden centers. Enjoy blooming beauty, tasty veggies, and happy herbs from containers wherever you wish. Ⓔ

Chapter 18

E Happier, Healthier Houseplants

Houseplants are a growing hobby for millions of people. Nearly seven out of ten households have living plants growing indoors on windowsills or as decorative accents. Houseplants can make living environments come alive in apartments, homes, condos, offices, or wherever you live and work. If they are healthy and happy, they'll make you happy, too!

Give Your Plants TLC

Too often our houseplants disappoint us. They don't bloom. They look sorrowful. Usually houseplants don't thrive because we don't understand their individual needs. Many are killed by the misplaced kindness of overwatering.

You can enjoy years of blooming beauty and fantastic foliage by paying proper attention to the needs of your houseplant and with a little TLC, tender loving care. Understanding and attending to their needs for proper soil, watering, light, heat, and food can make your houseplants flourish.

You have a wide choice for house plantscaping. Many species have variegated leaf colors, patterns, shapes, and sizes to satisfy every taste. You can select a variety of different plants to create the indoor plantscape that pleases you. Some plants love sun. Many prefer less direct sunlight. Others require shaded areas to perform best. You also can opt for foliage plants, plants that bloom periodically, or enjoy the glorious, but short-lived displays of potted bulbs like crocus, hyacinths, tulips, or daffodils for a blaze of color in winter.

Learn about Plant Needs

Whatever your preference, shop carefully and learn about each plant's needs so you can match the plants with the type of growing environment you can provide. In winter, hot dry homes have been called the indoor American desert. You can adjust for that with proper soil mix, watering, misting, and other culture techniques, but for sure success, begin with easy care plants as you begin your house plantscaping.

Because there are so many types of houseplants, it is impossible to provide the specific growing tips for each type. This chapter focuses on basic tips, advice, and cultural methods for most houseplants. Two of the best books that give you plant-by-plant tips are the *Woman's Day Book of House Plants* and the *New York Times Book of House Plants*. You can probably obtain them from most local libraries or bookstores.

Know Your Plant Factors

Light, water, temperature, humidity, ventilation, fertilization, and soil are chief factors affecting plant growth, and any one of these factors in incorrect proportions will prevent proper plant growth indoors. It pays to learn about each to give your plants their best chance to thrive and reward you for your tender loving care.

Light Them Right

Light is probably the most essential factor for houseplant growth. When examining light levels consider three aspects of light: intensity, duration, and quality.

Light intensity influences the manufacture of plant food, stem length, leaf color, and flowering. A plant grown in low light tends to be spindly, and the leaves are a light green or yellowish color. A similar plant grown in very bright light would be shorter, better branched, and have larger, dark green leaves.

Houseplants can be classified according to their light needs, such as high, medium, and low light requirements. When you buy houseplants, check the tag and put the plant where it gets the light it needs. Southern exposures have the most intense light. Eastern and western exposures receive about 60 percent of the intensity of southern exposures. Northern exposures receive only 20 percent of the light a southern exposure gets.

FACT

Always check the specific light needs for new plants. Many have been developed to thrive in those shaded areas where you wish to brighten a room with foliage.

Light and Location Are Key

Light and location are key considerations. Too much light and heat, especially on south-facing windows can harm plants. Feel the heat against your window on a sunny day. That demonstrates how much heat can be transmitted to plants, drying them out and sunburning them. Pay attention to houseplant needs, which vary by type of plant, and they'll reward you with healthy displays.

Temperature also is important. Avoid radiators or heating sources that can dry plants out. For sun-loving plants, pick a bright spot where day temperatures range from 65° to 75°F. Don't let cold air from air conditioners or drafty windows blow directly on plants. You don't like that. Plants don't either. Houseplants, like people, do best when they are comfortable and provided with the living conditions that suit their needs.

Save these light requirements of houseplants for reference:

- Cool temperature—50–60°F daytime; 45–55°F at night
- Medium temperature—60–65°F daytime; 55–60°F at night
- High temperature—70–80°F daytime; 65–70°F at night

The Right Pots for Houseplants

You have a wide choice of houseplant containers. A good container should be large enough to provide room for soil and roots, have sufficient headroom (the space between the soil level and the top of the pot) for proper watering, provide bottom drainage, and be attractive without competing with the plant it holds. Containers may be ceramic, plastic, fiberglass, wood, aluminum, copper, brass, and many other materials.

Clay and Ceramic Containers

Unglazed and glazed porous clay pots with drainage holes are sometimes still used by commercial houseplant growers and are frequently left with the plant when it is purchased. Ornate containers are often nothing but an outer shell to cover the plain clay pot.

Clay pots absorb and release moisture through their walls. Frequently the greatest accumulation of roots is next to the walls of the clay pot, because moisture and nutrients build up in the clay pores. Although easily broken, clay pots provide excellent aeration for plant roots and are considered by some to be the healthiest type of container for most plants.

Plastic, fiberglass plastic, and fiberglass containers are usually quite light and easy to handle. They've become the standard in recent years because they are relatively inexpensive and quite attractive in shape and color. Plastic pots are easy to sterilize or clean for reuse. Because they are not porous, plastic pots need less frequent watering and tend to accumulate fewer salts.

Talking to your plants is a good idea. People tended to laugh at that idea when it was first suggested, but there is a point to talking to plants. It's silly but fun. Most important, spending time enjoying your plants gives you time to really notice them and the signs they give you about their health and needs. Then you can spot and correct any problems they may have.

The Need for Repotting

Rapidly growing houseplants may need repotting. A green thumb rule for foliage plants is that they require repotting when their roots have filled the pot and are growing out the bottom. The new pot should be no more than 2 inches larger in diameter. If it has been used, wash it well with a solution of 1 part liquid bleach to 9 parts water. If the plant is root bound, cut and unwind any roots that encircle the plant.

Moisten the soil and carefully remove the rootball. A tap or two on a counter usually loosens it. Or, use a spatula to do so. Then, trim away the knotted, excess roots. Use a sharp pointed stick to loosen the old soil without damaging the basic roots. If the plant needs dividing, gently pull the roots apart and cut where two or more crowns are formed. Remove any dead or damaged roots. In the process, keep the roots moist. Also prune the tops of the plants to compensate for the root pruning.

Position the plant so the top of the old soil ball is slightly below the rim of the pot. Add the soil mix gradually while holding the plant. Move it gently to let the soil settle and pack the mix uniformly and firmly. After watering and settling, the soil level should be below the level of the pot to leave headroom. A properly potted plant has enough headroom to allow water to wash through the soil to thoroughly moisten it.

Double-Potting Tips

Many gardeners prefer decorative plant containers for indoor display, but these may not be the best for houseplants. In this case, you can give the plants better growing conditions by double-potting them. Use a clean clay pot for the plant. Then select a larger decorative container and place the potted plant into that unit. Fill the space between the clay pot and the outer container with sphagnum moss. Now when you water your houseplant, excess water can escape through the bottom and sides of the clay pot and moisten the sphagnum moss to provide humidity for the plant.

Roots Need the Right Foundation

Proper soil is important so that plant nutrients, water, and air can move through the soil and satisfy the needs of plant roots to nourish your plants. Soil mixes today are widely available for growing houseplants and repotting those that are overgrown and root bound. These combinations of soil, peat moss, and vermiculite are scientifically blended to insure proper growing conditions. Mixes should be loose for proper drainage and distribution of plant nutrients. Don't use ordinary garden soil. It can contain disease organisms and insect infestations.

QUESTION?

The most common question home gardeners ask is, "How often should I water my plants?"
There is no one answer to this question. Some plants like moist conditions, while others prefer drier conditions. It is up to you to learn the moisture needs of each plant and provide what they require as part of your TLC.

Water Well and Wisely

Watering is another basic factor in houseplant care that is often misunderstood. Overwatering kills more houseplants than any other single cause. People tend to see a few yellow leaves and believe their plants need more water. They add more and that can begin the process of drowning and rotting roots.

Differences in soil or potting medium and environment can also influence water needs. Watering as soon as the topsoil crust dries usually results in overwatering. Houseplant roots are usually in the bottom two-thirds of the pot; so do not water until the bottom two-thirds starts to dry out slightly.

You can't tell this by looking. You have to feel the soil. For a 6-inch pot, stick your index finger about 2 inches into the soil. If the soil feels damp, don't water. For smaller pots, go 1 inch into the soil.

Water the pot until water runs out of the bottom. This method serves two purposes. First, it washes out excess salts or fertilizer residue. Second, it guarantees that the bottom two-thirds of the pot, which contains most of the roots, receives sufficient water.

Watch the Temperature

Most houseplants tolerate normal temperature fluctuations and grow best between 70° and 80°F during the day and from 60° to 68°F at night. Most flowering houseplants prefer the same daytime range but grow best at nighttime temperatures from 55° to 60°F. The lower night temperature induces physiological recovery from moisture loss, intensifies flower color, and prolongs flower life.

FACT

A good rule of thumb is to keep the night temperature 10° to 15°F lower than the day temperature. A thermometer nearby will let you check that for the first week or so.

Consider Humidity

American homes, especially those heated with forced hot air can be arid. You can increase humidity for your houseplant in two ways: either by attaching a humidifier to your home heating or ventilating system or by placing gravel trays, in which an even moisture level is maintained, under the flowerpots or containers. The water in the gravel trays will increase the relative humidity in the vicinity of the containers. As the moisture around the pebbles evaporates, the relative humidity is raised.

Plants Like Nice Climates

Houseplants, especially flowering varieties, are sensitive to drafts or heat from registers. Forced air dries the plants rapidly, overtaxes their limited root systems, and may cause damage or plant loss. Houseplants are sensitive to natural or blended gas. Some plants refuse to flower, while others drop buds and foliage when exposed to gases. Blended gases are more toxic to houseplants than natural gases.

Increasing the atmospheric humidity in your home, as discussed in the previous section, is a good idea. Occasional light misting of foliage also helps tropical plants by cleaning the foliage and moistening it especially during winter when many homes are too dry for best plant growth.

Plants need clean leaves to grow well. Dust, especially in homes heated by hot air systems, can clog the pores of leaves. Periodic cleaning with mild soapy water and a clear water rinse keeps leaves clean and at their peak for best plant performance.

ALERT!

Never use outdoor garden soil to pot houseplants. It contains bacteria, fungi, and other potential problems for houseplants. When repotting, wash the container carefully and use only houseplant soil.

Feeding Their Growing Needs

To stay healthy, houseplants need a balanced diet just like you. Fortunately, many excellent, balanced houseplant fertilizers are available. Read the labels carefully. Too much plant food can be as harmful as too little. Read, heed, and follow fertilizing recommendations for the brand you use. More frequent feedings of lighter applications is best, unless you use special timed-release fertilizer.

Insects can be a problem for houseplants, especially when you add a new plant to your home décor. Wilted, discolored leaves and stunted branches are sure signs of pests. Check for insect problems before you buy a new plant, and every time you water or feed the ones you already have. Spotting damage early leads to faster cures. Mites, mealybugs, aphids, and other types of sucking or chewing insects can breed fast, especially in warm, humid conditions. Most pests attack growing tender tips and ends of branches. If you see insects, cleaning with soapy water or a cotton swab dipped in rubbing alcohol can stop their spread.

Modern multipurpose houseplant pesticides are valuable for controlling insect problems that may arise. As with fertilizer, apply a pesticide according to specific label directions. With pesticides, you are using a chemical or combination of chemicals to kill insects. A little goes a long way. Too much can harm plants.

Plant Selection Pointers

When you shop for houseplants, take time to pick the best. Select only those plants that appear to be free of insects and disease. Check the undersides of the foliage and the axils of leaves for signs of insects or disease. Select plants that look sturdy, clean, well-potted, shapely, and well-covered with leaves.

Choose plants with healthy foliage. Avoid plants that have yellow or chlorotic leaves, brown leaf margins, wilted or water-soaked foliage, spots or blotches, and spindly growth. In addition, avoid leaves with mechanical damage and those that have been treated with "leaf shines," which add an unnatural polish to the leaves. Plants that have new flowers and leaf buds along with young growth are usually of superior quality.

ALERT!

Beware of that urge to water your plants too often. Instead, check the moisture in the soil mix. Insert a toothpick. If it comes out with soil particles clinging to it, you probably have sufficient moisture.

Transporting Plants

When transporting plants, the two seasons of the year that most often cause damage to the plants are the hot summer and the cold winter months. In the summer, avoid placing plants in a car and leaving the car closed, because the inside temperature will rise and destroy the plant in a short period. If you have to travel for any distance at all, direct sun can burn the plant even though the air conditioner is on and the temperature is comfortable in the car. Shade the plant from direct sun while it is in the car.

During winter months, wrap plants thoroughly before leaving the store to carry them to your car. A short run from the store to the car in very low temperatures can kill or severely damage plants. Wrap plants thoroughly with newspaper or paper bags and place them in the front of the car and turn on the heater. Many foliage plants will be damaged considerably if the temperature drops much below 50°F, so maintain as warm a temperature as possible around these plants when transporting them from one location to another.

ALERT!

Watch for these signs of trouble. Reduced growth, brown leaf tips, dropping of lower leaves, small new growth, dead root tips, and wilting are all signs of high soluble salts. These fertilizer salts may accumulate on top of the soil forming a yellow to white crust. As the salts in the soil become more and more concentrated, plants find it harder and harder to take up water.

Houseplant Soil Mixes

The potting soil or medium in which a plant grows must be of good quality. It should be porous for root aeration and drainage but also capable of retaining water and nutrients. Most commercially prepared mixes are termed *artificial,* which means they contain no soil. High-quality artificial mixes generally contain slow-release fertilizers that take care of a plant's nutritional requirements for several months. You can find many good mixes at garden center departments and chain stores.

America's Favorite Houseplants

You probably have your own favorite houseplants. As you expand your growing horizons, it helps to take a look at other opportunities, whether with your landscape or with your houseplant decorating scheme. As you look ahead, here's a handy list of the most popular houseplants in America, according to sales and survey reports:

- African violet
- Agave
- Aloe
- Aluminum plant
- Amaryllis
- Asparagus fern
- Azalea
- Bird's-nest fern
- Cacti
- Caladium
- Christmas cactus
- Cineraria
- Crown-of-thorns
- Cyclamen
- Dracaena
- Gardenia
- Gloxinia
- Impatiens
- Ivies
- Kalanchoe
- Maidenhair fern
- Norfolk Island pine
- Orchids
- Oxalis
- Passionflower
- Philodendron
- Piggyback plant
- Poinsettia
- Polka-dot plant
- Pothos vine
- Rex begonia
- Rubber plant
- Sedum
- Shrimp plant
- Snake plant
- Spider plant
- Swedish ivy
- Ti plant
- Vase plant
- Wax plant
- Zebra plant

Houseplants are another wonderful growing adventure for gardeners. With the knowledge from this chapter you, too, can enjoy the beauty and wonder of houseplants. Try your green thumb at propagating more houseplants from cuttings. Grow extras for the office and to share with friends. Organize a houseplant swap day. Houseplants offer bouquets of fun and ways to meet new gardening friends.

Chapter 19
Let's Grow Together

Gardening offers many wonderful ways for people to grow together with their children, grandchildren, friends, neighbors, and others in the community. Think of gardening this year as your new great growing opportunity. In this chapter you'll find dozens of ideas for all ages, interests, and abilities.

Earn Money While Meeting People

There's gold in them thar hills of pumpkins, cucumbers, and melons. Here are some great growing ideas from innovative gardeners who have mined their gardens for substantial extra income. They've also enjoyed berry fine profits from fruitful landscapes, plus many other great growing projects. People today want and need ways to supplement their incomes and even launch profitable home-based businesses. Here are some green thumb ways to earn extra income from your gardening talents. Plus, you'll have the added bonus of getting to know your neighbors and others in the community!

Try Dried Flowers

Strawflowers are designed to become beautiful dried flowers. Order a few packets of seeds, grow the flowers, and try your hand at drying them. Then, see how they sell at a roadside stand, at flea markets, church fairs, and other events. If you like the feel of flower arranging, strawflowers can lead you to some regular extra income.

Fresh Veggie Stand

Fresh veggies are very popular, as any farmer will tell you. You can test the market right at curbside with your own small vegetable stand. People pay a premium for fresh produce that is fresher by miles than stuff trucked to supermarkets. They also pay a higher premium if you grow organically, without chemicals on the crops. Be sure to have a sign identifying what you offer, the price, and details about organic growing. Seal it in a plastic page so people can read it.

FACT

Freshly picked, sun-ripened berries are one of the most popular fruits people want to buy at roadside markets. Blackberries, blueberries, and red and black raspberries are easy to grow and bring top dollar for easy picking work.

Be sure to shade your vegetable stand so veggies don't bake in the hot sun. Sprinkle them periodically with water to keep them fresh. In the process, consider expanding from your curbside stand to a fresh veggie route. Kids like to earn money and they can, taking orders and delivering fresh-from-the-garden vegetables to neighbors on the way to or from school.

Unusual Plants

People like unusual plants. You can easily grow some plant oddities and sell them well. Curious ornamental and Indian corns are popular. People like them for fall decorations. Check seed catalogs and order the more unusual types. Try other colors and shapes in future years.

Think about gourds, too. You can grow a variety that are in demand for table decorations. Some grow in strange and unique shapes. Others you can grow, dry, paint, and sell as ornamental gourds. With the larger ones, try drying them out, drilling a hole in them, shaking out the seeds, and selling them as unique birdhouses.

Plant Cuttings

Plant cuttings are another moneymaking idea that veteran gardeners have found popular. The more unusual the plant the more you can charge, depending on the market in your area. Flower shows, church fairs, and other such events are logical places to have displays, take orders, and build a home plant-propagating sideline. You can also divide perennial plants and expand your line of unusual plants.

FACT

Many restaurants want flower arrangements. Several home gardeners grew flowers so profusely they took bouquets to local restaurants. By keeping the flowers affordable, they traded bouquets for lunches and dinners. That was a win/win deal for all concerned, including diners who enjoyed the attractive floral displays.

Part-Time Plant Businesses

Here are a few other ideas that may whet your appetite for growing your own part-time plant business with your children, for supplemental income, as a retirement hobby, or simply to meet and get to know others.

- Grow Tex-Mex, Russian, oriental, or other exotic foods
- Be a store décor person, setting up store window decorations of flowers
- Grow super sunflowers and offer them in buckets to local florists
- Collect old, rare, heirloom plant varieties for sale or collect and sell the seeds
- Arrange houseplant swaps or sales among friends as a church fundraiser or business

Brag Patch Fun

You and your children can grow the Great Pumpkin that Charlie Brown's friend Linus always wanted to see every Halloween. Here's a project that can help your family produce a prize-winning pumpkin of 200 pounds or more. You'll need the right giant pumpkin seeds: Big Max, Big Moon, or Prizewinner hybrid, plus lots of garden space. Pumpkins, like most vine crops, require room to roam.

Select a spot in full sun, away from tree roots. Before planting, work a 5-10-5 fertilizer into the soil, 3 to 5 pounds per 100 square feet. To get a head start on springtime, start seeds on a sunny, draft-free windowsill. The room temperature must be 65° to 70°F. Plant two to three seeds in peat pots filled with seed starting mix. After each seedling has produced its second set of leaves, cut off all but the sturdiest seedling in each container.

When the danger of frost is past, transplant the seedlings into the fertilized garden soil you prepared. Place peat pots deep enough so containers are completely covered with soil. Allow two plants per hill. Use black plastic mulch to cover the ground around your pumpkins. It attracts warmth from the sun, smothers weeds, conserves soil moisture, and protects developing fruits from damaging ground contact, soil bacteria, and soil insects. During dry days, water your plants thoroughly, soaking the soil to a depth of at least 6 inches, about once every ten days.

Learn the Great Pumpkin Secret

Now for the secret! To grow the biggest pumpkin possible, *remove all except one pumpkin from each vine.* That way, all the nutrients and water you apply go into making that one remaining pumpkin the biggest it can be. Some veteran gardeners recommend cutting a slice in the vine and gently pressing a fiberglass wick into it. The other end is inserted in a bottle of water buried in the ground and kept filled at all times. They say this helps give the single pumpkin left on the vine an extra push to giant size.

Fertilize your plants again when the pumpkins begin to form and again when the pumpkins are half grown. Follow directions on the fertilizer container.

Before Halloween arrives, you can harvest your giant pumpkin for school display or enter it in local fairs. Have it weighed and next year, improve your growing skills to try to beat your own record weight.

Grow a "Named" Pumpkin

You can also have fun by adding a name, creating a face, or putting a magic message on your pumpkin. It will come alive mysteriously to amaze your children and their friends. When your pumpkins are half grown, in about late August, use a nail or knife to scratch a face, or write a name or other design into the rind of your pumpkin. Make cuts about ¼ inch deep just into the rind, no deeper.

Be sure to leave 3 to 4 inches of stem attached to the fruit. Cure them for one to two weeks at 75° to 80°F and then store them in a dry, well-ventilated place at 50° to 60°F until you use them.

As the pumpkin grows to maturity, scar tissue will form over the cuts. That results in raised areas on the shell that seem to appear mysteriously and naturally. Harvest your pumpkins before the first frost when rinds are hard and have a deep, solid orange color.

Easy Care Family Adventures

The following projects can help you and your family, even your friends, study, learn, and perfect your abilities to produce and propagate new plants. You'll even have fun in the process.

Raspberry Delights

Raspberries are a real taste treat. Begin with just a few plants and see how you can make them multiply. Raspberries are especially easy to produce. Red varieties do it themselves. New sucker shoots sprout all around the plants from underground roots and runners.

For your first project, find and dig up these new sucker plants. Transplant them in the spring to another area to begin a new berry patch. Then, expand your propagating studies.

Try Tip Layering

Try simple tip layering to produce more plants. The best time to do this is in the fall when tips of canes have small, curled leaves. Bend the canes carefully and tuck these tips into the soil. Cover each tip well with a shovel full of garden soil. Use a stone to hold a cane down if it is springy and tends to snap out of the ground.

By late fall, laterals are usually well rooted. Leave them there until spring, covered with mulch and stakes to mark their spot. In spring, cut the old cane from the parent plant and dig up the newly rooted plant to begin a new berry patch.

Serpentine Layering

You can grow faster with serpentine layering. In the fall, select several of the longest canes from red, black, or purple raspberry plants. Bend them down and bury the tip. Then, bury another spot along the cane under a shovel full of soil. Sometimes canes of black raspberries are long enough to let you bury three areas. Cover each with a full shovel of soil, and weight the area with a rock or brick. By spring, you'll have many more plants from serpentine layering.

Air Layering Is Fun

You also can try air layering. Select several berry canes in summer to try this method. Push a knife blade through the cane. Then, insert a toothpick to hold the wound open. Wrap moist sphagnum moss around the area. Cover the moss with a plastic bag and tape it closed. By fall, you should see roots through the moss. Then, cut the cane from the parent plant and plant it.

Following Sunflowers

As more people have discovered the value of natural foods, sunflowers have gained wider popularity. One of the unusual habits of this fun plant is its ability to turn its flowers to follow the sun. That is most likely why it was named sunflower by the earliest American pioneers. You can study them and even trace their movements with these fun-in-the-sun projects.

See how many sunflower seeds you can grow. You are going to have two groups of sunflowers: fertilized and unfertilized plants. Count and weigh the number of seeds you plant from a package. Then, sow the seeds and grow several rows of sunflowers. Estimate how many seeds you expect your plants to produce. Fertilize, weed, and water the plants according to directions on the seed package. Don't add any fertilizer to the control group or row of plants.

When seed heads have matured and begun to bend with the weight of the seed crop, cut them off. Remove the seeds. Count and weigh them from your fertilized plants. Then, remove, count, and weigh the seeds from the unfertilized plants. Review your estimate of the number and weight of the seeds you thought your plants would produce. How accurate were you? The answer may really surprise you.

Sow and grow a crop of the largest sunflowers. When they mature, cut the seed heads and nail them to a post, a wall, or any place where birds can find them. Keep a daily diary of what types of birds come to feed, how many, and how long it takes for the birds to eat all the sunflower seeds you have grown.

School Science Fair Projects

Your family and children can enjoy school science fair projects that you grow in your garden. Here's an example. You can prove that sunflowers do follow the sun. You'll need a package of sunflower seeds, two tall stakes, string, and ruler. For more advanced studies, a camera and tripod give you amazing and accurate records. Select any sunflower variety. Mammoth and Giant size provide easier measurements and huge blooms with many more seeds.

Sow sunflower seeds and follow the package directions. As your plants grow, place a 5- to 6-foot stake on each side of the plants. Connect the stakes with string at the top and bottom. Then, tie more lines of string vertically to form a grid pattern. Using wire garden fencing to make this guide will let you measure and record the movement of sunflower blooms more accurately.

As plants flower, observe them and use your ruler to measure the changes every few hours as the blooms turn with the sun's movement across the sky, from morning to afternoon. Record your measurements and write your own scientific report of sunflower movements.

FACT

For a more accurate study, photograph the sunflowers' movement. Place three flat stones or bricks as a base for the tripod so it will stay in the same position every time you photograph the plants. Beginning in the morning, take a photo every hour from that same position, right up to late afternoon. You can use these photos for a plant science study as you describe the way sunflowers move and how much they really do in a day.

Discover Underground Mysteries

You can discover nature's underground mysteries and learn more about how plants grow with a root-watching box. It's easy to make. All you need are cedar or redwood boards, screws, a clear Plexiglas panel, soil mix, and seeds. Cut three 1-by-4-inch boards in 12-inch segments. Attach both sides to the bottom piece. Then cut a piece of plywood to fit the back.

Finally, cut a piece of clear Plexiglas or other rigid plastic sheet to cover the front. Screw them firmly in place. Use putty or window caulking to seal the seams so the box won't leak. Then, fill the box with planting mix. Any types of seeds will perform for you, but beans, corn, and radishes are larger and easier to see as they perform. Plant your seeds and water them. Keep the soil mix moist, and watch the plants carefully every day.

Measure Your Rooting Progress

Attach a ruler to the side of the box so you can measure root progress every day. Because root growth can surprise you, plan to check it morning, noon, and afternoon. Keep a daily record of root progress. Your diary can serve as your first scientific study of plant root growth.

You can expand your natural science growing horizons with two or more root-watching boxes. The goal is to compare plant growth from top to bottom with fertilized plants in one box and unfertilized plants in the other. You can use different quantities of fertilizer, or even organic nutrients in future scientific tests. Let your imagination set the pace for how extensive you wish to grow with these revealing root-watching experiments.

Be a Plant Scientist

Fill the boxes with identical soil mix and plant the same number, types, and varieties of seeds. Apply water regularly to the "control" box but don't use any fertilizer. To the other box, mix and apply regular feedings of plant fertilizer. Record the dates that you add the plant nutrients, how much, and what kind. Mark root progress daily and record the growth difference between the plants and their roots compared with those in the other box that had no nutrients. Write down your observations. You'll soon see how important fertilizer is to plant growth, even in these little root boxes.

Young Gardeners

Gardening is now ranked as America's number one outdoor activity and, no pun intended, is growing like a weed. Many parents find gardening an excellent way to spend quality time with their kids, teach environmental awareness and responsibility, and also have good old-fashioned family fun.

FACT

Gertrude Jekyll, the celebrated English garden writer, suggested that "autumn is the time to plant little gardens." Though vegetable gardens are often touted as the best way to plant the gardening seed in children, Ms. Jekyll felt that the pure fun of digging in the dirt was the real key.

Fall Colors and Fun Combine

With the brisk air and colorful tree foliage, autumn is a great time to introduce children to gardening. Raking fallen leaves into piles and rolling in them is a treat. That can lead to raking them up again and beginning a compost pile.

Fall is the right time to plant spring flowering bulbs. Kids love playing and digging in the dirt, so this is another ideal way to introduce them to the fun of gardening. Crocus, daffodils, hyacinths, and tulips all should be planted between September and ground freezing. Consider giving your children their own garden spot. Show them how to dig and plant the bulbs and mark their garden plot.

Come spring, you can enjoy that delight as these colorful spring-flower plants arise, shoot up, and bloom gloriously. It is a treat indeed to watch youngsters who discover their first flowers, come running in with the blooming news.

Great Oaks from Little Acorns Grow

Trees are one of nature's magnificent achievements. Don't wait for Arbor Day to introduce youngsters to the tradition of trees. Chances are they already know much about them since rain forest and environmental studies are so popular today. Think back and you may recall planting a tree when you were young or seeing others do it. Think how big that tree is today. Give a youngster the opportunity to plant his or her own tree. Think ahead to that day when you and your child can look at it and have happy family memories together.

When choosing a young tree, try to guide youngsters in positive research ways. Find out how tall the tree is likely to become when it grows to full size. Learn how fast it grows and if it might make a mess in your yard in spring or fall. Mulberry trees, for example, are lovely, grow quickly, and yield a sweet fruit. But unless you're planning to spend weeks each summer gathering fallen berries, you're buying a smelly mess. Gingko trees do well on city lots but also drop smelly, messy pods. Great oaks also litter the lawn below with bushels of acorns.

Here are some thinking points:

- Keep the tree's eventual growth in mind when choosing a site and paint a picture of the future tree to your young arborist
- Remember that most young trees should be planted in holes about 3 feet wide and 18 inches deep so the sapling roots can spread to get a firm roothold
- Arrange for good drainage by adding some gravel or other drainage material, especially if you have heavy clay soil
- Stake young trees for support for the first few years
- Provide adequate watering when planting and during the first six months of tree growth

Tool Up for Tots

Child-size rakes, hoes, and spades are available today from garden shops and catalog. You can find excellent sets at garden centers and in the garden departments of Home Depot and similar major chains. Gardeners Supply Company also has excellent tools for youngsters and seniors alike. Here's a handy list of tools for young gardeners:

- Trowel
- Basket or bucket
- Gardening gloves and hat
- Hoe
- Rake
- Small wheelbarrow
- Spade

Planting Fall Bulbs

Fall is perfect bulb-planting time for crocus, daffodils, and tulips. Unlike seeds, bulbs are not dormant. They are already living plants and are practically guaranteed to grow if you put them in the ground in the fall. Slice open a hyacinth, for example, and your child can see the "baby flower" in the middle, just waiting to burst forth in the spring.

You should plant bulbs in one of two ways: either laid out in quantity in large groups or placed in small groups in small holes. Trench planting is the ideal way to achieve a formal look or design patterns. You could write your children's names in different colored crocuses or tulips.

Naturalizing Comes Easy

Naturalizing is an easy technique that uses the small hole approach. Naturalized bulbs are meant to look as if nature planted them; *naturalizing* is a term for planting those types of bulbs that will come back year after year. Children can have a lot of fun with naturalizing, because the best way to achieve that "natural" look is to grab handfuls of bulbs, toss them out on the desired area, and plant them where they fall. Bulbs can actually be planted right on the lawn and will grow through the grass.

Planting Tips

Here are some planting tips for bulbs:

- Bulbs need good drainage so choose areas where water is not likely to collect; add compost to help improve drainage
- Plant large bulbs, such as tulips and daffodils, 8 inches deep, and small bulbs, such as snowdrops or crocuses, 5 inches deep
- Plant before the first ground-freezing frost
- Plant with the pointed side of the bulb up

Fooling Mother Nature

A great project for families is fooling Mother Nature by forcing bulbs to bloom indoors when the snow may still be on the garden ground outdoors. Bulb forcing is easy, just about foolproof, and a super way to keep little hands busy for hours on a rainy day. Bulbs can be potted up as "I made it myself" gifts for friends, teachers, or grandparents. Bulb forcing also gives youngsters a real feeling of accomplishment, especially when they hear the *ooohs* and *ahhhs* from grandparents as they see beautiful pots of blooming amaryllises!

You can obtain appropriate bulbs through catalogs, at garden and home centers, and even in the produce or floral department of many supermarkets. These bulbs need no special preparation and can be potted and grown as soon as you get them home. Some fun bulbs for easy forcing include colorful hyacinths, crocuses, and narcissi. They require a bit more attention, but they too can offer the young gardener an enchanting indoor experience. It's best to begin with the easiest, paperwhites.

FACT

The term *forcing* might be better expressed as *fooling*. For what you really do is fool the bulb into thinking that winter is over and it's time to flower. The two easiest bulbs to force are paperwhite narcissus and amaryllis. You also can force hyacinths and other daffodils.

Paperwhite Forcing Tips

Paperwhite types are especially easy to grow. They can be bought as loose bulbs or as part of a prepackaged forcing kit. They are often found in displays along with gravel, containers, and other bulbs for forcing.

Paperwhites are best forced in a shallow pot or bowl with no drainage holes in the bottom. Fill the pot two-thirds full with gravel, stones, or even marbles! Place as many bulbs as will fit on the gravel with the pointed side up. Then fill in gravel around them leaving the tops exposed. Add water up to the base of the bulbs and maintain water at this level. That's where the roots will get the water. Any higher up and you risk rotting bulbs.

Next, place the container in a cool place. Within a few days roots will appear. As they grow, they will sometimes push the bulbs upward. When the green shoots appear, move your pot to a cool, sunny spot.

Plant shoots will develop rapidly. In about three weeks you'll have masses of heavily scented sweet white flowers.

Amaryllis Forcing Tips

Amaryllis bulbs are very large but also are very easy to grow. Plant these big bulbs one to a pot. You can often find complete prepackaged kits. Begun early enough, amaryllises can be easily brought to flower for the holiday season. By varying start-up times, you can enjoy amaryllises blooming indoors from December through April. Here's how to do it.

Pick any attractive container with a drainage hole and saucer to catch the extra water that drains out. The pot circumference should be just a little larger than the bulb itself. Next, spread a shallow layer of gravel or other drainage material at the bottom of the pot. Add several inches of soil. Then place the bulb in the pot, pointed end up, with the neck and "shoulders" of the bulb just over the top of the container. Next, fill in with soil and gently pat down, leaving the neck of the bulb exposed.

Place the bulb in a cool bright spot. Water it sparingly at first. After the first sprouts appear in about two weeks, keep the soil moist but don't overwater. In about eight weeks, you and your young gardener will be proud to show off your plants with their huge, exotic-looking flowers of velvety red, pink, white, peach, orange, or even multicolor.

Keep in mind that amaryllis will grow tall and top-heavy. To keep your amaryllis upright as it blooms, try double-potting it by using a lightweight plastic flowerpot placed inside a heavier decorative container.

Forcing Other Bulbs

Forcing many other bulbs—especially hyacinths, crocuses, grape hyacinths, and narcissi, which many people call daffodils—is also easy. However they require some free space in a refrigerator or in an unheated garage or storeroom to duplicate the dormant period these bulbs need. Ask your garden center for the right bulbs or order forcing kits and bulbs from mail-order catalogs. Once you have tried a few easy ones, expand your horizons with new challenges for other fragrant, blooming displays to brighten your windowsills in winter. (E)

Chapter 20

Plant a Row
for the Hungry

The members of the Garden Writers Association of America decided to address the problem of hunger with an innovative program that they call "Plant a Row for the Hungry." This chapter will give you details about the program and how to put your gardening skills to use for the cause.

The Origin of PAR

Jeff Lowenfels, former president of the Garden Writers Association of America (GWAA), originally alerted members to the extent and pervasiveness of the hunger problem in North America. They accepted the challenge to urge home gardeners to help feed America's hungry.

Plant a Row for the Hungry, or PAR, was launched in 1995. Today that program has taken root across America. Millions of pounds of food have been grown and donated to food kitchens, pantries, and other facilities. Plant a Row for the Hungry has been a remarkably successful program, enlisting many thousands of backyard gardeners nationwide to plant extra rows to feed the hungry. You, too, can get involved in this worthwhile program.

PAR encourages America's home gardeners to grow an extra row beyond what they need for their own family. Think what might happen if each gardener planted one extra row and donated the harvest to a local food bank! With that thought in mind, GWAA members began writing to get the program the public attention it deserves. GWAA director Jacqui Heriteau created the first PAR program and continues to lead PAR as national program director.

A Grow and Share Plan

Conceived at the outset as a people-based program, PAR's success depends on the goodwill and efforts of thousands of gardeners and gardening groups. It began with members of GWAA who were supported by their editors, radio, and TV stations as they wrote to alert the public to the hunger problem in their region with suggestions for how they could help. In keeping with the PAR name, writers urged the planting of an extra row of vegetables through their newspaper columns, on their radio or TV shows, in newsletters, church bulletins, and public appearances.

Corporate Support

Corporate support for PAR campaigns became a key part of the program. For instance, soil amendment producer Fafard, Inc., of

Anderson, South Carolina, contributes Plant a Row garden row markers for distribution to participating gardeners to promote the campaign. Many other garden product companies add the Plant a Row logo on their packaging. Nurseries and garden centers participate by offering Plant a Row brochures and row markers at checkout counters.

FACT

Today there are citywide programs in many towns, plus statewide projects in Missouri and South Carolina. Many others are being organized. Many groups such as garden clubs, schools, service and civic organizations, and church congregations are participating as well.

An Amazing Success Story

Garden columnist Joan Jackson of the San Jose *Mercury News* pioneered the PAR program among her readership. She devoted many of her columns to describing the program and encouraging gardeners to sign a pledge to grow and contribute fresh produce. Jackson published addresses of collection sites and agencies that used the food. She tallied the weight of the food contributions over the season, saluted the donors by printing their names, and made many appearances at garden events. The response was overwhelming. By September of the first year, her readers had donated more than 30,000 pounds of fruit and vegetables to hunger relief agencies. That's just one success story. There are dozens more.

Extending the Campaign

The PAR effort has grown increasingly successful. After just a few years, the donated food is measured in tons. Even nongardeners have helped, as drivers and workers at collection sites to weigh and pack produce. In 1999, several new sponsors joined to expand the campaign. Lending its name and resources as a sponsor, Home & Garden TV (HGTV) provided wide media coverage as one of the nation's fastest-growing cable networks with more than 50 million viewers. HGTV is committed to this worthwhile public service campaign to feed the hungry. The Scotts Company has also become very active. It promotes PAR on every box of Miracle-Gro fertilizer, and Fafard, Inc., promotes PAR on millions of soil amendment bags.

The Key Is Simplicity

The key to the program's success is its simplicity. There are no governmental hassles or funding issues. The program is just a grass-roots effort by neighbors to help neighbors. The job of garden communicators is to generate awareness of the need and this unique way to meet it. Through newspapers, magazines, radio, TV, and other programs, garden writers reach an estimated 100 million gardeners in North America to encourage them to plant an extra row in their gardens for the hungry. From that encouragement, the gardeners take over, dig in, and grow the food in their garden rows in cities and towns across the country. With such a worthwhile goal, people of all ages are making new friends as they reach out to help fellow Americans in need.

Who are PAR participants? They are America's caring gardeners from all walks of life and from all regions of the United States and Canada, from rural and suburban residents to the inner cities. They include young children, teenagers, adults, and seasoned seniors. Some may be teachers or business executives. Others include local businesspeople, church members, Boy Scouts and Girl Scouts, and students of all ages, according to GWAA archives. Some garden alone; many garden with their families. Others are part of a group or PAR network and coordinate their planting to produce certain crops for local food banks. PAR gardens seem to be sprouting everywhere: in backyards, in community plots, in schoolyards, behind churches, and on apartment balconies and rooftops.

FACT

To learn more about Plant a Row or GWAA, you can visit the Plant a Row page on the GWAA Web site at ✑ *www.gwaa.org*. You also can obtain general information, brochures, and other information by calling toll-free ✆ (877) GWAA-PAR or e-mail at *PAR@GWAA.org*.

Help Feed the Hungry Locally

According to the U.S. Conference of Mayors, hunger continues to be a problem in most of the largest metropolitan areas across the country. Figures released during 2000 revealed an increase of food assistance requests in 1999 of 17 percent above the previous year. The largest groups suffering from hunger are working families and their children, especially single-parent families with one income. Senior citizens are another group that tends to have food needs.

Second Harvest Facts

A national food relief agency, America's Second Harvest, reports that their 200-plus food banks serving 50,000 people turned away more than one million requests for help last year. According to news reports, donations to food banks were down 40 percent during 2001 while requests for help were up 5 to 50 percent, depending on the areas surveyed. America's Second Harvest food banks serve thousands of individual food distribution agencies.

The Importance of Fresh Crops

Many participating gardeners are aware of the importance of fresh fruit and vegetables to families. Local food banks, soup kitchens, and similar programs usually have regular sources of bakery, packaged, and canned goods. However, getting fresh produce, which offers superior nutrition, has been difficult. PAR gardeners are filling that need. Typically they deliver their surplus harvest at designated collection points in their communities where it is recorded, delivered to a nearby food relief agency, and often used the same day.

Share Caring and Know-How

You can get involved wherever you live. Look for stories in your local media or call your local food pantry, Salvation Army office, or county extension agent. Sometimes gardeners get involved because they have excess crops and are trying to find a way to give it away. Virginia Davidson figured she had enough winter squash to last a year after the first 20 pounds came in. Her problem was what to do with the other 250 pounds! She called a local food rescue program in nearby Mechanicsburg, Pennsylvania, and learned about PAR. Now she and her office colleagues cultivate a rented garden plot where all the rows are planted for PAR.

Being part of PAR may have a similar impact on you. Participating gardeners continue to grow the crops that do best in their region so they can count on large harvests. They also sow extra of those crops that are most appreciated and wanted by food kitchen organizations. Some agencies prefer certain crops because they are popular with their clients or are especially high in nutrition. Others suggest foods that they use frequently.

Most agencies appreciate any veggies and fruits that will store on a shelf for a day or two if necessary. They generally want food that is high in nutrients. Many also welcome fresh herbs to flavor the various soups and stews that are included in their meals. During 2000, PAR gardeners donated more than a million pounds of fresh food to the hungry, making it their most productive year thus far.

Flowers are wanted, too, and PAR gardeners often donate flowers to food agencies as well as vegetables. There is something very appealing about a bouquet of fresh flowers on the table to make a nutritious meal especially wonderful.

Gardeners Get Something in Return

Here's one episode that tells part of the story. Darlene White of British Columbia recalls opening her car trunk, which was full of plums for the food bank, when a van drove up with a family of six, including four little kids. They were looking for some groceries. She recalls how the mom was really happy to take a pail full of plums to make jam. What made her day was the little boy who looked up at her with such a happy smile. In that moment, she had her quiet thanks for the small effort it took to make a contribution.

Other gardeners who participate in PAR say that they also receive far more than they give. Naturally, they already love gardening. Now they know that they are helping fight hunger, which makes the gardening experience even more worthwhile. Every participant has a heartwarming story to tell about wonderful incidents in the garden and moving encounters with the grateful. Perhaps Beth Bangert's experience in Calthan, Colorado, says it best. She delivered more than 6,000 pounds of fresh food to the needy, and the response was as if someone had opened the door to a toy store and said, "Go to it." She says her PAR project made her summer the best she's ever had.

Growing Guidelines for All

For everyone who wants to become involved in one of America's most useful growing projects here are key points to consider:

- Contact local food banks and soup kitchens or food recovery organizations for information on what they need
- Extend the main growing season by planting cool-weather crops spring and fall
- Space plantings so that produce ripens over several weeks rather than all at once
- Grow foods that will stay fresh with minimal care for a few days
- Pick promptly to stimulate more production
- Choose foods that travel well and withstand handling
- Be sure to deliver produce that is clean
- Store excess crops properly before taking them to a collection place
- Discard any damaged, old vegetables to prevent spoilage

With profuse thanks to Liz Ball for most of this worthwhile information, there is more to the ongoing PAR story. It gets better and you can be part of it.

Working for Nutrition

A million pounds of garden-fresh produce may sound like a huge amount of food. It stretches the imagination to think that backyard gardeners across North America would and could grow and donate that much extra food to help solve hunger in their communities. However, the dedicated members of Garden Writers Association of America (GWAA) who participated in the Plant a Row for the Hungry program knew it could be done.

One Million by the Millennium

After the first few years of experience planning, developing, and cultivating Plant a Row, their focused commitment to address the chronic problem of hunger led to setting an impressive goal: One Million by the Millennium. Thanks to welcome funding and public service announcements by Home & Garden TV (HGTV), they reached their goal. In fact, by January 2000, the tally had reached 1,051,000 pounds of food collected and distributed to food assistance programs across the United States and Canada.

PAR program director Jacqui Heriteau and her committee organized a monumental national campaign among garden writers and multimedia communicators. Their messages reached out and inspired home gardeners in cities and small towns alike in a growing community effort to generate food donations. That led to the next phase of the PAR effort, which is to spread the word about how many more citizens can build networks, enlist public support, organize more local efforts, and build even more PAR food campaigns, coast to coast.

Launching PARtnering Plans

Gardeners already have the habit of sharing. They routinely give away seeds, seedlings, cuttings, and harvested fruits and vegetables to neighbors, friends, and fellow gardeners. It is but a small step from this generosity to a community food collection depot with a PAR network.

Unfortunately, a problem still remains for an estimated 36 million people who worry every day about where their next meal will come from. Fortunately, the solution of a Plant a Row network to help provide fresh, nutritious food is as close as their neighbors—school kids, businesspeople, and civic, service, and church groups. The link between the gardener and the food kitchen is the network of volunteers.

FACT

There is no single model or example for a PAR food-raising network or organization. They are as diverse as those who set them up, grow the food, and distribute it to the needy. In fact, one of the most important lessons PAR taught is that it is very easy to grow an extra row or two. That's one beauty of the program.

Where to Get Details and Help

You, too, can discover the joys of gardening and being a PAR person. As thousands before you have discovered, there is a richly rewarding experience in growing bounty from the good earth and making some of it available for those who need food. To get in on a good thing, just call ✆ (877) 492-2727 toll free for additional information. There is no cost or obligation, but it may open a garden gate or door wide for great growing experiences.

PAR Networks

A Plant a Row network can be a single garden writer or gardener, backed by a newspaper, TV, or radio station, or a civic, service, or garden organization. PAR networks can be formed within an individual company or business, in a neighborhood or condo group, a union or church, or any similar organization.

It might involve a single garden that is created and managed especially for a giveaway harvest. It might involve coordinating many individual gardeners who purposely grow excess food to donate. One basic fact stands out: The more elements of the community that are involved, the more successful the network and the more food that can be raised. Not everyone has to be a gardener or even a food person. There are many useful jobs for volunteers with all kinds of skills.

Look for PAR News

At the heart of every effort is the publicity provided by a garden communicator and the local media. Initially, a mention of PAR on radio, on TV, at a lecture, or in the newspaper stimulates public interest. That's where the Garden Writers of America members do their best work, communicating garden news locally at the grass-roots level, so to speak.

Subsequently at every stage, publicity supports the local network efforts. Where do you find volunteers to staff the network? Think about civic or service clubs, Scouts, churches, extension agents, Master Gardeners, local businesspeople, garden clubs, Future Farmers/4-H clubs, school service clubs, athletic teams, nearby arboretums, a public garden's staff, your neighbors, and so on. PAR national spokesman Jim Wilson says that he never ceases to be amazed at the creativity of the many networks of volunteers across the country. They work hard and they work smart.

Building Your Own Network

Here are some basic checkpoints that can lead to greater success than you imagine. These steps have been proved productive, so it pays to tap that track record. Begin to build your network about three to four months before the beginning of the growing season by enlisting key people to form a PAR committee. This leadership team will establish a strategy, recruit volunteer workers, and set up and run the food donation campaign. Typically, the leadership of a network is composed of the following positions:

Local PAR coordinator: This person oversees and coordinates all volunteer efforts. If you are reading this chapter, you may be the best candidate for this job! Call a planning meeting, hand out brochures, and show Jim Wilson's PAR video.

Food assistance liaison: A representative of a local food pantry or established food assistance program such as Second Harvest is a key member of the network team. He or she can describe the need, suggest which crops are most appreciated, and facilitate delivery of the donated harvest. This person is also a great source of information for publicity.

Publicist: You don't need to be a GWAA member or even a garden writer to fill this position. This person keeps network activities in the public consciousness through contacts with local media. He or she generates a stream of stories about local PAR efforts by explaining the need, describing the campaign as it develops, soliciting contributions, publishing collection weights, promoting special events, and preparing stories about the donated food and its use. A typical publicity effort would be to arrange a photo of the first donation, of its use in a soup kitchen, or of volunteers at the collection sites.

Collection organizer: This person enlists gardeners and local farmers who might have excess from their fields and orchards into the PAR effort. He or she identifies sponsors, establishes locations to distribute promotional materials and collect food, and organizes volunteers to run them.

Events organizer: This person must be a celebration expert; in other words, a "beater of the drum" or pep rally leader. He or she creates events to spur excitement and pride in the PAR effort at the beginning and end of the season and at high points during the collection period. Maryalice Koehne, a PAR activist in Milwaukee, noted that her group finds that sponsoring events is a great excuse for invitations, which are invaluable public relations tools. She also notes that gardeners love to party. If you come up with events that are fun, you are sure to attract an enthusiastic group around you and the project.

Next Vital Step–Make a Call

Once a network of enthusiastic volunteer leaders is in place and they determine a strategy, the real work begins. As the growing season approaches, it is time to implement the strategy and launch the actual campaign for food donations. GWAA and PAR's national sponsors and its media partner HGTV have established a national PAR program office, with a toll-free telephone number. It provides support to local networks throughout their food campaigns. Feel free to contact them at any time for printed materials, advice, and encouragement. GWAA offers support supplies. Help is just a phone call away at the PAR headquarters,

✆ (877) GWAA-PAR or e-mail *PAR@gwaa.org.* A variety of useful tools, which have been creatively designed to support the program, are available. These tools include the following:

- **Ad slick/Logo**—Two-color or black-and-white artwork or electronic version
- **Donor receipts**—For gift records and use of contributors for in-kind tax deductions
- **Marketing brochure**—General information to interest people in participating
- **Public service announcement (VHS or Beta)**—For local TV stations
- **Quarterly PAR newsletter**—For network organizers and the media
- **Row markers**—Giant markers for PAR gardeners or a giant statement at an event, collection site, photo opportunity; small markers for gardens or giveaways for publicity and starter kits
- **Sharing Your Harvest brochure for donors**—Details on how to contribute and what to grow
- **Starting Your Own Campaign brochure**—Guidelines on how to start a network
- **Video**—Hosted by Jim Wilson (for loan or purchase), about a half hour long
- **Workbook and press kit**—To help enlist media coverage, or organize a committee

The Plant a Row program is another dramatic demonstration of how individuals can make a difference. With the details from this chapter, you can make an important contribution to your town. It's actually fun and opens doors to new friendships as well. Ⓔ

Chapter 21

E Preserve Your Garden's Bounty

When you have grown the tastiest, most nutritious vegetables and fruits in your garden, it makes good sense to find ways to save and savor them for more delicious meals all year long. Many gardeners have found the answers: freezing, drying, pickling, canning, and preserving.

Enjoy Tastier Eating

You can easily make those tasty garden-fresh pleasures last throughout the year. True, you won't have the delicate, picked-minutes-ago flavor of vegetables rushed from outdoor plot to kitchen pot, but you can come mighty close when you freeze, pickle, can, and preserve them. It really isn't that difficult. Many modern gardeners can still remember "the good old days" back on the farm. They didn't go shopping for vegetables. They "picked" them from the freezer or storage shelves in the basement.

Most gardeners, especially beginners, become a bit ambitious. Unless you hold yourself in check, you will produce more squash than you'll ever eat in summer. The same goes for tomatoes. They'll taste great in the middle of winter if you preserve them.

Berries in particular—if you grow them as property borders and edible hedges—can bear profusely. If you don't give them away, sell them, or eat them, there is an answer called "Freezer Jam" that is fun and easy to make.

This chapter isn't intended to provide full details on freezing or other types of food preserving; it's merely here to help you focus on ways that will work best for you.

FACT

Unless you are a rarity, you will probably grow more of some veggies than you can pick and use at once. It is nice to share them with others, and give to food pantries and shelters, but you still may have surplus. That's a fact of garden life. Preserve your bounty and you'll enjoy it when winter arrives.

Freezing Pointers

Of all the vegetable and fruit preserving methods, freezing is the fastest and, for most people, the easiest and best. Freshly picked crops frozen on cookie trays and put into freezer containers when solid also are rated among the best-tasting rewards of home gardeners.

Appliance manufacturers provide fliers about using their products. So do the makers of pressure cookers and the Ball and Kerr jar companies. Entire books have been written about preserving food, and you should consult them whenever you do your food preserving. It is best to learn to do these processes correctly to avoid any spoilage.

Assemble Your Supplies

You can get brochures about home freezing from your county extension agent. To begin freezing, obtain and assemble your supplies.

Plastic zippered freezer pouches are handy and less expensive, but they do have drawbacks. They don't stack well, can sometimes leak, and are more difficult to fill neatly than square rigid containers. If you have limited freezer space, use square containers; you lose space in the freezer with round containers. However, if you have an upright or chest freezer, recycle your round margarine and other containers. Just be sure that you seal them tightly.

Most gardeners prefer rigid plastic containers. They cost more initially, but they are handier and reusable. Those that have smaller bottoms than tops are best. After sealing the container, apply the lid, depress its center with your thumb, and "burp" one corner, tucking it back to seal the container with a little vacuum.

Don't overfill rigid containers. Leave some space when filling them with vegetables—about ½ inch for dry packs (those veggies frozen without extra liquid). For a wet pack (vegetables you are freezing in liquid), allow ½ inch for pints and a full inch for quart containers. Remember that as food freezes, it expands; if you pack it too full, the contents could pop the lid off.

If you use plastic freezer bags, seal them well. Heat sealing is best. Your next choice should be zippered tops, which is what most people use today. Tying with twist-ties is fine if you can get the bags closed tightly to avoid freezer burn. Be sure to eliminate as much air as possible.

You can also use glass jars. But if you overfill them, they can break, leaving produce and glass pieces inside your freezer. Leave sufficient head room and use new tops to seal them properly.

Family-Size Portions

Pack food in containers that provide the right size portion for your family. Containers with slightly wider tops allow you to pop the contents into a saucepan for heating. Newer types of microwave-proof containers are also available. It still is wise to let them thaw a bit and follow directions about use in the microwave oven. One or two mistakes will cure anyone of bad habits!

Before you put containers away, mark them. Keep a felt-tip pen handy. While veggies are cooling in an ice bath after blanching (the process of partly cooking vegetables before preserving them), label the containers with the food name and date. This may sound fundamental, but foods can look very similar in a freezer container. If you defrost containers for supper and find you have cantaloupe balls and beets for supper, you'll remember to label next time. You should also plan to eat the foods you froze first. Even when you freeze properly, food left too long in a freezer can get freezer burn, which reduces the flavor considerably.

FACT

Use simple labeling such as: Broccoli, 9/14/year, #1 of 12 packs. A chart on the freezer door will help you keep track of your frozen vegetable inventory. Let "first in, first out" be your guide.

Freezing Tips

Read your freezer book first. Then, assemble all ingredients for blanching and packaging. After washing and cutting your produce, boil the water in your blanching pot. Pop the veggies in and watch the timing. You don't want to cook the vegetables, only blanch them. Some gardeners don't bother to blanch, but it is a good practice. Blanching catches and holds the flavor in the vegetables. It also slightly precooks the vegetables, so it takes less time to prepare meals when you take the containers out of the freezer.

After blanching, chill the vegetables twice the length of time they were blanched. Chilling stops the cooking process and helps preserve the best flavor. For details, consult your favorite cookbook, as well as your own freezer guide.

Other Preserving Methods

This chapter isn't intended as a detailed guide for drying, canning, pickling, or preserving. It is best to use the instructions in your cookbook or books that address these specific topics. Instead, this chapter is intended to give you some basic tips from veteran gardeners to help you save and savor your garden's bounty all year long.

Jams, Jellies, and Fruit Pies

Making jams and jellies can become an art. You need a large kettle or big cooking pot. For making jelly, you'll need closely woven cheese-cloth or unbleached muslin, a measuring spoon, cups, bowls, a colander, and other usual kitchen tools. Jams are easier and have more substance to them, too.

Many gardeners prefer to use their surplus berries and other fruits for pies. Today all you need are the premade piecrusts, the fruit, a mixing bowl, sugar, and tapioca. The tapioca is useful to prevent runny or overly juicy pies. Naturally, you can make your own crusts but when berries come ripe it pays to get them quickly into pies or jams rather than take extra time to blend and roll out piecrusts.

ESSENTIAL

Strawberry and rhubarb pies, blackberry pies, and raspberry tarts are all treats you earn when you garden fruitfully. So are delights such as peach cobbler, apple pies that have nuances of flavor from different types of apples, and a variety of more exotic desserts you can make and freeze or put by in jars.

Keep the Process Tidy

When you freeze, make jam or jelly, pickle or preserve, keep things as clean as possible. Wash the produce, even from your garden. You don't want any little "nasties" getting frozen into your food. Cut away any poor quality portions of vegetables. Discard any overripe fruit. Watch tomatoes especially. Those soft bad spots can ruin an entire lot with their bitter taste. Blanching is important to stop any bacteria that could impart off-flavors to your processed vegetables.

Tried-and-True Storage Systems

Sometimes storing veggies is a lot easier than you think. Leave some of them right in the ground. Old-time gardeners vow that a touch of frost in the ground actually improves the flavor of parsnips, some carrots, and onions.

Actually, carrots and turnips can be left in the soil even after frost. A light covering of grass clippings avoids frost heaving that could crack them. Parsnips can stay in the ground all winter. To pull a few, just pour a bucket of hot water on the ground and pull up those you need. Cabbages can be covered with straw or hay and left outside until it gets really cold.

Devoted veggie gardeners report that root cellars are coming back. Not the old kind with dirt floors, but cool basements or garage areas. You can build a replica root cellar by nailing pieces of Styrofoam on 2-by-4s and making shelves to hold squash, turnips, cabbages, parsnips, and carrots. Winter squash and root crops store rather well in cool dry areas between 40° and 50°F.

FACT

Herbs also can be hung from beams in family rooms or dry basements. They add a nice aroma to rooms, dry well as decorator accents, and are there when you want them for cooking.

Onions are easy to save. Simply pull them up, shake off the soil, and tie them in bundles to dry; hang them in your garage or basement. It is a good idea to let them dry in the sun for a few days before bringing them indoors. Because there are so many different types of onions, you can try a variety of them; see which you prefer and save the surplus for use all year long.

Canning Still Works Wonders

Canning is an old-time American tradition. Farmers grew their own food and filled shelves with hundreds of glass jars of all types of canned vegetables. Some people still stock their basements with their homegrown veggies. Canning actually means preserving the food by precooking it and storing it in vacuum-sealed jars.

A Longer Process

To can food, sterilize the container and make sure the vegetables are cooked according to instructions in your cookbook or pressure cooker guide. Since there have been many cases of spoilage because of improper preparation or canning procedures, you may wish to forego this type of food storage.

However, as more gardeners focus on natural gardening without chemicals and seek what they believe is a safer food supply, there may indeed be a swing back to canning vegetables. Perhaps the number of canning jars showing up each summer and fall in hardware and grocery store chains is an indication of a refocus on home food storage. Canning doesn't require an extra freezer and electric costs or worries about power outages.

Generally speaking, freezing is much easier. Most refrigerators have freezer space for saving some veggies when you have a surplus.

FACT

Putting up quarts of delicious bread and butter pickles or dill pickles can be a family fun experience. *The Joy of Cooking* is a reliable reference for a variety of pickle recipes, or you can follow the recipes in your own favorite cookbook. The Ball and Kerr glass jar companies also have useful details available on request.

Plan to Pickle

Another ages-old food saving system is making pickles. Cucumbers are notorious for their abundance. Newer hybrids that resist disease and bear abundantly are available for pickle making. In fact, new varieties have fewer seeds and are being featured as pickling varieties in mail-order catalogs and seed racks.

Drying Surprises

Drying herbs has become one of America's fasting growing gardening activities. As more people seek to reduce the salt and fats in their diets, foods can seem rather bland. That has led to a surge in herb gardening and an upswing in drying herbs for year-round use. You can find more details about that process in Chapter 16.

As you become a more productive gardener, you'll undoubtedly enjoy more abundant crops and a fair amount of surplus. Share and trade with neighbors. Give to the food pantry or church food collection facility in your town. And think of ways to save some of your delicious veggies for future dining delights.

Appendices

Appendix A
Glossary

Appendix B
Great Gardens to Visit

Appendix C
Gardening Supply Companies

Appendix A
Glossary

A

acid soil: Soil with a pH value less than 7.0 on the pH scale of 1 (acid) to 14 (alkaline).

alkaline soil: Soil with a pH greater than 7.0 on a soil test.

annual: A plant that completes its life cycle from seed to mature plant to seed again in one growing season.

B

bacteria: Microscopic, one-celled organisms that lack chlorophyll, multiply by fission, and live on nonliving organic matter, helping to break it down into humus.

biennial: A plant that requires two growing seasons to complete its life cycle and then dies; vegetative growth takes place the first year and flowering and fruiting the second year.

blood meal: An organic source of nitrogen that contains approximately 10 to 12 percent nitrogen.

bud: Naked or scale-covered embryonic tissue that will eventually develop into a vegetative shoot, stem, or flower.

bulb: An underground stem that stores energy in modified leaves, as found in bulbs of daffodils and tulips.

C

chemical fertilizer: Fertilizer produced without carbon or derived from nonliving material.

compost: The end product of aerobic *decomposition* of *organic matter*, such as plant residues, weeds, manures, lawn clippings, and other natural materials.

corm: An underground stem that stores energy in modified stem tissue, as in a crocus corm.

cultivar: A term synonymous with *variety*, except that it refers only to cultivated plants.

D

decomposition: Breakdown of organic materials into their constituent parts as a result of the action of bacteria and microorganisms.

drip irrigation: A system of adding water to a garden soil in a slow, gentle stream from sources such as a perforated hose or one with a bubbler or slow release action; prevents soil from being disturbed and reduces water runoff.

F

foliar fertilizing: Applying plant nutrients directly to leaves, which will absorb them to feed the plant, rather than to the soil.

forcing: A process of making plants or bulbs bloom at a time that is not natural for them.

G

genus: Closely related plants grouped together under a single name, known as the *genus. Species* are plants within a genus that can be separated from one another by recognizable individual characteristics. Each different plant is assigned a specific epithet. Taken together, the genus and specific epithet form the species name.

germination: Growth of a plant embryo or the sprouting of a seed.

H

habitat: The region in which a plant is found growing wild.

humus: The stable organic constituent of soil that persists after the *decomposition* process of *organic matter.*

I, L

insecticide: Also called pesticide, a substance that kills insects by poisoning, suffocating, or paralyzing them; varieties include stomach poisons, contact poisons, and fumigants.

legume: A plant that is characterized botanically by fruit called a *legume* or a pod, including alfalfa, clover, peas, and beans that are associated with nitrogen-fixing bacteria that can take nitrogen from the air and fix it within the plant.

loam: A soil type made up of a mixture of sand, silt, and clay with various subdivisions that include sandy loam to clay loam.

O, P

organic matter: Technically, compounds containing carbon; in general, material that was once living.

peat moss: Partially decomposed vegetative material from sphagnum moss that is useful as mulch or a soil additive to increase moisture-holding ability and porosity.

perennial: A woody or herbaceous plant that lives from year to year; the plant's life cycle doesn't end with flowering or fruiting.

petal: One of the showy, usually colorful portions of a flower.

petiole: The stalk of a leaf.

pH: Represents the hydrogen ion concentration by which scientists measure soil acidity; the pH acidity scale measures from 1 (acid) to 14 (alkaline), with 7 as a neutral point.

phosphorus: An essential macronutrient for plant growing; its major function is promoting root formation in plants.

pistil: The female reproductive structure of a plant; found in the flower.

pollen: Minute grains that carry male reproductive cells; they are borne on anthers of the bloom.

potash: Or potassium; another essential macronutrient of plants; important for plant maturity, flower development, and hardiness.

R

rhizome: A horizontal underground stem that gives rise to roots and shoots.

rototilling: Garden soil preparation done with a rototiller that turns the soil to create a fine seedbed and area for planting.

S

seed: A fertilized, ripened ovule (egg) that can grow into a new plant.

sepal: One part of a whorl of green leafy structures that is located on the flower stem just below the petals.

soil: Basically a natural layer of mineral and organic materials that covers the surface of the earth at various depths and that supports plant life. *Soil* is created by the action of climate, water, and time, and the interactions of living organisms and microorganisms on the parent material.

species: A group of individuals forming a subdivision of a *genus* with similar characteristics but differing from the genus too slightly to form another genus.

stamen: The reproductive organ of the male pollen-bearing flower; the top part is the anther.

stigma: The terminal part of the reproductive organ of the female flowering plant that receives pollen.

T, V

terminal bud: The bud that is borne at the tip of a stem.

tuber: A swollen, underground stem modified to store large quantities of food for the plant.

variety: A group of individuals forming a subdivision of a *species* with similar characteristics but differing from the species too slightly to form another species.

Appendix B
Great Gardens to Visit

All-America Selections Display Gardens

Alabama

Bellingrath Gardens and Home
12401 Bellingrath Highway
Theodore, AL 36582

Birmingham Botanical Gardens
2612 Lane Park Road
Birmingham, AL 35223

Alaska

Alaska State Fair, Inc.
2075 Glenn Highway
Palmer, AK 99645

Georgeson Botanical Garden
West Tanana Drive
AFES, University of Alaska
Fairbanks, AK 99775

Municipality of Anchorage Horticulture Section
5200 DeBarr Road
Russian Jack Springs Park
Anchorage, AK 99508

Arkansas

University of Arkansas Ornamental Display Garden
979 West Maple
Fayetteville, AR 72701

California

City of Chino Civic Center
13220 Central Avenue
Chino, CA 91710

College of Sequoias Farm
2245 South Linwood
Visalia, CA 93277

Pan American Seed Company
335 South Briggs Road
Santa Paula, CA 93060

Pier 39, Inc.
Beach and Embarcadero
San Francisco, CA 94133

Sea World
500 Sea World Drive
San Diego, CA 92109

Seminis Vegetable Seeds, Inc.
37437 State Highway 16
Woodland, CA 95695

University of California Coop. Ext. Garden of the Sun
1944 North Winery Avenue
Fresno, CA 93703

Colorado

City of Aurora Parks Department
151 Potomac Street
Aurora, CO 80011

Colorado State University
High School Park
Corner of College and Lake Street
Fort Collins, CO 80523

Denver Botanic Gardens
909 York Street
Denver, CO 80206

Happiness Gardens
4226 Ammons Street
also West 28th and Benton
Wheat Ridge, CO 80033

Horticultural Art Society, Inc.
Monument Valley Park
Corner of Mesa and Glen
Colorado Springs, CO 80904

Welby Gardens
2761 East 74th Avenue
Denver, CO 80229

Connecticut

Bartlett Arboretum
151 Brookdale Road
Stamford, CT 06903

Elizabeth Park
Asylum and Prospect Avenue
Hartford, CT 06119

District of Columbia

Potomac Job Corps Center
#1 D.C. Village Lane, SW
Washington, D.C. 20032

U.S. Botanic Garden
245 First Street, SW
Washington, D.C. 20024

Florida

Marie Selby Botanical Gardens
811 South Palm Avenue
Sarasota, FL 34236

Mounts Botanical Garden
559 North Military Trail
West Palm Beach, FL 33415

Pensacola Junior College
Biology Department
1000 College Boulevard
Pensacola, FL 32504

Georgia

Callaway Gardens
Highway 27
Pine Mountain, GA 31822

Cloister Hotel Resort Trial Garden
100 Hudson Place
Sea Island, GA 31561

Oak Hill Gardens
Berry College
Mount Berry, GA 30149

State Botanical Garden of Georgia
2450 South Milledge Avenue
Athens, GA 30605

Idaho
Brigham Young University-Idaho
Thomas Ricks Demonstration Garden
500 South Center Street
Rexburg, ID 83460

Illinois
Alwerdt's Gardens
1 mile south of I-70 Exit 82
Altamont, IL 62411

Bird Haven Greenhouse
225 North Gougar Road
Joliet, IL 60432

Cantigny Gardens
1S151 Winfield Road
Wheaton, IL 60187

Chicago Botanic Garden
1000 Lake Cook Road
Glencoe, IL 60022

Illinois Central College
Agriculture Land Laboratory
One College Drive
East Peoria, IL 61635

Mabery Gelvin Botanical Gardens
Route 47
Mahomet, IL 61853

Triton College Botanical Garden
Triton College
2000 5th Avenue
River Grove, IL 60171

Washington Park Botanical Garden
Corner Fayette and Chatham Road
Springfield, IL 62705

Indiana
Foster Gardens
3900 Old Mill Road
Fort Wayne, IN 46807

Hamilton Co. Master Gardeners
2003 East Pleasant Street
Noblesville, IN 46060

Iowa
Amana Colonies Community Gardens
Village Perimeter
South Amana, IA 52334

Des Moines Botanical Center
909 East River Drive
Des Moines, IA 50316

Dubuque Arboretum Botanical Gardens
3800 Arboretum Drive
Dubuque, IA 52001

Iowa State University Home Demonstration Garden
Armstrong Research & Demonstration Farm
53020 Hitchcock Avenue
Lewis, IA 51544

Iowa State University Reiman Gardens
1407 Elwood Drive
Ames, IA 50011

Noelridge Park
4900 Council Street, NE
Cedar Rapids, IA 52402

Vander Veer Botanical Park
215 West Central Park Avenue
Davenport, IA 52803

Kansas

Botanica, The Wichita Gardens
701 Amidon
Wichita, KS 67203

NWK Research-Extension Center
105 Experiment Farm Road
Colby, KS 67701

Kentucky

Kentucky Fair & Expo. Center
Phillips Lane and Freedom Way
Louisville, KY 40209

University of Kentucky Arboretum
Alumni Drive
Lexington, KY 40546

Louisiana

Hodges Gardens
Highway 171 South
Many, LA 71449

New Orleans Botanical Garden
Victory Avenue City Park
New Orleans, LA 70119

Maine

University of Maine Rogers Farm
Bennoch Road
Stillwater, ME 04489

Maryland

Brookside Gardens
1800 Glenallen Avenue
Wheaton, MD 20902

Cylburn Arboretum
4915 Greenspring Avenue
Baltimore, MD 21209

Massachusetts

Berkshire Botanical Garden
5 West Stockbridge Road
Stockbridge, MA 01262

Massachusetts Horticultural Society
New England Trial Garden
Elm Bank Reservation
900 Washington Street
Wellesley, MA 02482

Newton Centre Green
Langley Road, Centre Street, Beacon Street
Newton, MA 02459

University of Massachusetts
Durfee Conservatory, French Hall
Amherst, MA 01003

Michigan
Dow Gardens
Eastman (US-10) and West St. Andrews
Midland, MI 48640

Fernwood Botanic Gardens
13988 Rangeline Road
Niles, MI 49120

Frankenmuth Mutual Insurance Co.
One Mutual Avenue
Frankenmuth, MI 48787

Michigan State University
Hidden Lake Gardens
Route M-50
Tipton, MI 49287

Michigan State University
Horticulture Demonstration Gardens
Horticulture Building
East Lansing, MI 48824

Minnesota
Lyndale Park Gardens
4125 East Lake Harriet Parkway
Minneapolis, MN 55409

Minnesota Landscape Arboretum
3675 Arboretum Drive
Chanhassen, MN 55317

University of Minnesota
North Central Res. & Outreach Ctr.
1861 Highway 169 East
Grand Rapids, MN 55744

University of Minnesota
West Central Res. & Outreach Ctr.
State Highway 329
Morris, MN 56267

University of Minnesota, St. Paul
Corner of Gortner and Folwell Avenue
St. Paul, MN 55108

Mississippi
Mississippi State University
Coastal R & E Center
711 West North Street
Poplarville, MS 39470

Mississippi State University
Truck Crops Experiment Station
Highway 51 South
Crystal Springs, MS 39059

Missouri
Loose Park Gardens
5200 Pennsylvania Avenue
Kansas City, MO 64114

Missouri Botanical Garden
4344 Shaw Boulevard
St. Louis, MO 63110

Powell Gardens
1609 NW U.S. Highway 50
Kingsville, MO 64061

St. Louis County Government Center
41 South Central Avenue
Clayton, MO 63105

Southeast Missouri State University
University Horticulture Display Gardens
New Madrid Drive Cape
Girardeau, MO 63701

University of Missouri
Department of Horticulture
I-87 Agriculture Building
Columbia, MO 65211

Nebraska
Bluebird Nursery, Inc.
520 Cherry Street
Clarkson, NE 68629

Metro Community College
Fort Omaha Campus
30th and Fort Streets
Omaha, NE 68111

State Fair Park Arboretum
1800 State Fair Park Drive
Lincoln, NE 68504

New Hampshire
Balsams Grand Resort Hotel
Route 26
Dixville Notch, NH 03576

Fuller Gardens
10 Willow Avenue
North Hampton, NH 03862

University of New Hampshire Trial Garden
Prescott Park, Marcy Street
Portsmouth, NH 03801

New Jersey
Deep Cut Gardens
352 Red Hill Road
Middletown, NJ 07748

Frelinghuysen Arboretum
53 E. Hanover Avenue
Morristown, NJ 07962

Hunterdon County Arboretum
1020 Highway 31
Lebanon, NJ 08833

Ramapo College of New Jersey
505 Ramapo Valley Road
Mahwah, NJ 07430

Rutgers University
Lacey Display Garden
Route 1 and Ryders Lane
New Brunswick, NJ 08901

Skylands Botanical Garden
Ringwood State Park
1304 Sloatsburg Road
Ringwood, NJ 07456

New York
Boldt Castle Formal Gardens
Thousand Islands Bridge Authority
Alexandria Bay, NY 13607

Brooklyn Botanic Garden
1000 Washington Avenue
Brooklyn, NY 11225

Buffalo & Erie County Botanical Gardens
2655 South Park Avenue
Buffalo, NY 14218

Cornell Cooperative Extension of Dutchess County
Dutchess County Fairgrounds
Route 9
Rhinebeck, NY 12572

Cornell Cooperative Extension of Nassau County
1425 Old Country Road
Plainview, NY 11803

Cutler Botanic Gardens
840 Upper Front Street
Binghamton, NY 13905

Dickman Farms Gardens
13 Archie Street
Auburn, NY 13021

Erie Basin Marina Park
Joan Fuzak Memorial Gardens
1 Erie Street
Buffalo, NY 14202

Mohonk Mountain House
Mountain Rest Road
New Paltz, NY 12561

Old Westbury Gardens
71 Old Westbury Road
Old Westbury, NY 11568

The Potager
116 Sullivan Street
Wurtsboro, NY 12790

Queens Botanical Garden Society, Inc.
45-50 Main Street
Flushing, NY 11355

Sonnenberg Gardens
151 Charlotte Street
Canandaigua, NY 14424

North Carolina
North Carolina State University
JC Raulston Arboretum
4301 Beryl Road
Raleigh, NC 27695

Reynolda Gardens of Wake Forest University
100 Reynolda Village
Winston-Salem, NC 27106

North Dakota

International Peace Garden
Route 1
Dunseith, NC 58329

North Dakota State University
1300 18th Street North
Fargo, ND 58105

Ohio

Dawes Arboretum
7770 Jacksontown Road SE
Newark, OH 43056-9380

Gardenview Horticultural Park
16711 Pearl Road
Strongsville, OH 44136

Kingwood Center
900 Park Avenue West
Mansfield, OH 44906

Krohn Conservatory
1501 Eden Park Drive
Cincinnati, OH 45202

Miami University Formal Gardens
Botany Department Gardens
Boyd Hall, Fisher Drive
Oxford, OH 45056

Mill Creek Metro Parks
Fellows Riverside Gardens
123 McKinley Avenue
Youngstown, OH 44509

Ohio State University
Agricultural Technical Institute
Route 250 and U.S. 83
Wooster, OH 44691

Rockefeller Park Greenhouse Gardens
750 East 88th Street
Cleveland, OH 44108

Spring Grove Cemetery and Arboretum
4521 Spring Grove Avenue
Cincinnati, OH 45232

Toledo Botanical Garden
5403 Elmer Drive
Toledo, OH 43615

Wilson's Hillview Display Garden
10923 Lambs Lane NE
Newark, OH 43055

Oklahoma

Oklahoma State University
400 North Portland
Oklahoma City, OK 73107

Oregon

Clackamas Community College
19600 South Molalla Avenue
Oregon City, OR 97045

Josephine County Fairgrounds
1451 Fairgrounds Road
Grants Pass, OR 97527

Nichols Garden Nursery
1190 Old Salem Road NE
Albany, OR 97321

Pennsylvania
Longwood Gardens
U.S. Route 1 South
Kennett Square, PA 19348

Pennsylvania State University
Dept. of Horticulture, 101 Tyson Building
University Park, PA 16802

Rodale Research Center
611 Siegfriedale Road
Kutztown, PA 19530

Temple University
Ambler Research Gardens
580 Meetinghouse Road
Ambler, PA 19002-3994

South Carolina
Clemson University
The SC Botanical Garden
Highway 76-28 and Perimeter Road
Clemson, SC 29634

South Dakota
South Dakota State University
McCrory Gardens, SDSU
6th Street and 20th Avenue
Brookings, SD 57007

Tennessee
University of Tennessee
Agriculture Campus, Neyland Drive
Knoxville, TN 37901

Texas
Dallas Arboretum & Botanical Garden
8617 Garland Road
Dallas, TX 75218

Harris County Ext. Service Display
#2 Abercrombie Drive
Agricultural Extension Grounds
Bear Creek Park
Houston, TX 77084

Houston Civic Garden Center
1500 Hermann Drive
Houston, TX 77004

Montgomery County Extension
Master Gardener Test Gardens
9020 FM 1484
Conroe, TX 77303

Moody Gardens
One Hope Boulevard
Galveston, TX 77554

San Antonio Botanical Gardens
555 Funston Place
San Antonio, TX 78209

Texas Discovery Gardens
3601 Martin Luther King Drive
Dallas, TX 75210

Utah
Utah State University Botanical Gardens
USU Research Farm
Main Street and Burton Lane
Kaysville, UT 84037

Vermont
Vermont Community Botanical Garden
1100 Dorset Street South
Burlington, VT 05403

Waterfront Park
College Street at Lakefront
Burlington, VT 05405

Virginia
American Horticultural Society
7931 East Boulevard Drive
Alexandria, VA 22308

J. Sargeant Reynolds Community College
Western Campus Route 6 & Route 522
Goochland, VA 23063

Norfolk Botanical Garden Society
Azalea Garden Road
Norfolk, VA 23518

Virginia Tech
Hampton Roads AREC
1444 Diamond Springs Road
Virginia Beach, VA 23455

Virginia Tech University Horticulture Gardens
Washington Street
Blacksburg, VA 24061

Virginia Western Community College
The Community Arboretum
3095 Colonial Avenue SW
Roanoke, VA 24015

Washington
Manito Park & Botanical Gardens
4 West 21st Avenue
Spokane, WA 99203

Molbak's
13625 NE 175th Street
Woodinville, WA 98072

Seymour Botanical Conservatory
316 South G Street
Tacoma, WA 98405

Washington State University Coop. Extension
Jennings Park
7027 51st Avenue NE
Marysville, WA 98270

West Virginia
Oglebay Resort & Conference Center
Route 88 North
Wheeling, WV 26003

Wisconsin
A. R. Albert Horticultural Garden
Hancock Ag. Research Station

N3909 County Highway V
Hancock, WI 54943

Boerner Botanical Gardens
5879 South 92nd Street
Hales Corners, WI 53130

Jung Seed Company
335 South High Street
Randolph, WI 53957

Vincent High School
Agribusiness/Natural Resources
7501 North Granville Road
Milwaukee, WI 53224

West Madison Research Station
University of Wisconsin
Mineral Point Road
Madison, WI 53706

Major Arboretums

Arboretum at Arizona State University
ASU Visitors Information Center
P.O. Box 872512, 826 East Apache Boulevard
Tempe, AZ 85287-2512
(480) 965-8467
▶ A great place to see unique collections and learn more about native and indigenous plant materials

The Arnold Arboretum at Harvard University
125 Arborway
Jamaica Plain, MA 02130-3519

(617) 524-1718
✐ www.arboretum.harvard.edu
▶ One of America's most distinguished arboretums; vast stores of knowledge are available

The Dallas Arboretum
8525 Garland Road
Dallas, TX 75218
(214) 327-8263
✐ www.dallasarboretum.org
▶ Features superbly landscaped acres of towering trees, fragrant gardens, and lush lawns

Minnesota Landscape Arboretum
3675 Arboretum Drive
P.O. Box 39
Chanhassen, MN 55317-0039
(952) 443-1400
✐ www.arboretum.umn.edu
▶ Includes information on the Andersen Horticultural Library, a rich resource for gardeners, botanists, and horticultural specialists

North Carolina Arboretum
100 Frederick Law Olmsted Way
Asheville, NC 28806
(828) 665-2492
✐ www.ncarboretum.org/
▶ Emphasizes education, research, conservation, and garden demonstrations about landscape, architecture, and plant sciences

Strybing Arboretum and Gardens
Golden Gate Park
Ninth Avenue at Lincoln Way

San Francisco, CA 94122

(415) 661-1316

✑ www.strybing.org

▶ Located within Golden Gate Park; contains extensive plant collections and references to help gardeners

United States National Arboretum

3501 New York Avenue, NE

Washington, D.C. 20002-1958

(202) 245-2726

✑ www.usna.usda.gov

▶ A must-see national treasure with many resources for gardeners

University of Nebraska Botanical Garden and Arboretum

1340 North 17th Street

Lincoln, NE 68588

(402) 472-2679

✑ www.unl.edu/unlbga

▶ Has an expanding collection of unusual plants designed to help in teaching, research, and public service

University of Wisconsin Arboretum

University of Wisconsin–Madison

1207 Seminole Highway

Madison, WI 53711-3726

(608) 263-7888

http://wiscinfo.doit.wisc.edu/arboretum/index.htm

▶ Features information on the arboretum's history, public events, and resources for naturalists

Biblical Gardens

Arizona

Paradise Valley United Methodist Church

4455 East Lincoln Drive

Paradise Valley, AZ 85253

Temple Beth Shalom

Jewish Community Center of Sun City

12202 101st Avenue

Sun City, AZ 85361

California

Alta Sierra Biblical Gardens

16343 Auburn Road

Grass Valley, CA 95945

Biblical Garden of B'nai Shalom

74 Eckley Lane

Walnut Creek, CA 94596

Church of the Wayfarer

Corner of Lincoln and 7th

Carmel by the Sea, CA 93921

Ojai Presbyterian Church

304 North Foothill Road

Ojai, CA 93023

St. Gregory's Episcopal Church Biblical Garden

6201 East Willow Street

Long Beach, CA 90815-2296

Strybing Arboretum
Golden Gate Park
San Francisco, CA 94122

Connecticut
Concordia Lutheran Church
40 Pitkin Street
Manchester, CT 06040

Florida
Highlands-Presbyterian Church
1001 NE 16th Avenue
Gainesville, FL 32601

St. James Lutheran Church
110 Avenue Phoenetia
Coral Gables, FL 33134

Indiana
Warsaw Biblical Garden
Warsaw Community Development Corp.
P.O. Box 1223, Route 15
Warsaw, IN 46580

Kentucky
St. Michael's Church
2025 Bellefonte
Lexington, KY 40503

Maine
Biblical Garden
Prince of Peace Lutheran Church
209 Eastern Avenue
Augusta, ME 04330

Massachusetts
Church of the Holy Spirit
9 Morgan's Way
Orleans, MA 02653

Michigan
Messiah Lutheran Church
5740 West Holt Road
Holt, MI 48842

Missouri
St. John's Lutheran Church
Babbtown, MO 63131

New Hampshire
St. Thomas Church
5 Hale Street
Dover, NH 03820

New York
The Biblical Garden
Cathedral of St. John the Divine
1047 Amsterdam Avenue
New York, NY 10025

Schervier Nursing Care Center
2975 Independence Avenue
Riverdale, NY 10463

Oklahoma
St. John's Episcopal Church
P.O. Box 2088
Norman, OK 73070

Pennsylvania

Phipps Conservatory, Schenley Park
613 Oxford Boulevard
Pittsburgh, PA 15243

Rodef Shalom Biblical Botanical Garden
4905 Fifth Avenue
Pittsburgh, PA 15213

Shir Ami Temple—Bucks County Jewish Congregation
101 Richboro Road
Newtown, PA 18940

Rhode Island

Temple Beth-El Synagogue
70 Orchard Avenue
Providence, PA 02903

South Carolina

Magnolia Plantation and Gardens
3550 Ashley River Road
Charleston, SC 29414

Tennessee

First Presbyterian Church
4815 Franklin Road
Nashville, TN 37220

Vermont

Fair Haven Biblical Garden
First Congregational Church
19 West Street
Fair Haven, VT 05743

Virginia

Temple Sinai Biblical Gardens
11620 Warwick Boulevard
Newport News, VA 23601

Appendix C
Gardening Supply Companies

Antonelli Brothers
2545 MN Capitola Road
Santa Cruz, CA 95062
▶ Leading begonia specialists with probably more varieties than any other firm

Appalachian Gardens
P.O. Box 82
Waynesboro, PA 17268
▶ Offers an appealing and unique selection of rare trees and shrubs

Burgess Seed/Plant Company
904 Four Seasons Road
Bloomington, IL 61701
▶ Bulbs and seeds

Burpee
300 Park Avenue
Warminster, PA 18974
✍ www.burpee.com
▶ One of America's oldest and most famed seed and plant firms; offers seeds, bulbs, and gardening products

Charley's Greenhouses
1599 Memorial Highway
Mt. Vernon, WA 98273
▶ America's premier mail-order firm for greenhouses and greenhouse supplies; a worthwhile catalog for those who want to garden year-round

The Cook's Garden
P.O. Box 535

Londonderry, VT 05148
✍ www.cooksgarden.com
▶ Specializes in salad veggie varieties

Clyde Robin Seed Company
P.O. Box 2366
Castro Valley, CA 9454
▶ Specializes in wildflowers with collections that apply to all parts of the country

Dixondale Farms
P.O. Box 127
Carizzo Springs, TX 78834
▶ Specializes in onions; more types and tastes than you can imagine

Drip Rite Irrigation
4235 Pacific Street, Suite H
Rocklin, CA 95490
▶ Specializes in a wide range of irrigation supplies for all types of gardening

Duncraft
P.O. Box 9020
Penacook, NH 03303
✍ www.duncraft.com
▶ One of America's leading producers of birdhouses, feeders, and so on

Dutch Gardens
P.O. Box 200
Adelphia, NJ 07710
▶ Colorful catalog packed with hundreds of types of Dutch bulbs

Earthmade
1502 Meridian Road
Jasper, IN 47547
▶ Tools and accessories

Ferry Morse Seed Company
P.O. Box 488
Fulton, KY 42041
▶ Respected, old-time and reliable supplier of
seeds, bulbs, and plants

Gardener's Supply Company
128 Intervale Road
Burlington, VT 05401
✍ www.gardeners.com
▶ Widest range of gardening tools, devices, and
gardening supplies available

Gardens Alive!
5100 Schenley Place
Lawrenceburg, IN 47025
✍ www.gardensalive.com
▶ Foremost mail-order organic gardening product
source

Harris Seeds
60 Saginaw Drive
Rochester, NY 14692
▶ Old-line seed firm

High Country Gardens
2902 Rufina Street
Sante Fe, NM 87505
▶ Features western plants of all types

Ed Hume Seeds, Inc.
P.O. Box 1450
Kent, WA 98035
▶ Features short growing season varieties

Hydrangeas Plus
P.O. Box 389
Aurora, OR 97002

Johnny's Selected Seeds
RR 1, Box 2580
Albion, ME 04910
✍ www.johnnyseeds.com
▶ One of the most innovative and farsighted new
firms with a wide variety list

Lilypons Water Gardens
P.O. Box 10
Buckeystown, MD 21717
▶ Long-time specialist in great water garden plants
and products

Mantis
1028 Street Road
Southampton, PA 18966
▶ Manufactures lightweight, very handy rototillers
and tools

Miller Nurseries
5060 West Lake Road
Canandaigua, NY 14224
✍ www.millernurseries.com
▶ A long-time major source for quality berries and
fruit trees

Monticello
P.O. Box 316
Charlottesville, VA 22902
✍ www.monticello.org
▶ Offers Thomas Jefferson's historic and heirloom plants

Nichols Garden Nursery
1190 North Pacific Highway NE
Albany, OR 97321
✍ www.nicholsgardennursery.com
▶ Offers oriental and other ethnic exotic varieties, as well as good growing and using tips

Northwoods Nursery
27635 South Oglesby Road
Canby, OR 97013
▶ Rare fruits, nuts, and other specialties

Park Seed
1 Parkton Avenue
Greenwood, SC 29647
✍ www.parkseed.com
▶ Major U.S. seed firm, many new hybrids, landscape shrubs, and trees

Raintree Nursery
391 M. Butts Road
Morton, WA 98356
▶ Source for many special berries, fruits, and vines

Ronniger's Seed & Potato Company
P.O. Box 307
Ellensburg, WA 98926
▶ Tasty and exotic potatoes and onions

Roris Gardens
8195 Bradshaw Road

Sacramento, CA 95829
▶ Iris specialists

Royal River Roses
P.O. Box 370
Yarmouth, ME 04096
▶ Rare, hardy, and old-time roses

Select Seeds Antique Flowers
180 Stickney Road
Union, CT 06076
▶ Features hard-to-find heirloom seeds and plants

Stark Bro's Nurseries & Orchards Co.
Highway 54 West
Louisiana, MO 63353
✍ www.strakbros.com
▶ A great source for fruit trees

Van Bourgondien
P.O. Box 1000
Babylon, NY 11702
✍ www.dutchbulbs.com
▶ A major Dutch bulb specialist run by the Bulb Lady

Vessey's Seeds Ltd.
P.O. Box 9000
Calais, ME 04619
▶ Features short-season U.S. and Canadian varieties

Wildseed Farms
525 Wildflower Hills
Fredericksburg, TX 78624
▶ Wildflower specialists

Index

THE EVERYTHING LANDSCAPING BOOK

By Allan A. Swenson

Have you ever wondered why your neighbors' property is always so beautiful? It's not as difficult as you think! In *The Everything® Landscaping Book*, noted gardener Allan A. Swenson walks you through his quick and easy steps to beautifying your home and increasing its value by up to 10 percent. *The Everything® Landscaping Book* shows you how to "frame" your home with vibrant flowerbeds, blossoming bushes, and shady trees. Whether you're a novice, or longtime homeowner, you can learn to create a water garden, plant window boxes, and color-coordinate your landscape design like a professional.

Trade paperback,
$14.95 ($22.95 CAN)
1-58062-861-3, 320 pages

OTHER *EVERYTHING*® BOOKS BY ADAMS MEDIA CORPORATION

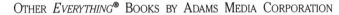

BUSINESS

Everything® **Business Planning Book**
Everything® **Coaching & Mentoring Book**
Everything® **Home-Based Business Book**
Everything® **Leadership Book**
Everything® **Managing People Book**
Everything® **Network Marketing Book**
Everything® **Online Business Book**
Everything® **Project Management Book**
Everything® **Selling Book**
Everything® **Start Your Own Business Book**
Everything® **Time Management Book**

COMPUTERS

Everything® **Build Your Own Home Page Book**
Everything® **Computer Book**

Everything® **Internet Book**
Everything® **Microsoft® Word 2000 Book**

COOKING

Everything® **Bartender's Book, $9.95**
Everything® **Barbecue Cookbook**
Everything® **Chocolate Cookbook**
Everything® **Cookbook**
Everything® **Dessert Cookbook**
Everything® **Diabetes Cookbook**
Everything® **Low-Carb Cookbook**
Everything® **Low-Fat High-Flavor Cookbook**
Everything® **Mediterranean Cookbook**
Everything® **One-Pot Cookbook**
Everything® **Pasta Book**
Everything® **Quick Meals Cookbook**
Everything® **Slow Cooker Cookbook**

Everything® **Soup Cookbook**
Everything® **Thai Cookbook**
Everything® **Vegetarian Cookbook**
Everything® **Wine Book**

HEALTH

Everything® **Anti-Aging Book**
Everything® **Dieting Book**
Everything® **Herbal Remedies Book**
Everything® **Hypnosis Book**
Everything® **Menopause Book**
Everything® **Stress Management Book**
Everything®**Vitamins, Minerals, and Nutritional Supplements Book**
Everything® **Nutrition Book**

HISTORY

Everything® **American History Book**

All Everything® books are priced at $12.95 or $14.95, unless otherwise stated. Prices subject to change without notice.
Canadian prices range from $11.95–$22.95 and are subject to change without notice.

Everything® **Civil War Book**
Everything® **World War II Book**

HOBBIES

Everything® **Bridge Book**
Everything® **Candlemaking Book**
Everything® **Casino Gambling Book**
Everything® **Chess Basics Book**
Everything® **Collectibles Book**
Everything® **Crossword and Puzzle Book**
Everything® **Digital Photography Book**
Everything® **Drums Book (with CD),**
 $19.95, ($31.95 CAN)
Everything® **Family Tree Book**
Everything® **Games Book**
Everything® **Guitar Book**
Everything® **Knitting Book**
Everything® **Magic Book**
Everything® **Motorcycle Book**
Everything® **Online Genealogy Book**
Everything® **Playing Piano and**
 Keyboards Book
Everything® **Rock & Blues Guitar**
 Book (with CD), $19.95,
 ($31.95 CAN)
Everything® **Scrapbooking Book**

HOME IMPROVEMENT

Everything® **Feng Shui Book**
Everything® **Gardening Book**
Everything® **Home Decorating Book**
Everything® **Landscaping Book**
Everything® **Lawn Care Book**
Everything® **Organize Your Home Book**

KIDS' STORY BOOKS

Everything® **Bedtime Story Book**
Everything® **Bible Stories Book**
Everything® **Fairy Tales Book**
Everything® **Mother Goose Book**

NEW AGE

Everything® **Astrology Book**

Everything® **Divining the Future Book**
Everything® **Dreams Book**
Everything® **Ghost Book**
Everything® **Meditation Book**
Everything® **Numerology Book**
Everything® **Palmistry Book**
Everything® **Spells and Charms Book**
Everything® **Tarot Book**
Everything® **Wicca and Witchcraft Book**

PARENTING

Everything® **Baby Names Book**
Everything® **Baby Shower Book**
Everything® **Baby's First Food Book**
Everything® **Baby's First Year Book**
Everything® **Breastfeeding Book**
Everything® **Get Ready for Baby Book**
Everything® **Homeschooling Book**
Everything® **Potty Training Book,**
 $9.95, ($15.95 CAN)
Everything® **Pregnancy Book**
Everything® **Pregnancy Organizer,**
 $15.00, ($22.95 CAN)
Everything® **Toddler Book**
Everything® **Tween Book**

PERSONAL FINANCE

Everything® **Budgeting Book**
Everything® **Get Out of Debt Book**
Everything® **Get Rich Book**
Everything® **Investing Book**
Everything® **Homebuying Book, 2nd Ed.**
Everything® **Homeselling Book**
Everything® **Money Book**
Everything® **Mutual Funds Book**
Everything® **Online Investing Book**
Everything® **Personal Finance Book**

PETS

Everything® **Cat Book**
Everything® **Dog Book**
Everything® **Dog Training and Tricks**
Everything® **Horse Book**
Everything® **Puppy Book**
Everything® **Tropical Fish Book**

REFERENCE

Everything® **Astronomy Book**
Everything® **Car Care Book**
Everything® **Christmas Book, $15.00,**
 ($21.95 CAN)
Everything® **Classical Mythology Book**
Everything® **Divorce Book**
Everything® **Etiquette Book**
Everything® **Great Thinkers Book**
Everything® **Learning French Book**
Everything® **Learning German Book**
Everything® **Learning Italian Book**
Everything® **Learning Latin Book**
Everything® **Learning Spanish Book**
Everything® **Mafia Book**
Everything® **Philosophy Book**
Everything® **Shakespeare Book**
Everything® **Tall Tales, Legends, &**
 Other Outrageous Lies Book
Everything® **Toasts Book**
Everything® **Trivia Book**
Everything® **Weather Book**
Everything® **Wills & Estate Planning**
 Book

RELIGION

Everything® **Angels Book**
Everything® **Buddhism Book**
Everything® **Catholicism Book**
Everything® **Judaism Book**
Everything® **Saints Book**
Everything® **World's Religions Book**
Everything® **Understanding Islam Book**

SCHOOL & CAREERS

Everything® **After College Book**
Everything® **College Survival Book**
Everything® **Cover Letter Book**
Everything® **Get-a-Job Book**
Everything® **Hot Careers Book**
Everything® **Job Interview Book**
Everything® **Online Job Search Book**
Everything® **Resume Book, 2nd Ed.**
Everything® **Study Book**

All Everything® books are priced at $12.95 or $14.95, unless otherwise stated. Prices subject to change without notice.
Canadian prices range from $11.95–$22.95 and are subject to change without notice.

WE HAVE EVERYTHING . . . .

SPORTS/FITNESS

Everything® **Bicycle Book**
Everything® **Fishing Book**
Everything® **Fly-Fishing Book**
Everything® **Golf Book**
Everything® **Golf Instruction Book**
Everything® **Pilates Book**
Everything® **Running Book**
Everything® **Sailing Book, 2nd Ed.**
Everything® **T'ai Chi and QiGong Book**
Everything® **Total Fitness Book**
Everything® **Weight Training Book**
Everything® **Yoga Book**

TRAVEL

Everything® **Guide to Las Vegas**
Everything® **Guide to New England**
Everything® **Guide to New York City**
Everything® **Guide to Washington D.C.**

Everything® **Travel Guide to The Disneyland Resort®, California Adventure®, Universal Studios®, and the Anaheim Area**
Everything® **Travel Guide to the Walt Disney World® Resort, Universal Studios®, and Greater Orlando, 3rd Ed.**

WEDDINGS & ROMANCE

Everything® **Creative Wedding Ideas Book**
Everything® **Dating Book**
Everything® **Jewish Wedding Book**
Everything® **Romance Book**
Everything® **Wedding Book, 2nd Ed.**
Everything® **Wedding Organizer, $15.00** ($22.95 CAN)

Everything® **Wedding Checklist,** $7.95 ($11.95 CAN)
Everything® **Wedding Etiquette Book,** $7.95 ($11.95 CAN)
Everything® **Wedding Shower Book,** $7.95 ($12.95 CAN)
Everything® **Wedding Vows Book,** $7.95 ($11.95 CAN)
Everything® **Weddings on a Budget Book, $9.95** ($15.95 CAN)

WRITING

Everything® **Creative Writing Book**
Everything® **Get Published Book**
Everything® **Grammar and Style Book**
Everything® **Grant Writing Book**
Everything® **Guide to Writing Children's Books**
Everything® **Writing Well Book**

ALSO AVAILABLE:
THE EVERYTHING® KIDS' SERIES!

Each book is 8" x 91/4", 144 pages, and two-color throughout.

Everything® **Kids' Baseball Book, 2nd Edition, $6.95** ($11.95 CAN)
Everything® **Kids' Bugs Book, $6.95** ($10.95 CAN)
Everything® **Kids' Cookbook, $6.95** ($10.95 CAN)
Everything® **Kids' Joke Book, $6.95** ($10.95 CAN)
Everything® **Kids' Math Puzzles Book, $6.95** ($10.95 CAN)
Everything® **Kids' Mazes Book, $6.95** ($10.95 CAN)
Everything® **Kids' Money Book, $6.95** ($11.95 CAN)

Everything® **Kids' Monsters Book, $6.95** ($10.95 CAN)
Everything® **Kids' Nature Book, $6.95** ($11.95 CAN)
Everything® **Kids' Puzzle Book $6.95,** ($10.95 CAN)
Everything® **Kids' Science Experiments Book, $6.95** ($10.95 CAN)
Everything® **Kids' Soccer Book, $6.95** ($11.95 CAN)
Everything® **Kids' Travel Activity Book, $6.95** ($10.95 CAN)

Available wherever books are sold!
To order, call 800-872-5627, or visit us at everything.com

Everything® is a registered trademark of Adams Media Corporation.